Entertainment Directory

VANCOUVER
TRAVEL GUIDE

SHOPS, RESTAURANTS, ATTRACTIONS & NIGHTLIFE

The Most Positively
Reviewed and Recommended
by Locals and Travelers

EGP
Editorial

VANCOUVER
TRAVEL GUIDE
SHOPS, RESTAURANTS, ATTRACTIONS & NIGHTLIFE

VANCOUVER TRAVEL GUIDE 2022
Shops, Restaurants, Arts, Entertainment & Nightlife

© Howard P. Quinn
© E.G.P. Editorial

ISBN-13: 9798749388039

Copyright ©
All rights reserved.

INDEX

SHOPS
Top 500 Shops - 9

RESTAURANTS
Top 500 Restaurants - 53

ARTS & ENTERTAINMENT
Top 500 Arts & Entertainment - 97

NIGHTLIFE SPOTS
Top 400 Nightlife Spots - 138

VANCOUVER TRAVEL GUIDE
Shops, Restaurants, Arts, Entertainment and Nightlife

*This directory is dedicated to Vancouver Business Owners and Managers
who provide the experience that the locals and tourists enjoy.
Thanks you very much for all that you do and thank for being the "People Choice".*

*Thanks to everyone that posts their reviews online and
the amazing reviews sites that make our life easier.*

*The places listed in this book are the most positively reviewed
and recommended by locals and travelers from around the world.*

*Thank you for your time and enjoy the directory that is
designed with locals and tourist in mind!*

TOP 500 SHOPS
The Most Recommended by Locals & Trevelers
(From #1 to #500)

Shops, Restaurants, Attractions & Nightlife / Vancouver Travel Guide

#1
Granville Island
Category: Shopping Center
Average price: Modest
Area: Granville Island/False Creek
Address: 1689 Johnston St
Vancouver, BC V6H 3R9
Phone: (604) 685-8335

#2
The Gourmet Warehouse
Category: Kitchen & Bath, Appliances
Average price: Modest
Area: Grandview-Woodlands
Address: 1340 Hastings Street E
Vancouver, BC V5L 1S3
Phone: (604) 253-3022

#3
Urban Source
Category: Art Supplies
Average price: Inexpensive
Area: Mount Pleasant
Address: 3126 Main St
Vancouver, BC V5T 3G7
Phone: (604) 875-1611

#4
The Soap Dispensary
Category: Cosmetics & Beauty Supply
Average price: Modest
Area: Riley Park
Address: 3623 Main Street
Vancouver, BC V5V 3N6
Phone: (604) 568-3141

#5
The Regional Assembly of Text
Category: Cards & Stationery
Average price: Modest
Area: Riley Park
Address: 3934 Main St
Vancouver, BC V5V 3P2
Phone: (604) 877-2247

#6
MacLeod's Books
Category: Bookstore
Average price: Modest
Area: Downtown
Address: 455 Pender St W
Vancouver, BC V6B 1V2
Phone: (604) 681-7654

#7
Community Thrift and Vintage
Category: Thrift Store
Average price: Modest
Area: Downtown Eastside
Address: 331 Carrall Street
Vancouver, BC V6B
Phone: (604) 682-8535

#8
Walrus
Category: Home Decor
Average price: Modest
Area: South Cambie, Riley Park
Address: 3408 Cambie St
Vancouver, BC V5Z 2W8
Phone: (604) 874-9770

#9
Yokoyaya123
Category: Department Store, Discount Store
Average price: Inexpensive
Area: Downtown
Address: 1199-88 W Pender St
Vancouver, BC V6B 6N9
Phone: (604) 682-8073

#10
Livestock
Category: Shoe Store
Average price: Modest
Area: Downtown, Gastown
Address: 239 Abbott St
Vancouver, BC V6B 2K7
Phone: (604) 685-1433

#11
Oak + Fort
Category: Women's Clothing
Average price: Modest
Area: Downtown, Gastown
Address: 355 Water Street
Vancouver, BC V6B 1B8
Phone: (604) 566-9199

#12
Front & Company
Category: Used, Vintage, Accessories, Women's Clothing
Average price: Modest
Area: Riley Park
Address: 3772 Main Street
Vancouver, BC V5V 3N7
Phone: (604) 879-8431

#13
Chocolate Mousse Kitchenware Etc
Category: Kitchen & Bath
Average price: Modest
Area: West End
Address: 1553 Robson St
Vancouver, BC V6G 1C3
Phone: (604) 682-8223

#14
Button Button
Category: Arts & Crafts
Average price: Modest
Area: Downtown, Gastown
Address: 318 Homer Street
Vancouver, BC V6B 2V2
Phone: (604) 687-0067

#15
Welk's
Category: Department Store
Average price: Inexpensive
Area: Riley Park
Address: 3511 Main Street
Vancouver, BC V5V 3N4
Phone: (604) 873-3330

#16
Dilly Dally
Category: Toy Store
Average price: Modest
Area: Grandview-Woodlands, The Drive
Address: 1161 Commercial Drive
Vancouver, BC V5L 3X3
Phone: (604) 252-9727

#17
Community Thrift and Vintage
Category: Thrift Store
Average price: Inexpensive
Area: Downtown, Gastown
Address: 41 W Cordova Street
Vancouver, BC V6C 3N8
Phone: (604) 682-1004

#18
Dutil
Category: Men's Clothing, Women's Clothing
Average price: Expensive
Area: Downtown, Gastown
Address: 303 Cordova St W
Vancouver, BC V6B 1E5
Phone: (604) 688-8892

#19
Nice Shoes
Category: Shoe Store
Average price: Modest
Area: Kensington-Cedar Cottage
Address: 3568 Fraser St
Vancouver, BC V5V 4C6
Phone: (604) 558-3000

#20
Pacific Centre
Category: Shopping Center
Average price: Modest
Area: Downtown
Address: 701 Georgia Street W
Vancouver, BC V7Y 1G5
Phone: (604) 688-7235

#21
Deadly Couture
Category: Lingerie, Adult, Accessories
Average price: Modest
Area: Downtown
Address: 317A Cambie St
Vancouver, BC V6B 2N4
Phone: (604) 688-3766

#22
Pulpfiction Books
Category: Bookstore
Average price: Inexpensive
Area: Mount Pleasant
Address: 2422 Main St
Vancouver, BC V5T 3E2
Phone: (604) 876-4311

#23
Free Geek Vancouver
Category: Community Service, Computers, Tutoring Center
Average price: Inexpensive
Area: Grandview-Woodlands
Address: 1820 Pandora Street
Vancouver, BC V5L 1M5
Phone: (604) 879-4335

#24
Spool of Thread
Category: Fabric Store, Sewing & Alterations
Average price: Modest
Area: Mount Pleasant
Address: 649 E 15th Avenue
Vancouver, BC V5T 2R6
Phone: (604) 879-3031

#25
The Vancouver Pen Shop
Category: Office Equipment
Average price: Modest
Area: Downtown
Address: 512 Hastings Street W
Vancouver, BC V6B 1L6
Phone: (604) 681-1612

#26
Tanglewood Books
Category: Bookstore
Average price: Inexpensive
Area: Kitsilano
Address: 2306 Broadway W
Vancouver, BC V6J 1W6
Phone: (604) 736-8876

#27
Paper-Ya
Category: Cards & Stationery
Average price: Modest
Area: Granville Island/False Creek
Address: 9 - 1666 Johnston St
Vancouver, BC V6H 3S2
Phone: (604) 684-2531

#28
Barefoot Contessa
Category: Women's Clothing, Accessories
Average price: Modest
Area: Grandview-Woodlands, The Drive
Address: 1928 Commercial Dr
Vancouver, BC V5N 4A7
Phone: (604) 255-9035

#29
8th & Main
Category: Jewelry, Men's Clothing, Women's Clothing
Average price: Modest
Area: Mount Pleasant
Address: 2403 Main Street
Vancouver, BC V5T 3E1
Phone: (604) 559-5927

#30
ReFind
Category: Antiques, Furniture Store
Average price: Modest
Area: Riley Park
Address: 4609 Main Street
Vancouver, BC V5T 3B8
Phone: (778) 855-0969

#31
My Sister's Closet
Category: Used, Vintage
Average price: Inexpensive
Area: Downtown, Granville Entertainment District
Address: 1092 Seymour St
Vancouver, BC V6B 3M6
Phone: (604) 687-0770

#32
Goorin Bros.
Category: Accessories, Hats
Average price: Expensive
Area: Downtown, Yaletown
Address: 1188 Hamilton St
Vancouver, BC V6B 2S2
Phone: (604) 683-1895

#33
The Umbrella Shop
Category: Accessories
Average price: Modest
Area: Granville Island/False Creek
Address: 1550 Anderson Street
Vancouver, BC V6H 3Y5
Phone: (604) 697-0919

#34
Kimprints
Category: Home Decor, Gift Shop
Average price: Modest
Area: Downtown, Gastown
Address: 41 Powell St
Vancouver, BC V6A 1E9
Phone: (604) 685-0443

#35
John Fluevog
Category: Shoe Store
Average price: Expensive
Area: Downtown, Gastown
Address: 65 Water Street
Vancouver, BC V6B 1A1
Phone: (604) 688-6228

#36
The Cross Decor and Design
Category: Furniture Store, Interior Design
Average price: Expensive
Area: Downtown, Yaletown
Address: 1198 Homer Street
Vancouver, BC V6B 2X6
Phone: (604) 689-2900

#37
Ming Wo Cookware
Category: Kitchen & Bath
Average price: Modest
Area: Chinatown
Address: 23 E Pender St
Vancouver, BC V6A 1S9
Phone: (604) 683-7268

#38
Roden Gray
Category: Men's Clothing
Average price: Exclusive
Area: Downtown, Gastown
Address: 8 Water Street
Vancouver, BC V6B 1A4
Phone: (604) 689-7302

#39
Honey Gifts
Category: Lingerie, Adult
Average price: Modest
Area: South Cambie, Riley Park
Address: 3448 Cambie St
Vancouver, BC V5Z 2W8
Phone: (604) 708-8065

#40
Provide
Category: Home Decor
Average price: Expensive
Area: Downtown
Address: 529 Beatty Street
Vancouver, BC V6B 0G2
Phone: (604) 632-0095

#41
The lululemon Lab
Category: Sports Wear, Women's Clothing, Yoga
Average price: Expensive
Area: Fairview Slopes
Address: 511 W Broadway
Vancouver, BC V5Z 1E6
Phone: (604) 708-1126

#42
Nouvelle Nouvelle
Category: Fashion
Average price: Modest
Area: Downtown, Gastown
Address: 209 Abbott Street
Vancouver, BC V6B 2K7
Phone: (604) 682-2234

#43
Old Faithful Shop
Category: Home Decor
Average price: Expensive
Area: Downtown, Gastown
Address: 320 W Cordova Street
Vancouver, BC V6B 1E8
Phone: (778) 327-9376

#44
Blubird Clothing
Category: Women's Clothing
Average price: Expensive
Area: West End, Downtown
Address: 1055 Alberni St
Vancouver, BC V6E
Phone: (604) 257-0700

#45
Discount Foam & Furniture
Category: Furniture Store
Average price: Modest
Area: Sunset
Address: 6035 Fraser St
Vancouver, BC V5W 2Z8
Phone: (604) 324-2927

#46
Roots
Category: Fashion
Average price: Modest
Area: West End, Downtown
Address: 1001 Robson St
Vancouver, BC V6E 1A9
Phone: (604) 683-4305

#47
Revolucion
Category: Tobacco Shop, Accessories, Men's Clothing
Average price: Modest
Area: Downtown, Yaletown
Address: 1063 Mainland Street
Vancouver, BC V6B 5P9
Phone: (604) 662-4427

#48
Umbrella Shop
Category: Shopping Center
Average price: Expensive
Area: Downtown
Address: 526 Pender Street W
Vancouver, BC V6B 1V3
Phone: (604) 669-1707

Shops, Restaurants, Attractions & Nightlife / Vancouver Travel Guide

#49
Art Knapp
Category: Home Decor, Fashion
Average price: Modest
Area: Downtown
Address: 1401 Hornby Street
Vancouver, BC V6Z 1W8
Phone: (604) 662-3303

#50
Hitz Boutique
Category: Sports Wear,
Men's Clothing, Women's Clothing
Average price: Modest
Area: Downtown, Gastown
Address: 316 Cordova St W
Vancouver, BC V6B 1E8
Phone: (604) 662-3334

#51
Ultra-Love Products
Category: Lingerie, Adult
Average price: Modest
Area: West End
Address: 1151 Davie Street
Vancouver, BC V6E 1N2
Phone: (604) 687-2337

#52
Bird on a Wire Creations
Category: Jewelry, Gift Shop,
Home Decor
Average price: Modest
Area: Mount Pleasant
Address: 2535 Main Street
Vancouver, BC V5T 3E5
Phone: (604) 874-7415

#53
Much & Little
Category: Home Decor,
Women's Clothing
Average price: Modest
Area: Mount Pleasant
Address: 2541 Main Street
Vancouver, BC V5T 3E5
Phone: (604) 709-9034

#54
One Of A Few
Category: Jewelry, Women's Clothing
Average price: Expensive
Area: Downtown, Gastown
Address: 354 Water St
Vancouver, BC V6B 1B6
Phone: (604) 605-0685

#55
Van Caissey
Category: Accessories, Men's Clothing,
Women's Clothing
Average price: Modest
Area: Mount Pleasant
Address: 125 W Broadway
Vancouver, BC V5Y 1P4
Phone: (778) 228-8359

#56
Shine Consignment Clothing
Category: Used, Vintage,
Women's Clothing
Average price: Inexpensive
Area: Kitsilano
Address: 2970 Broadway W
Vancouver, BC V6K 2G8
Phone: (604) 738-0738

#57
Brooklyn Clothing
Category: Men's Clothing, Shoe Store
Average price: Expensive
Area: Downtown
Address: 418 Davie Street
Vancouver, BC V6B 2G3
Phone: (604) 683-2929

#58
New World Designs
Category: Women's Clothing,
Shoe Store
Average price: Modest
Area: Downtown, Gastown
Address: 306 Cordova Street W
Vancouver, BC V6B 1E8
Phone: (604) 687-3443

#59
Banyen Books & Sound
Category: Bookstore
Average price: Modest
Area: Kitsilano
Address: 3608 4th Avenue W
Vancouver, BC V6R 1P1
Phone: (604) 732-7912

#60
The Bay
Category: Department Store
Average price: Modest
Area: Downtown
Address: 674 Granville Street
Vancouver, BC V6C 1Z6
Phone: (604) 681-6211

#61
Costco Wholesale
Category: Home Decor, Appliances
Average price: Modest
Area: Downtown
Address: 605 Expo Blvd
Vancouver, BC V6B 1V4
Phone: (604) 622-5050

#62
Wonderbucks Wonderful Living
Category: Home Decor, Kitchen & Bath
Average price: Inexpensive
Area: Grandview-Woodlands, The Drive
Address: 1803 Commercial Dr
Vancouver, BC V5N 4A6
Phone: (604) 253-0515

#63
Dressew Supply
Category: Fabric Store
Average price: Inexpensive
Area: Downtown
Address: 337 W Hastings Street
Vancouver, BC V6B 1H6
Phone: (604) 682-6196

#64
Fine Finds Boutique
Category: Women's Clothing, Accessories, Gift Shop
Average price: Modest
Area: Downtown, Yaletown
Address: 1014 Mainland St
Vancouver, BC V6B 2T4
Phone: (604) 669-8325

#65
Salmagundi West
Category: Antiques, Home Decor
Average price: Modest
Area: Downtown, Gastown
Address: 321 Cordova Street W
Vancouver, BC V6B 1E5
Phone: (604) 681-4648

#66
Shop Cocoon
Category: Women's Clothing, Jewelry
Average price: Modest
Area: South Cambie, Riley Park
Address: 3345 Cambie Street
Vancouver, BC V5Z 2W6
Phone: (778) 232-8532

#67
Ace Cycles
Category: Bikes
Average price: Modest
Area: Kitsilano
Address: 3155 Broadway W
Vancouver, BC V6K 2H2
Phone: (604) 738-9818

#68
Vancouver Art Gallery Store
Category: Arts & Crafts, Jewelry, Newspapers & Magazines
Average price: Modest
Area: Downtown
Address: 750 Hornby Street
Vancouver, BC V6Z 2H7
Phone: (604) 662-4706

#69
Drexoll Games
Category: Toy Store, Hobby Shop
Average price: Modest
Area: Kitsilano
Address: 2860 W 4th Ave
Vancouver, BC V6K 1R2
Phone: (604) 733-6511

#70
Three Bags Full
Category: Arts & Crafts
Average price: Modest
Area: Riley Park
Address: 4458 Main St
Vancouver, BC V5V 3R3
Phone: (604) 874-9665

#71
Mountain Equipment Co-op
Category: Sporting Goods
Average price: Modest
Area: Mount Pleasant
Address: 130 Broadway W
Vancouver, BC V5Y 1P3
Phone: (604) 872-7858

#72
Scarlet
Category: Lingerie, Adult
Average price: Expensive
Area: Downtown
Address: 460 Granville St
Vancouver, BC V6C 1V4
Phone: (604) 605-1601

Shops, Restaurants, Attractions & Nightlife / Vancouver Travel Guide

#73
Oakridge Centre
Category: Shopping Center
Average price: Expensive
Area: Oakridge
Address: 650 41st Avenue W
Vancouver, BC V5Z 2M9
Phone: (604) 261-2511

#74
Forsya Boutique & Gallery
Category: Women's Clothing,
Art Gallery
Average price: Modest
Area: Mount Pleasant
Address: 2206 Main Street
Vancouver, BC V5T 3C7
Phone: (604) 568-8667

#75
Meadow Gifts and Apparel
Category: Gift Shop, Women's Clothing
Average price: Modest
Area: Downtown, Gastown
Address: 104 Water Street
Vancouver, BC V6B 1B2
Phone: (604) 620-5802

#76
Burcu's Angels
Category: Used, Vintage
Average price: Expensive
Area: Mount Pleasant, Riley Park
Address: 221 16th Ave E
Vancouver, BC V5T 2T5
Phone: (604) 874-1030

#77
Umeboshi Footwear
Category: Shoe Store
Average price: Expensive
Area: Riley Park
Address: 3638 Main St
Vancouver, BC V5V 3N5
Phone: (604) 909-8225

#78
Barefoot Contessa
Category: Accessories,
Women's Clothing
Average price: Modest
Area: Riley Park
Address: 3715 Main Street
Vancouver, BC V5V 3N8
Phone: (604) 879-1137

#79
Headphone Bar
Category: Electronics
Average price: Expensive
Area: Mount Pleasant
Address: 245 W Broadway
Vancouver, BC V5Y 1P5
Phone: (604) 569-0694

#80
Got Craft?
Category: Arts & Crafts
Average price: Inexpensive
Area: Grandview-Woodlands
Address: 1880 Triumph Street
Vancouver, BC V5L 4C3
Phone: (604) 628-2151

#81
Ride On Again Bikes
Category: Bikes
Average price: Modest
Area: Kitsilano
Address: 2255 Broadway W
Vancouver, BC V6K 2E4
Phone: (604) 736-7433

#82
Eye Candy Optical
Category: Optometrists,
Eyewear & Opticians
Average price: Modest
Area: Kitsilano
Address: 4th Avenue W
Vancouver, BC V6J 1M3
Phone: (604) 731-1956

#83
Long & McQuade
Category: Musical Instruments,
Electronics
Average price: Modest
Area: Strathcona
Address: 368 Terminal Avenue
Vancouver, BC V6A 3W9
Phone: (604) 734-4886

#84
Lynn Steven
Category: Women's Clothing
Average price: Expensive
Area: Downtown, Gastown
Address: 225 Carrall St
Vancouver, BC V6B 2J2
Phone: (604) 899-0808

Shops, Restaurants, Attractions & Nightlife / Vancouver Travel Guide

#85
BeautyMark
Category: Cosmetics & Beauty Supply, Skin Care, Makeup Artists
Average price: Modest
Area: Downtown, Yaletown
Address: 1268 Pacific Blvd
Vancouver, BC V6B 2S2
Phone: (604) 642-2294

#86
Plenty
Category: Women's Clothing, Men's Clothing
Average price: Modest
Area: West End
Address: 1107 Robson Street
Vancouver, BC V6E 1B5
Phone: (604) 689-4478

#87
Scout
Category: Women's Clothing
Average price: Expensive
Area: Mount Pleasant
Address: 152 E 8th Avenue
Vancouver, BC V5T 1R7
Phone: (604) 879-7903

#88
Winners
Category: Department Store
Average price: Modest
Area: Mount Pleasant
Address: 491 W 8th Ave
Vancouver, BC V5Y 3Z5
Phone: (604) 879-3701

#89
Independent Goldsmith
Category: Jewelry
Average price: Modest
Area: Fairview Slopes
Address: 555 12th Avenue W
Vancouver, BC V5Z 3X7
Phone: (604) 872-5330

#90
Malene Grotrian Designs
Category: Women's Clothing, Formal Wear
Average price: Expensive
Area: Downtown
Address: 207 W Hastings Street
Vancouver, BC V6B 1H7
Phone: (604) 568-0666

#91
Lace Embrace Atelier
Category: Women's Clothing, Lingerie, Bridal
Average price: Expensive
Area: Mount Pleasant, Riley Park
Address: 219 E 16th Avenue
Vancouver, BC V5T 2T5
Phone: (604) 737-1119

#92
Inform Interiors
Category: Furniture Store, Home Decor
Average price: Exclusive
Area: Downtown, Gastown
Address: 50 Water St
Vancouver, BC V6B 1A4
Phone: (604) 682-3868

#93
Gravity Pope Store
Category: Shoe Store
Average price: Expensive
Area: Kitsilano
Address: 2205 4th Avenue W
Vancouver, BC V6K 1N9
Phone: (604) 731-7673

#94
Anthropologie
Category: Furniture Store, Home Decor, Accessories
Average price: Expensive
Area: Fairview Slopes, South Granville
Address: 2912 Granville Street
Vancouver, BC V6H 3J7
Phone: (604) 734-2529

#95
Lunapads International
Category: Natural Feminine Hygiene Products
Average price: Modest
Area: Kensington-Cedar Cottage
Address: 3433 Commercial Street
Vancouver, BC V5N 4E8
Phone: (888) 590-2299

#96
L'atelier Home
Category: Home Decor
Average price: Modest
Area: Downtown, Gastown
Address: 452 W Cordova Street
Vancouver, BC V6B 4K2
Phone: (604) 684-9933

#97
Williams Sonoma
Category: Kitchen & Bath
Average price: Expensive
Area: Fairview Slopes, South Granville
Address: 2903 Granville St
Vancouver, BC V6H 3J6
Phone: (778) 330-2581

#98
City Square Shopping Centre
Category: Shopping Center
Average price: Modest
Area: Fairview Slopes
Address: 555 W 12th Avenue
Vancouver, BC V5Z 3X7
Phone: (604) 876-5165

#99
JQ Clothing
Category: Women's Clothing, Accessories, Jewelry
Average price: Inexpensive
Area: Grandview-Woodlands, The Drive
Address: 2120 Commercial Drive
Vancouver, BC V5N 4B4
Phone: (604) 215-7833

#100
Juillet Spa & Wedding
Category: Day Spa, Massage, Bridal
Average price: Modest
Area: Kitsilano
Address: 2525 Arbutus Street
Vancouver, BC V6J 4S2
Phone: (604) 736-2111

#101
Misch
Category: Accessories, Women's Clothing
Average price: Expensive
Area: Fairview Slopes, South Granville
Address: 2960 Granville St
Vancouver, BC V6H 3J7
Phone: (604) 731-1017

#102
Umbrella Shop
Category: Accessories
Average price: Modest
Area: Fairview Slopes
Address: 1106 Broadway W
Vancouver, BC V6H 1G5
Phone: (604) 669-9444

#103
Dollarama
Category: Discount Store
Average price: Inexpensive
Area: Downtown
Address: 668 Seymour St
Vancouver, BC V6B 3K4
Phone: (604) 662-7543

#104
Woo Vintage Clothing
Category: Used, Vintage, Men's Clothing, Women's Clothing
Average price: Expensive
Area: Riley Park
Address: 4393 Main Street
Vancouver, BC V5V 3P9
Phone: (604) 687-8200

#105
Yolo Repair
Category: Electronics Repair, Mobile Phones
Average price: Modest
Area: Downtown, Yaletown
Address: 1058 Mainland Street
Vancouver, BC V6B 2T4
Phone: (604) 558-1700

#106
Army & Navy
Category: Sporting Goods, Department Store
Average price: Inexpensive
Area: Gastown, Downtown Eastside
Address: 36 Cordova St W
Vancouver, BC V6B 1C9
Phone: (604) 682-6644

#107
Blim
Category: Art Supplies, Art School, Venues & Event Space
Average price: Modest
Area: Chinatown
Address: 115 Pender St E
Vancouver, BC V6A 1T6
Phone: (604) 872-8180

#108
Baaad Anna's
Category: Knitting Supplies
Average price: Modest
Area: Hastings-Sunrise
Address: 2667 E Hastings
Vancouver, BC V5K
Phone: (604) 255-2577

Shops, Restaurants, Attractions & Nightlife / Vancouver Travel Guide

---

#109
Bamboo Village Oriental FolkArt & Craft
Category: Antiques, Home Decor, Furniture Store
Average price: Modest
Area: Chinatown
Address: 135 Pender Street E
Vancouver, BC V6A 1T6
Phone: (604) 662-3300

#110
The Granville Island Toy
Category: Toy Store
Average price: Modest
Area: Granville Island/False Creek
Address: 1496 Cartwright Street
Vancouver, BC V6H 3Y5
Phone: (604) 684-0076

#111
Ayden Gallery
Category: Art Gallery
Average price: Modest
Area: Downtown
Address: 88 W Pender Street
Vancouver, BC V6B 6N9
Phone: (604) 376-6947

#112
Kids Market
Category: Shopping Center
Average price: Modest
Area: Granville Island/False Creek
Address: 1496 Cartwright St
Vancouver, BC V6H 3Y5
Phone: (604) 689-8447

#113
Eastside Vapes
Category: Tobacco Shop, Vape Shop
Average price: Modest
Area: Kensington-Cedar Cottage
Address: 1231 Kingsway Avenue
Vancouver, BC V5V 3E2
Phone: (604) 876-1117

#114
Purr Clothing
Category: Women's Clothing
Average price: Modest
Area: Kitsilano, Fairview Slopes
Address: 2928 Granville Street
Vancouver, BC V6J 3J7
Phone: (604) 742-9880

#115
Hermes
Category: Leather Goods
Average price: Exclusive
Area: West End, Downtown
Address: 755 Burrard Street
Vancouver, BC V6Z 1X6
Phone: (604) 681-9965

#116
Turnabout
Category: Used, Vintage, Accessories, Women's Clothing
Average price: Expensive
Area: Shaughnessy, South Granville
Address: 3109 Granville Street
Vancouver, BC V6H 3K1
Phone: (604) 734-5313

#117
The Perfume Shoppe
Category: Cosmetics & Beauty Supply
Average price: Exclusive
Area: Downtown
Address: 757 Hastings Street W
Vancouver, BC V6C 1A1
Phone: (604) 299-8463

#118
Urban Fare
Category: Specialty Food, Florist, Grocery
Average price: Expensive
Area: Downtown, Yaletown
Address: 177 Davie St
Vancouver, BC V6Z 2Y1
Phone: (604) 975-7550

#119
El Kartel
Category: Shoe Store, Men's Clothing, Women's Clothing
Average price: Expensive
Area: Downtown, Granville Entertainment District
Address: 1007 Granville Street
Vancouver, BC V6Z 1L2
Phone: (604) 683-2171

#120
Lazy Susan's
Category: Used, Vintage
Average price: Inexpensive
Area: Riley Park
Address: 3647 Main Street
Vancouver, BC V5V 3N6
Phone: (604) 873-9722

Shops, Restaurants, Attractions & Nightlife / Vancouver Travel Guide

#121
Walmart Supercentre
Category: Department Store, Grocery, Pharmacy
Average price: Inexpensive
Area: Renfrew-Collingwood
Address: 3585 Grandview Highway
Vancouver, BC V5M
Phone: (604) 435-6905

#122
Lee's Electronic Components
Category: Electronics
Average price: Inexpensive
Area: Riley Park
Address: 4522 Main Street
Vancouver, BC V5V 3R5
Phone: (604) 875-1993

#123
Beadworks
Category: Art Supplies, Jewelry
Average price: Modest
Area: Granville Island/False Creek
Address: 1666 Johnston St
Vancouver, BC V6H 3S2
Phone: (604) 682-2323

#124
Sikora's Classical Records
Category: Music & DVDs
Average price: Modest
Area: Downtown
Address: 432 Hastings St W
Vancouver, BC V6B 1L1
Phone: (604) 685-0625

#125
Hudson House Trading Company
Category: Department Store
Average price: Modest
Area: Downtown, Gastown
Address: 321 Water St
Vancouver, BC V6B 1B8
Phone: (604) 687-4781

#126
Restoration Hardware
Category: Home Decor, Furniture Store
Average price: Expensive
Area: Fairview Slopes, South Granville
Address: 2555 Granville Street
Vancouver, BC V6H 3G7
Phone: (604) 731-3918

#127
Two of Hearts Boutique
Category: Women's Clothing
Average price: Expensive
Area: Riley Park
Address: 3728 Main St
Vancouver, BC V5V 3N7
Phone: (604) 568-0998

#128
Room In Order
Category: Home Decor
Average price: Expensive
Area: West End
Address: 1055 Davie Street
Vancouver, BC V6E 1M5
Phone: (604) 684-8884

#129
Pineapple Repairs
Category: Electronics Repair, Mobile Phones
Average price: Inexpensive
Area: Downtown
Address: #25 - 601 W Cordova Street
Vancouver, BC V6B 1E1
Phone: (778) 889-7642

#130
F As In Frank
Category: Used, Vintage
Average price: Modest
Area: Mount Pleasant
Address: 2425 Main Street
Vancouver, BC V5T 3C9
Phone: (604) 568-5130

#131
WorkShop Salon
Category: Hair Salon, Barbers, Cosmetics & Beauty Supply
Average price: Expensive
Area: Downtown
Address: 522 Beatty Street
Vancouver, BC V6B 2L3
Phone: (604) 558-0299

#132
Mintage
Category: Used, Vintage, Men's Clothing, Women's Clothing
Average price: Modest
Area: Grandview-Woodlands, The Drive
Address: 1714 Commercial Drive
Vancouver, BC V5N 4A3
Phone: (604) 646-8243

#133
Value Village
Category: Thrift Store
Average price: Inexpensive
Area: Fraserview
Address: 6415 Victoria Dr
Vancouver, BC V5P 3X5
Phone: (604) 327-4434

#134
Moe's Home Collection
Category: Furniture Store, Home Decor, Interior Design
Average price: Modest
Area: Strathcona
Address: 1728 Glen Dr
Vancouver, BC V6A 4L5
Phone: (604) 687-5599

#135
Adhesif
Category: Women's Clothing
Average price: Modest
Area: Mount Pleasant
Address: 2202 Main St
Vancouver, BC V5T 3C7
Phone: (778) 231-4930

#136
Vancouver Art Gallery
Category: Museum, Art Gallery
Average price: Modest
Area: Downtown
Address: 750 Hornby Street
Vancouver, BC V6Z 2H7
Phone: (604) 662-4700

#137
Stepback
Category: Furniture Store, Antiques
Average price: Modest
Area: Kitsilano
Address: 2936 W Broadway
Vancouver, BC V6K 2G8
Phone: (604) 731-7525

#138
Vancouver Special
Category: Home Decor
Average price: Expensive
Area: Riley Park
Address: 3612 Main St
Vancouver, BC V5V
Phone: (604) 568-3673

#139
Ten Thousand Villages
Category: Home Decor, Jewelry, Musical Instruments
Average price: Modest
Area: Granville Island/False Creek
Address: 1660 Duranleau Street
Vancouver, BC V6H 3S4
Phone: (604) 633-0440

#140
Change Lingerie
Category: Lingerie
Average price: Modest
Area: Kitsilano
Address: 2815 W Broadway
Vancouver, BC V6K 2G6
Phone: (604) 742-0557

#141
Neptoon Records & CD's
Category: Music & DVDs
Average price: Modest
Area: Riley Park
Address: 3561 Main Street
Vancouver, BC V5V 3N4
Phone: (604) 324-1229

#142
Hill's of Kerrisdale
Category: Men's Clothing, Women's Clothing
Average price: Expensive
Area: Kerrisdale, Arbutus Ridge
Address: 2125 W 41st Ave
Vancouver, BC V6M 1Z3
Phone: (604) 266-9177

#143
Pulpfiction Books
Category: Bookstore
Average price: Modest
Area: Kitsilano
Address: 2754 Broadway W
Vancouver, BC V6K 2H2
Phone: (604) 873-4311

#144
Erin Templeton
Category: Leather Goods, Used, Vintage, Accessories
Average price: Modest
Area: Chinatown
Address: 511 Carrall St
Vancouver, BC V6B 2J8
Phone: (604) 682-2451

#145
All-Court Stringing Racquet Sports Store
Category: Sporting Goods, Tennis, Badminton
Average price: Modest
Area: Grandview-Woodlands
Address: 1217 Nanaimo Street
Vancouver, BC V5L 4T5
Phone: (778) 835-0672

#146
Holt Renfrew
Category: Department Store
Average price: Exclusive
Area: Downtown
Address: 737 Dunsmuir Street
Vancouver, BC V7Y 1K2
Phone: (604) 681-3121

#147
Golden Age Collectables
Category: Comic Books, Bookstore
Average price: Modest
Area: Downtown, Granville Entertainment District
Address: 852 Granville Street
Vancouver, BC V6Z 1K3
Phone: (604) 683-2819

#148
Parliament Interiors
Category: Interior Design, Home Decor
Average price: Expensive
Area: Downtown, Gastown
Address: 115 Water St
Vancouver, BC V6B
Phone: (604) 689-0800

#149
m0851
Category: Leather Goods
Average price: Exclusive
Area: West End, Downtown
Address: 1035 Alberni Street
Vancouver, BC V6E
Phone: (604) 688-9575

#150
The Sound Room
Category: Electronics
Average price: Expensive
Area: Kitsilano
Address: 2025 Broadway W
Vancouver, BC V6J 1Z6
Phone: (604) 736-7771

#151
Lola Home & Apparel
Category: Women's Clothing, Accessories, Home Decor, Lingerie
Average price: Expensive
Area: Downtown, Yaletown
Address: 1076 Hamilton St
Vancouver, BC V6B 2R9
Phone: (604) 633-5017

#152
The Block
Category: Women's Clothing, Men's Clothing
Average price: Expensive
Area: Downtown, Gastown
Address: 350 W Cordova St
Vancouver, BC V6B 1E8
Phone: (604) 685-8885

#153
Birks
Category: Jewelry
Average price: Expensive
Area: Downtown
Address: 698 Hastings St W
Vancouver, BC V6B 1P1
Phone: (604) 669-3333

#154
Valhalla Pure Outfitters
Category: Sporting Goods
Average price: Expensive
Area: Mount Pleasant
Address: 88 W Broadway
Vancouver, BC V5Y 1P2
Phone: (604) 872-8872

#155
Cigar Connoisseurs
Category: Tobacco Shop
Average price: Modest
Area: Downtown, Gastown
Address: 346 Water St
Vancouver, BC V6B 1B6
Phone: (604) 682-4427

#156
Book Warehouse
Category: Bookstore
Average price: Modest
Area: Fairview Slopes
Address: 632 W Broadway
Vancouver, BC V5Z 1G1
Phone: (604) 872-5711

Shops, Restaurants, Attractions & Nightlife / Vancouver Travel Guide

#157
Superbest Photos
Category: Photography Store
Average price: Inexpensive
Area: Downtown
Address: 925 W Georgia Street
Vancouver, BC V6C 3L2
Phone: (604) 682-2555

#158
Maiwa Supply
Category: Art Supplies, Knitting Supplies
Average price: Expensive
Area: Granville Island/False Creek
Address: 1663 Duranleau St
Vancouver, BC V6H
Phone: (604) 669-3939

#159
Pacific Boarder
Category: Sports Wear, Outdoor Gear
Average price: Expensive
Area: Fairview Slopes
Address: 1793 W 4th Avenue
Vancouver, BC V6J 1M2
Phone: (604) 734-7245

#160
Pallucci Furniture
Category: Furniture Store
Average price: Inexpensive
Area: Mount Pleasant
Address: 32 E Broadway
Vancouver, BC V5T 1V6
Phone: (604) 568-4855

#161
Salvatore Ferragamo
Category: Shoe Store, Accessories, Arts & Crafts, Women's Clothing
Average price: Exclusive
Area: Downtown
Address: 918 Robson St
Vancouver, BC V6Z 2E7
Phone: (604) 669-4495

#162
The Wildlife Thrift Store
Category: Thrift Store
Average price: Inexpensive
Area: Downtown, Granville Entertainment District
Address: 1295 Granville St
Vancouver, BC V6Z 1M5
Phone: (604) 682-0381

#163
Mayfair News
Category: Newspapers & Magazines
Average price: Modest
Area: Fairview Slopes, South Granville
Address: 1535 Broadway W
Vancouver, BC V6J 1W6
Phone: (604) 738-8951

#164
Lens & Shutter
Category: Photography Store
Average price: Expensive
Area: Kitsilano
Address: 2912 Broadway W
Vancouver, BC V6K 2G8
Phone: (604) 428-0838

#165
Homewerx
Category: Kitchen & Bath, Home Decor
Average price: Expensive
Area: West End
Address: 1053 Davie Street
Vancouver, BC V6E 1M5
Phone: (604) 682-2204

#166
West Point Cycles
Category: Bikes, Bike Rental
Average price: Expensive
Area: Point Grey
Address: 3771 10th Ave W
Vancouver, BC V6R 2G5
Phone: (604) 224-3536

#167
True Value Vintage Clothing
Category: Women's Clothing, Used, Vintage, Jewelry
Average price: Modest
Area: Riley Park
Address: 4578 Main Street
Vancouver, BC V5V 3R5
Phone: (604) 876-2218

#168
Tiny Finery
Category: Jewelry, Fashion
Average price: Modest
Area: Grandview-Woodlands
Address: 2162 E Hastings Street
Vancouver, BC V5L 1V2
Phone: (604) 569-2171

#169
Essentia Mattress
Category: Mattresses
Average price: Expensive
Area: Kitsilano
Address: 2144 West 4th Avenue
Vancouver, BC V6K 1N7
Phone: (604) 738-0321

#170
Vikings Dragons & Fairies
Category: Jewelry, Gift Shop
Average price: Modest
Area: Downtown
Address: 88 W Pender Street
Vancouver, BC V6B 6N9
Phone: (604) 569-0194

#171
Wishlist Boutique
Category: Cosmetics & Beauty Supply, Accessories, Gift Shop
Average price: Modest
Area: Kitsilano
Address: 2811 West Broadway
Vancouver, BC V6K 2G6
Phone: (604) 676-8070

#172
Pink Elephant Clothing
Category: Thrift Store
Average price: Inexpensive
Area: Grandview-Woodlands, The Drive
Address: 1748 Commercial Drive
Vancouver, BC V5N 4A3
Phone: (604) 568-0741

#173
MCC Thrift Furniture & Appliance Shop
Category: Thrift Store
Average price: Inexpensive
Area: Sunset
Address: 5914 Fraser Street
Vancouver, BC V5W 2Z7
Phone: (604) 325-1612

#174
Aritzia
Category: Accessories, Women's Clothing
Average price: Expensive
Area: West End
Address: 1110 Robson Street
Vancouver, BC V6E 1B2
Phone: (604) 684-3251

#175
Staccato Menswear
Category: Men's Clothing
Average price: Expensive
Area: Kitsilano
Address: 1842 - West 1st Ave
Vancouver, BC V6J 1G5
Phone: (604) 731-4343

#176
Wanderlust
Category: Bookstore, Luggage
Average price: Modest
Area: Kitsilano
Address: 1929 4th Ave W
Vancouver, BC V6J 1M7
Phone: (604) 739-2182

#177
Grand & Toy
Category: Office Equipment
Average price: Modest
Area: Downtown
Address: 595 Burrard St
Vancouver, BC V7X 1H3
Phone: (604) 408-3577

#178
Devil May Wear
Category: Women's Clothing, Accessories
Average price: Modest
Area: Riley Park
Address: 3957 Main Street
Vancouver, BC V5V 3P3
Phone: (604) 216-2515

#179
Rags & Dishes
Category: Kitchen & Bath
Average price: Modest
Area: Riley Park
Address: 4213 Main St
Vancouver, BC V5V 3P8
Phone: (604) 879-2592

#180
RollerGirl
Category: Shoe Store, Sports Wear
Average price: Expensive
Area: Mount Pleasant
Address: 185 E 11th Ave
Vancouver, BC V5T 2C1
Phone: (604) 708-8602

Shops, Restaurants, Attractions & Nightlife / Vancouver Travel Guide

---

#181
Zelen Shoes
Category: Shoe Store
Average price: Modest
Area: Downtown, Granville Entertainment District
Address: 894 Granville St
Vancouver, BC V6Z 1K3
Phone: (888) 699-3536

#182
Robin's Pharmacy
Category: Drugstore
Average price: Inexpensive
Area: Grandview-Woodlands, The Drive
Address: 908 Commercial Dr
Vancouver, BC V5L 3W7
Phone: (604) 876-3784

#183
The Rock Shop
Category: Fashion
Average price: Modest
Area: Downtown, Granville Entertainment District
Address: 1076 Granville St
Vancouver, BC V6Z 1L5
Phone: (604) 685-9228

#184
Outdoor Innovations
Category: Fabric Store
Average price: Modest
Area: Riley Park
Address: 1005 Kingsway Ave
Vancouver, BC V3C 6R8
Phone: (604) 873-6992

#185
Changes Clothing & Jewellery Bar
Category: Used, Vintage, Jewelry
Average price: Modest
Area: Point Grey
Address: 4454 10th Ave W
Vancouver, BC V6R 2H9
Phone: (604) 222-1505

#186
Model Express
Category: Shoe Store, Women's Clothing, Accessories
Average price: Inexpensive
Area: Downtown, Downtown Eastside
Address: 55 W Hastings Street
Vancouver, BC V6B 1G4
Phone: (604) 685-5052

#187
Zulu Records
Category: Music & DVDs
Average price: Modest
Area: Kitsilano
Address: 1972 4th Ave W
Vancouver, BC V6J 1M5
Phone: (604) 738-3232

#188
Louis Vuitton
Category: Leather Goods, Women's Clothing
Average price: Exclusive
Area: Downtown
Address: 730 Burrard St
Vancouver, BC V6C 2W6
Phone: (604) 696-9404

#189
Nicole Bridger
Category: Women's Clothing
Average price: Expensive
Area: Kitsilano
Address: 2151 W 4th Ave
Vancouver, BC V6K 4S2
Phone: (604) 730-1129

#190
Kirpal Appliances
Category: Appliances, Appliances & Repair
Average price: Modest
Area: Oakridge
Address:
Vancouver, BC V6M 2P8
Phone: (604) 324-7086

#191
Urban Yarns
Category: Specialty School, Arts & Crafts, Knitting Supplies
Average price: Expensive
Area: Point Grey
Address: 4437 West 10th Avenue
Vancouver, BC V6R 2H8
Phone: (604) 228-1122

#192
Tiffany & Company
Category: Jewelry
Average price: Exclusive
Area: Downtown
Address: 723 Burrard St
Vancouver, BC V6Z 2P1
Phone: (604) 630-1300

#193
Pebble
Category: Baby Gear & Furniture
Average price: Modest
Area: Kitsilano
Address: 2675 Arbutus Street
Vancouver, BC V6J 3Y4
Phone: (604) 568-6923

#194
Crate and Barrel
Category: Home & Garden
Average price: Expensive
Area: Oakridge
Address: 650 W 41st Avenue
Vancouver, BC V5Z 2M9
Phone: (604) 269-4300

#195
Barbara-Jo's Books to Cooks
Category: Bookstore, Cooking School
Average price: Modest
Area: Granville Island/False Creek
Address: 1740 2nd Ave W
Vancouver, BC V6J 1H6
Phone: (604) 688-6755

#196
VanCell
Category: Electronics Repair, Mobile Phones, Mobile Phone Repair
Average price: Modest
Area: Renfrew-Collingwood
Address: 3292 E 29th Avenue
Vancouver, BC V5R 1W6
Phone: (778) 859-3565

#197
DeSerres
Category: Home Decor, Art Supplies
Average price: Modest
Area: Renfrew-Collingwood
Address: 2811 Grandview Hwy
Vancouver, BC V5M 2E1
Phone: (604) 681-7351

#198
Kingsgate Mall
Category: Shopping Center
Average price: Inexpensive
Area: Mount Pleasant
Address: 370 Broadway E
Vancouver, BC V5T 4G5
Phone: (604) 665-3962

#199
YWCA Thrift Store
Category: Thrift Store
Average price: Inexpensive
Area: Riley Park
Address: 4399 Main St
Vancouver, BC V5V 3R1
Phone: (604) 675-9996

#200
L'Occitane en Provence
Category: Cosmetics & Beauty Supply
Average price: Expensive
Area: Downtown
Address: 755 Burrard St
Vancouver, BC V6Z 1X6
Phone: (604) 688-1198

#201
London Drugs
Category: Drugstore
Average price: Modest
Area: West End
Address: 1187 Robson Street
Vancouver, BC V6E 1B5
Phone: (604) 448-4819

#202
Opus Art Supplies
Category: Art Supplies
Average price: Modest
Area: Downtown
Address: 207 W Hastings Street
Vancouver, BC V6B 1H7
Phone: (604) 678-5889

#203
Signed Sealed Delivered
Category: Cards & Stationery
Average price: Modest
Area: Kitsilano
Address: 1988 4th Ave W
Vancouver, BC V6J 1M5
Phone: (604) 732-0020

#204
Strategies Games & Hobbies
Category: Hobby Shop, Toy Store
Average price: Modest
Area: Riley Park
Address: 3878 Main St
Vancouver, BC V5V 3N9
Phone: (604) 872-6911

Shops, Restaurants, Attractions & Nightlife / Vancouver Travel Guide

#205
The Travel Bug
Category: Bookstore
Average price: Modest
Area: Kitsilano
Address: 3065 Broadway W
Vancouver, BC V6K 2G9
Phone: (604) 737-1122

#206
International Diving Centre
Category: Diving, Sports Wear
Average price: Modest
Area: Kitsilano
Address: 2572 Arbutus Street
Vancouver, BC V6J 3Y2
Phone: (604) 736-2541

#207
SPCA Thrift Store
Category: Shopping
Average price: Inexpensive
Area: Kitsilano
Address: 3626 Broadway W
Vancouver, BC V6R 2B7
Phone: (604) 736-4136

#208
Lululemon Athletica
Category: Sports Wear, Women's Clothing, Yoga
Average price: Expensive
Area: Oakridge
Address: 650 W 41st Avenue
Vancouver, BC V5Z 2M9
Phone: (604) 677-1134

#209
Apple Store
Category: Electronics, Computers, Mobile Phones
Average price: Expensive
Area: Downtown
Address: 701 W Georgia St
Vancouver, BC V7Y 1G5
Phone: (778) 373-1800

#210
Used House of Vintage Fashion
Category: Used, Vintage
Average price: Modest
Area: Downtown, Granville Entertainment District
Address: 831 Granville Street
Vancouver, BC V6Z 1K7
Phone: (604) 694-0322

#211
NCIX
Category: Computers, Mobile Phones, IT Service& Computer Repair
Average price: Modest
Area: Fairview Slopes
Address: 1711 Broadway W
Vancouver, BC V6J 1Y2
Phone: (604) 739-9985

#212
The Victoria Lamp Shade Shop
Category: Home Decor
Average price: Modest
Area: Kitsilano
Address: 1926 W 4th Ave
Vancouver, BC V6J 1M5
Phone: (604) 733-4900

#213
Book'mark The Library Store
Category: Cards & Stationery, Bookstore
Average price: Modest
Area: Downtown
Address: 350 Georgia St W
Vancouver, BC V6B 6B1
Phone: (604) 331-4040

#214
International Village
Category: Shopping Center
Average price: Modest
Area: Downtown
Address: 88 Pender Street W
Vancouver, BC V6B 6N9
Phone: (604) 806-0799

#215
Twigg & Hottie
Category: Accessories, Women's Clothing
Average price: Expensive
Area: Riley Park
Address: 3671 Main Street
Vancouver, BC V5V 3N6
Phone: (604) 879-8595

#216
Arbutus Jewellers
Category: Jewelry, Watch Repair
Average price: Modest
Area: Kitsilano
Address: 4255 Arbutus Street
Vancouver, BC V6J 1Z1
Phone: (604) 676-2383

Shops, Restaurants, Attractions & Nightlife / Vancouver Travel Guide

#217
London Drugs
Category: Electronics, Drugstore
Average price: Modest
Area: Downtown Eastside
Address: 351 Abbott Street
Vancouver, BC V6B 0G6
Phone: (604) 448-4878

#218
Exhibit Apparel
Category: Men's Clothing
Average price: Modest
Area: Mount Pleasant
Address: 2601 Main St
Vancouver, BC V5T 3E7
Phone: (604) 727-5272

#219
Peking Lounge
Category: Furniture Store, Antiques
Average price: Expensive
Area: Chinatown
Address: 83 E Pender Street
Vancouver, BC V6A 1S9
Phone: (604) 844-1559

#220
Sasso Moda
Category: Women's Clothing
Average price: Expensive
Area: Downtown
Address: 595 W Georgia Street
Vancouver, BC V6B 2A3
Phone: (604) 689-1996

#221
Forever 21
Category: Fashion
Average price: Inexpensive
Area: West End, Downtown
Address: 1032 Robson Street
Vancouver, BC V6Z 2V7
Phone: (604) 687-2101

#222
Spank
Category: Shoe Store
Average price: Expensive
Area: Grandview-Woodlands, The Drive
Address: 1181 Commercial Drive
Vancouver, BC V5L 3Y2
Phone: (604) 568-1229

#223
Eddie's Hang-Up Display
Category: General Display Supplies
Average price: Modest
Area: Mount Pleasant
Address: 60 3rd Avenue W
Vancouver, BC V5Y 1E4
Phone: (604) 708-3100

#224
Silk Weaving Studio
Category: Arts & Crafts
Average price: Expensive
Area: Granville Island/False Creek
Address: 1531 Johnston St
Vancouver, BC V6H 3R9
Phone: (604) 687-7455

#225
Ride On Sports
Category: Bikes
Average price: Inexpensive
Area: Riley Park
Address: 3469 Main St
Vancouver, BC V5V 3M9
Phone: (604) 738-7734

#226
Humpty Dumpty Books & Music
Category: Bookstore, Toy Store
Average price: Modest
Area: Granville Island/False Creek
Address: 1496 Cartwright St
Vancouver, BC V6H 3Y5
Phone: (604) 683-7009

#227
Dollar Tree
Category: Department Store
Average price: Modest
Area: Sunset
Address: 6464 Fraser Street
Vancouver, BC V5W 3A4
Phone: (604) 321-4428

#228
Scratch Records
Category: Music & DVDs
Average price: Modest
Area: Downtown Eastside
Address: 1 E Hastings Street
Vancouver, BC V6A 1M9
Phone: (604) 687-6355

#229
Venetian Blind Service Centre
Category: Home Decor
Average price: Modest
Area: Mount Pleasant
Address: 331 7th Avenue W
Vancouver, BC V5Y 1M2
Phone: (604) 874-1121

#230
Quick Nickel
Category: Accessories,
Women's Clothing, Discount Store
Average price: Inexpensive
Area: West End
Address: 1778 Davie Street
Vancouver, BC V6G 1W2
Phone: (604) 689-8910

#231
Kites & Puppets Granville Island
Category: Toy Store
Average price: Modest
Area: Granville Island/False Creek
Address: 1496 Cartwright St
Vancouver, BC V6H 3Y5
Phone: (604) 685-9877

#232
UGG Australia
Category: Shoe Store
Average price: Expensive
Area: Fairview Slopes, South Granville
Address: 2633 Granville Street
Vancouver, BC V6H 3H2
Phone: (604) 245-0040

#233
Kestrel Books
Category: Bookstore
Average price: Inexpensive
Area: Kitsilano
Address: 3642 4th Ave W
Vancouver, BC V6R 1P1
Phone: (604) 872-2939

#234
Canucks Team Store
Category: Sports Wear
Average price: Modest
Area: Downtown
Address: 800 Griffiths Way
Vancouver, BC V6B 6G1
Phone: (604) 899-7590

#235
High Sun Mattress Factory & Furniture
Category: Furniture Store, Mattresses
Average price: Inexpensive
Area: Kensington-Cedar Cottage
Address: 2111 Kingsway
Vancouver, BC V5N 2T4
Phone: (604) 717-1198

#236
The Hach
Category: Cards & Stationery
Average price: Modest
Area: Riley Park
Address: 197 E 17th Avenue
Vancouver, BC V5V 1A5
Phone: (604) 566-9611

#237
Gam Gallery
Category: Art Gallery, Music Venues
Average price: Inexpensive
Area: Downtown Eastside
Address: 110 E Hastings Street
Vancouver, BC V6A 1N4
Phone: (778) 235-6928

#238
EQ3
Category: Furniture Store,
Interior Design
Average price: Modest
Area: Fairview Slopes, South Granville
Address: 2301 Granville Street
Vancouver, BC V6H 3G4
Phone: (604) 681-5155

#239
Hip Baby
Category: Children's Clothing, Toy Store
Average price: Expensive
Area: Kitsilano
Address: 2110 W 4th Avenue
Vancouver, BC V6K 1N6
Phone: (604) 736-8020

#240
Buchan's Kerrisdale Stationery
Category: Cards & Stationery, Gift Shop
Average price: Expensive
Area: Kerrisdale, Arbutus Ridge
Address: 2141 41st Avenue W
Vancouver, BC V6M 1Z6
Phone: (604) 261-8510

#241
Chong Lee Market
Category: Grocery, Personal Shopping
Average price: Modest
Area: Renfrew-Collingwood
Address: 3308 22nd Avenue E
Vancouver, BC V5M 2Z3
Phone: (604) 432-6880

#242
Photo Express
Category: Photography Store
Average price: Modest
Area: Oakridge
Address: 650 W 41st Avenue, Suite 626
Vancouver, BC V5Z 2N0
Phone: (604) 267-3324

#243
Lord's Shoes
Category: Shoe Store
Average price: Modest
Area: Fairview Slopes, South Granville
Address: 2932 Granville St
Vancouver, BC V6H 3J7
Phone: (604) 730-2914

#244
Lavan Body Mind & Soap
Category: Cosmetics & Beauty Supply
Average price: Expensive
Area: Downtown, Granville Entertainment District
Address: 840 Granville Street
Vancouver, BC V6Z 1K3
Phone: (604) 568-8807

#245
Limelight Video
Category: Videos, Video Game Rental
Average price: Inexpensive
Area: Point Grey
Address: 2505 Alma St
Vancouver, BC V6R 3R8
Phone: (604) 228-1478

#246
Shoppers Drug Mart
Category: Drugstore
Average price: Modest
Area: Fairview Slopes, South Cambie
Address: 3277 Cambie St
Vancouver, BC V5Z 2W3
Phone: (604) 708-9090

#247
Subdivision Clothing
Category: Men's Clothing
Average price: Exclusive
Area: Downtown, Gastown
Address: 2-306 Water St
Vancouver, BC V6B 1B6
Phone: (604) 662-8518

#248
Future Shop
Category: Electronics, Computers
Average price: Modest
Area: Fairview Slopes
Address: 1740 Broadway W
Vancouver, BC V6J 1Y1
Phone: (604) 739-3000

#249
Tierra Del Sol
Category: Clothing Store
Average price: Inexpensive
Area: Grandview-Woodlands, The Drive
Address: 2020 Commercial Dr
Vancouver, BC V5N 4A9
Phone: (604) 254-5188

#250
Fairmont Optical
Category: Eyewear & Opticians
Average price: Modest
Area: Fairview Slopes
Address: 812 W Broadway Avenue
Vancouver, BC V5Z 1J8
Phone: (604) 879-9401

#251
The Shop Vancouver
Category: Coffee & Tea, Men's Clothing
Average price: Expensive
Area: Chinatown
Address: 432 Columbia Street
Vancouver, BC V6A 3X3
Phone: (604) 568-7273

#252
Boudoir
Category: Women's Clothing
Average price: Expensive
Area: Downtown, Yaletown
Address: 1230 Hamilton Street
Vancouver, BC V6B 2S8
Phone: (604) 676-7281

#253
Public Myth
Category: Women's Clothing, Sports Wear
Average price: Modest
Area: Mount Pleasant
Address: 190 W 3rd Avenue
Vancouver, BC V5Y 1E9
Phone: (604) 737-8565

#254
St Moritz Watch Corporation
Category: Wholesale Store, Watches
Average price: Modest
Area: Fairview Slopes
Address: 1140 7th Ave W
Vancouver, BC V6H 1B4
Phone: (604) 734-2316

#255
Spank Clothing
Category: Fashion
Average price: Expensive
Area: Downtown, Granville Entertainment District
Address: 856 Granville St
Vancouver, BC V6Z 1K3
Phone: (604) 677-3202

#256
The Tux Store
Category: Bridal, Men's Clothing, Formal Wear
Average price: Modest
Area: Fairview Slopes
Address: 1393 W 6th Avenue
Vancouver, BC V6H 0B1
Phone: (604) 732-5868

#257
Club Monaco
Category: Men's Clothing, Women's Clothing, Accessories
Average price: Expensive
Area: West End, Downtown
Address: 1034 Robson St
Vancouver, BC V6E 1A7
Phone: (604) 687-8618

#258
Doctor Vigari Gallery
Category: Art Gallery
Average price: Expensive
Area: Grandview-Woodlands, The Drive
Address: 1816 Commercial Dr
Vancouver, BC V5N 4A5
Phone: (604) 255-9513

#259
Santoku Equipment Office
Category: Kitchen & Bath
Average price: Expensive
Area: Downtown, Yaletown
Address: 1118 Homer St
Vancouver, BC V6B 6L5
Phone: (604) 568-7660

#260
Lee Valley Tools
Category: Hardware Store, Hobby Shop
Average price: Modest
Area: Sunset
Address: 1180 SE Marine Dr
Vancouver, BC V5X 2V6
Phone: (604) 261-2262

#261
Atex Fabrics
Category: Fabric Store
Average price: Inexpensive
Area: Downtown, Downtown Eastside
Address: 150 Hastings St W
Vancouver, BC V6B 1G8
Phone: (604) 669-3455

#262
Dream Apparel & Articles for People
Category: Women's Clothing, Accessories
Average price: Expensive
Area: Downtown, Gastown
Address: 356 Water Street
Vancouver, BC V6B 4Y2
Phone: (604) 683-7326

#263
Dollarama
Category: Discount Store
Average price: Inexpensive
Area: Kensington-Cedar Cottage
Address: 2201 Kingsway
Vancouver, BC V5N 5A1
Phone: (604) 430-1508

#264
West Coast Sports
Category: Outdoor Gear
Average price: Modest
Area: Fairview Slopes
Address: 1675 4th Avenue W
Vancouver, BC V6J 1L8
Phone: (604) 732-4810

#265
Red Rose Antiques
Category: Antiques, Furniture Store
Average price: Modest
Area: Riley Park
Address: 4285 Main St
Vancouver, BC V5V 3P8
Phone: (604) 875-8588

#266
Beauty Bar
Category: Cosmetics & Beauty Supply
Average price: Expensive
Area: Kitsilano
Address: 2142 W 4th Ave
Vancouver, BC V6K 1N6
Phone: (604) 733-9000

#267
Inhabit Interiors
Category: Home Decor
Average price: Expensive
Area: Downtown, Yaletown
Address: 1188 Hamilton Street
Vancouver, BC V6B 2S2
Phone: (604) 662-7408

#268
Lonsdale Leather
Category: Leather Goods
Average price: Modest
Area: Mount Pleasant
Address: 32 5th Avenue W
Vancouver, BC V5Y 1H5
Phone: (604) 873-6556

#269
Superior Dollar Store
Category: Discount Store
Average price: Inexpensive
Area: Kensington-Cedar Cottage
Address: 2637 Commercial Drive
Vancouver, BC V5N 4C3
Phone: (604) 879-3196

#270
H&M
Category: Men's Clothing, Women's Clothing
Average price: Modest
Area: Downtown
Address: 609 Granville St
Vancouver, BC V7Y 1G5
Phone: (604) 692-0308

#271
The Hang Out Place
Category: Home Decor
Average price: Modest
Area: Granville Island/False Creek
Address: 1652 Duranleau St
Vancouver, BC V6H 3S4
Phone: (604) 623-3477

#272
Vincent Park
Category: Women's Clothing, Accessories
Average price: Modest
Area: Riley Park
Address: 4278 Main St
Vancouver, BC V5V
Phone: (604) 879-6665

#273
Vancouver Telescope Centre
Category: Hobby Shop
Average price: Modest
Area: Fairview Slopes
Address: 2580 Burrard Street
Vancouver, BC V6J 3J7
Phone: (604) 737-4303

#274
Nineteen Ten
Category: Home & Garden
Average price: Modest
Area: Riley Park
Address: 4366 Main Street
Vancouver, BC V5V 3R1
Phone: (604) 558-0210

#275
Executive Hotel Vintage Park
Category: Shopping, Hotel
Average price: Modest
Area: Downtown
Address: 1379 Howe St
Vancouver, BC V6Z 1R7
Phone: (604) 688-7678

#276
iRepair
Category: Electronics Repair, Mobile Phones, Mobile Phone Repair
Average price: Modest
Area: Downtown
Address: 88 W Pender Street, Unit 2115
Vancouver, BC V6B 6N9
Phone: (778) 987-2571

#277
Shoppers Drug Mart
Category: Drugstore
Average price: Modest
Area: Downtown, Granville Entertainment District
Address: 1295 Seymour St
Vancouver, BC V6B 3N6
Phone: (604) 801-5708

#278
Safeway
Category: Deli, Drugstore, Grocery
Average price: Modest
Area: West End
Address: 1766 Robson Street
Vancouver, BC V6G 1E2
Phone: (604) 683-6155

#279
Freybe Factory Outlets
Category: Outlet Store, Meat Shop
Average price: Inexpensive
Area: Grandview-Woodlands
Address: 1927 Hastings St E
Vancouver, BC V5L 1T5
Phone: (604) 255-6922

#280
Running Room
Category: Sports Wear
Average price: Expensive
Area: Fairview Slopes
Address: 2317 Cambie Street
Vancouver, BC V5Z 2T9
Phone: (604) 558-0093

#281
Courtney Boutique
Category: Accessories, Women's Clothing
Average price: Modest
Area: Kerrisdale, Arbutus Ridge
Address: 2184 W 41st Avenue
Vancouver, BC V6M 1Z1
Phone: (604) 261-7633

#282
Bed
Category: Home Decor
Average price: Expensive
Area: Kitsilano
Address: 2907 W Broadway
Vancouver, BC V6K 2G6
Phone: (604) 736-3482

#283
Salvation Army Thrift Store
Category: Thrift Store
Average price: Inexpensive
Area: Marpole
Address: 8384 Granville Street
Vancouver, BC V6P
Phone: (604) 267-4942

#284
Why Knot's Curiosities
Category: Fashion
Average price: Expensive
Area: Downtown, Gastown
Address: 319 Cambie Street
Vancouver, BC V6B 2N4
Phone: (604) 669-2565

#285
The Boardroom Snowboard Shop
Category: Sporting Goods
Average price: Modest
Area: Fairview Slopes
Address: 1745 4th Ave W
Vancouver, BC V6J 1M2
Phone: (604) 734-7669

#286
Fresh Out
Category: Women's Clothing
Average price: Modest
Area: Mount Pleasant, Strathcona
Address: 336 E 1 Ave
Vancouver, BC V5T 4R6
Phone: (778) 928-5959

#287
Carson Books & Records
Category: Bookstore, Vinyl Records
Average price: Inexpensive
Area: Dunbar-Southlands
Address: 4275 Dunbar St
Vancouver, BC V6S 2G1
Phone: (604) 222-8787

#288
Wander
Category: Home Decor, Furniture Store
Average price: Modest
Area: Grandview-Woodlands, The Drive
Address: 1146 Commercial Drive
Vancouver, BC V5L 3X2
Phone: (604) 253-1711

#289
Amy's Jr Loonie Toonie Town
Category: Discount Store
Average price: Inexpensive
Area: West End
Address: 1050 Davie St
Vancouver, BC V6E 1M3
Phone: (604) 682-2033

#290
Harry Rosen Gentleman's Apparel
Category: Men's Clothing
Average price: Expensive
Area: Oakridge
Address: 650 41st Avenue W
Vancouver, BC V5Z 2M9
Phone: (604) 266-1172

#291
The House of McLaren
Category: Gift Shop, Candy Store, Fashion
Average price: Modest
Area: Downtown, Gastown
Address: 131 Water St
Vancouver, BC V6B 4M3
Phone: (604) 681-5442

#292
Dare to Wear
Category: Adult, Lingerie
Average price: Modest
Area: Downtown, Granville Entertainment District
Address: 1028 Granville St
Vancouver, BC V6Z 1L5
Phone: (604) 801-5482

#293
Splash Toy Shop
Category: Children's Clothing, Toy Store, Flowers & Gifts
Average price: Modest
Area: Dunbar-Southlands
Address: 4243 Dunbar Street
Vancouver, BC V6S 2G1
Phone: (604) 228-8697

#294
DeSerres
Category: Arts & Crafts
Average price: Modest
Area: Fairview Slopes, South Granville
Address: 1431 W Broadway
Vancouver, BC V6J 5L1
Phone: (604) 733-1331

#295
Chapters
Category: Bookstore
Average price: Modest
Area: Fairview Slopes, South Granville
Address: 2505 Granville St
Vancouver, BC V6H 3G7
Phone: (604) 731-7822

#296
One Stop Shop Cards and Games
Category: Hobby Shop, Videos, Video Game Rental
Average price: Modest
Area: Downtown
Address: 88 Pender Street W
Vancouver, BC V6B 6N6
Phone: (778) 373-0365

#297
City Square
Category: Shopping Center
Average price: Modest
Area: Fairview Slopes
Address: 555 12th Ave W
Vancouver, BC V5Z 3X7
Phone: (604) 872-5254

#298
Oliver and Lilly's
Category: Women's Clothing
Average price: Expensive
Area: Fairview Slopes, South Granville
Address: 1575 W 6th Avenue
Vancouver, BC V6J 2B5
Phone: (604) 736-7774

#299
Blumen
Category: Florist
Average price: Modest
Area: Mount Pleasant
Address: 438 W 8th Avenue
Vancouver, BC V5Y 1N7
Phone: (604) 708-0882

#300
Peekaboo Baby Boutique
Category: Children's Clothing
Average price: Expensive
Area: Dunbar-Southlands
Address: 4229 Dunbar Street
Vancouver, BC V6S 2G1
Phone: (604) 228-0804

#301
Kaboodles Toy Store
Category: Toy Store
Average price: Expensive
Area: South Cambie, Riley Park
Address: 3404 Cambie St
Vancouver, BC V5Y 2A9
Phone: (604) 558-1117

#302
Murata Japanese Tableware & Gifts
Category: Kitchen & Bath
Average price: Modest
Area: Mount Pleasant
Address: 15 Broadway E
Vancouver, BC V5T 1V4
Phone: (604) 874-1777

#303
Pedal Bike Depot
Category: Bikes
Average price: Modest
Area: Mount Pleasant
Address: 1830 Ontario Street
Vancouver, BC V5T 2W6
Phone: (604) 708-4992

#304
Show Off
Category: Women's Clothing
Average price: Modest
Area: Riley Park
Address: 3712 Main St
Vancouver, BC V5V 3N7
Phone: (604) 677-5377

#305
Samson Tailors
Category: Men's Clothing, Sewing & Alterations
Average price: Modest
Area: Downtown, Granville Entertainment District
Address: 1240 Seymour Street
Vancouver, BC V6B 6J3
Phone: (604) 682-7848

#306
Image Optometry
Category: Optometrists, Eyewear & Opticians
Average price: Inexpensive
Area: Fairview Slopes
Address: 716 West Broadway
Vancouver, BC V5Z 1G8
Phone: (604) 310-3937

#307
Sweet Scents Floral Design
Category: Florist
Average price: Expensive
Area: Point Grey
Address: 3714 W 10th Avenue
Vancouver, BC V6R 2G7
Phone: (604) 222-3331

#308
The Art of Loving
Category: Adult
Average price: Expensive
Area: Kitsilano
Address: 1819 W 5th Avenue
Vancouver, BC V6J 1P5
Phone: (604) 742-9988

#309
Make at Granville Island
Category: Arts & Crafts, Men's Clothing, Women's Clothing
Average price: Modest
Area: Granville Island/False Creek
Address: 1648 Duranleau St
Vancouver, BC V6H 3S4
Phone: (604) 684-5105

#310
The New Eclectic
Category: Home Decor
Average price: Expensive
Area: Fairview Slopes, South Granville
Address: 2329 Granville St
Vancouver, BC V6H 3G4
Phone: (604) 733-9797

#311
Urban Outfitters
Category: Men's Clothing, Women's Clothing, Shoe Store
Average price: Modest
Area: Downtown, Granville Entertainment District
Address: 830 Granville St
Vancouver, BC V6Z 1K3
Phone: (604) 685-1970

#312
Legends Retro-Fashion
Category: Used, Vintage, Costumes
Average price: Inexpensive
Area: Riley Park
Address: 4366 Main St
Vancouver, BC V5V 3P9
Phone: (604) 875-0621

#313
Studio FX
Category: Cosmetics & Beauty Supply
Average price: Expensive
Area: Downtown
Address: 925 W Georgia Street
Vancouver, BC V6C 3L2
Phone: (604) 685-5509

#314
Harry Rosen Gentleman's Apparel
Category: Fashion for Men
Average price: Exclusive
Area: Downtown
Address: 701 W Georgia St
Vancouver, BC V7Y 1K8
Phone: (604) 683-6861

#315
Vancouver Chinatown Night Market
Category: Specialty Food
Average price: Inexpensive
Area: Chinatown, Strathcona
Address: Keefer St & Main St
Vancouver, BC V6A
Phone: (604) 682-8998

#316
Flowerz
Category: Flowers & Gifts
Average price: Expensive
Area: Kitsilano
Address: 2883 W Broadway
Vancouver, BC V6J 5L1
Phone: (604) 742-1000

#317
Bisou Bridal
Category: Women's Clothing, Bridal
Average price: Exclusive
Area: Mount Pleasant
Address: 440 W 2nd Avenue
Vancouver, BC V5Y 1E2
Phone: (604) 696-0880

#318
Half Moon Bookstore
Category: Bookstore, Comic Books
Average price: Modest
Area: Marpole
Address: 519 Marine Drive SW
Vancouver, BC V6P 5X8
Phone: (604) 301-9075

#319
Obsessions
Category: Cards & Stationery
Average price: Expensive
Area: Downtown
Address: 595 Howe Street
Vancouver, BC V6C 2T5
Phone: (604) 633-0091

#320
Payless ShoeSource
Category: Shoe Store
Average price: Modest
Area: Downtown, Granville Entertainment District
Address: 804 Granville St
Vancouver, BC V6Z
Phone: (604) 683-4894

#321
Adidas Vancouver Heritage Store
Category: Sports Wear
Average price: Expensive
Area: Downtown, Granville Entertainment District
Address: 848 Granville St
Vancouver, BC V6Z 1K3
Phone: (778) 371-9117

#322
Cocoon Home Designs
Category: Furniture Store, Interior Design
Average price: Modest
Area: Mount Pleasant
Address: 75 7th Ave W
Vancouver, BC V5Y 1L4
Phone: (604) 708-1174

#323
Ming Wo Cookware
Category: Kitchen & Bath
Average price: Modest
Area: Kitsilano
Address: 2170 4th Ave W
Vancouver, BC V6K 1N6
Phone: (604) 737-2624

#324
Turnabout Consignment
Category: Used, Vintage
Average price: Modest
Area: Kitsilano
Address: 3112 W Broadway
Vancouver, BC V6K 2H1
Phone: (604) 731-7762

#325
Boboli
Category: Accessories,
Women's Clothing, Men's Clothing
Average price: Exclusive
Area: Fairview Slopes, South Granville
Address: 2776 Granville Street
Vancouver, BC V6H 3J3
Phone: (604) 257-2300

#326
Mr Mattress
Category: Mattresses
Average price: Modest
Area: Grandview-Woodlands
Address: 1315 Venables Street
Vancouver, BC V5L 2G1
Phone: (604) 255-2113

#327
Beijing Trading Company
Category: Health Food Store
Average price: Modest
Area: Chinatown
Address: 89 E Pender St
Vancouver, BC V6A 1S9
Phone: (604) 684-3563

#328
Gandy's Home Hardware Store
Category: Hardware Store
Average price: Modest
Area: Kitsilano
Address: 2262 W 4th Ave
Vancouver, BC V6K 1N8
Phone: (604) 733-8014

#329
Kissing Crows Cyclery
Category: Bike Rental, Bikes
Average price: Exclusive
Area: Riley Park
Address: 4562 Main Street
Vancouver, BC V5V 3R4
Phone: (604) 872-5477

#330
Murale
Category: Cosmetics & Beauty Supply
Average price: Expensive
Area: Oakridge
Address: 650 West 41st Avenue
Vancouver, BC V5Z 2M9
Phone: (604) 264-8035

#331
Home Hardware Store
Category: Hardware Store
Average price: Modest
Area: Grandview-Woodlands, The Drive
Address: 1575 Commercial Dr
Vancouver, BC V5L 3Y1
Phone: (604) 253-1747

#332
Blue Sky Clothing Company
Category: Women's Clothing
Average price: Modest
Area: Grandview-Woodlands, The Drive
Address: 1312 Commercial Drive
Vancouver, BC V5L
Phone: (604) 566-9976

#333
Little Earth Children's Store
Category: Children's Clothing,
Toy Store, Used, Vintage
Average price: Inexpensive
Area: Grandview-Woodlands, The Drive
Address: 1020 Commercial Drive
Vancouver, BC V5L 3W9
Phone: (778) 737-7004

#334
Circle Craft Co-Operative Shop & Gallery
Category: Art Gallery, Art Supplies
Average price: Expensive
Area: Granville Island/False Creek
Address: 1666 Johnston St
Vancouver, BC V6H 3S2
Phone: (604) 669-8021

#335
Albion Books
Category: Bookstore, Music & DVDs
Average price: Modest
Area: Downtown
Address: 523 Richards St
Vancouver, BC V6B 2Z5
Phone: (604) 662-3113

#336
Sports Junkies
Category: Bikes, Outdoor Gear,
Sports Wear
Average price: Modest
Area: Mount Pleasant
Address: 102 Broadway W
Vancouver, BC V5Y 1P3
Phone: (604) 879-6000

#337
Kali
Category: Accessories, Women's Clothing
Average price: Modest
Area: Grandview-Woodlands, The Drive
Address: 1000 Commercial Dr
Vancouver, BC V5L 3W9
Phone: (604) 215-4568

#338
Running Room
Category: Sporting Goods, Shoe Store
Average price: Modest
Area: West End
Address: 679 Denman St
Vancouver, BC V6G 2L3
Phone: (604) 684-9771

#339
Tenth & Proper Boutique
Category: Women's Clothing
Average price: Expensive
Area: Point Grey
Address: 4483 10th Avenue W
Vancouver, BC V6R 2H8
Phone: (604) 222-1115

#340
Denman Place Mall
Category: Shopping Center
Average price: Inexpensive
Area: West End
Address: 1030 Denman St
Vancouver, BC V6G 2M6
Phone: (604) 684-9254

#341
Beansprouts
Category: Children's Clothing, Used, Vintage
Average price: Modest
Area: Riley Park
Address: 4305 Main Street
Vancouver, BC V5V 3R1
Phone: (604) 871-9782

#342
Tees
Category: Men's Clothing, Women's Clothing
Average price: Modest
Area: Downtown, Gastown
Address: 227 Abbott Street
Vancouver, BC V6B 2K7
Phone: (604) 738-0654

#343
RowanSky
Category: Leather Goods, Shoe Store, Accessories
Average price: Expensive
Area: Downtown, Gastown
Address: 334 Cordova St W
Vancouver, BC V6B 1E8
Phone: (604) 568-2075

#344
New Vintage Kicks
Category: Shoe Store, Men's Clothing
Average price: Expensive
Area: Downtown, Yaletown
Address: 1028 Hamilton St
Vancouver, BC V6B
Phone: (778) 858-4665

#345
Abantu Beauty Products
Category: Wigs, Cosmetics, Beauty Supply
Average price: Expensive
Area: Killarney
Address: 3596 Kingsway
Vancouver, BC V5R 5L7
Phone: (604) 431-8008

#346
Wee Ones Reruns
Category: Children's Clothing, Used, Vintage
Average price: Modest
Area: Mount Pleasant
Address: 612 Kingsway
Vancouver, BC V5T 3K4
Phone: (604) 708-0956

#347
Canterbury Tales Bookstore
Category: Bookstore
Average price: Modest
Area: Grandview-Woodlands, The Drive
Address: 2010 Commercial Drive
Vancouver, BC V5N 4A9
Phone: (604) 568-3511

#348
Canucks Playoff Team Store
Category: Sports Wear
Average price: Expensive
Area: Downtown
Address: 653 Robson Street
Vancouver, BC V6B 5J3
Phone: (604) 662-8583

#349
Change
Category: Lingerie
Average price: Modest
Area: Mount Pleasant
Address: 2358 Cambie Street
Vancouver, BC V5Z
Phone: (604) 873-1056

#350
Halfmoon Yoga Products
Category: Sporting Goods, Yoga
Average price: Expensive
Area: Mount Pleasant
Address: Vancouver, BC V5Y 1E9
Phone: (604) 731-7099

#351
Della Optique
Category: Optometrists,
Eyewear & Opticians
Average price: Expensive
Area: Kitsilano
Address: 2589 Broadway W
Vancouver, BC V6K 2E9
Phone: (604) 742-3937

#352
Dream Designs
Category: Kitchen & Bath, Sports Wear
Average price: Expensive
Area: Grandview-Woodlands, The Drive
Address: 956 Commercial Drive
Vancouver, BC V5L
Phone: (604) 254-5012

#353
Biz Books Film & Theatre Store
Category: Computers, Bookstore
Average price: Modest
Area: Gastown, Downtown Eastside
Address: Vancouver, BC V6B 1E8
Phone: (604) 669-6431

#354
Mavi Jeans
Category: Women's Clothing,
Men's Clothing
Average price: Modest
Area: Kitsilano
Address: 2112 4th Ave W
Vancouver, BC V6K 1N6
Phone: (604) 738-6284

#355
Aqua La Vie En Rose
Category: Sports Wear,
Women's Clothing, Lingerie
Average price: Modest
Area: Kitsilano
Address: 2127 4th Ave W
Vancouver, BC V6K 1N7
Phone: (778) 328-9840

#356
Tinland Cookware
Category: Kitchen & Bath
Average price: Inexpensive
Area: Chinatown
Address: 260 E Pender Street
Vancouver, BC V6A 1T7
Phone: (604) 608-0787

#357
Finlandia Natural Pharmacy
Category: Health & Medical, Drugstore
Average price: Modest
Area: Fairview Slopes
Address: 1111 W Broadway
Vancouver, BC V6H 1G1
Phone: (604) 733-5323

#358
Winners
Category: Women's Clothing,
Men's Clothing
Average price: Modest
Area: Downtown
Address: 798 Granville St
Vancouver, BC V6Z 3C3
Phone: (604) 683-1058

#359
Laurel Prescriptions
Category: Drugstore
Average price: Expensive
Area: Fairview Slopes
Address: 888 8th Avenue W
Vancouver, BC V5Z 3Y1
Phone: (604) 873-5511

#360
Lely's Books Etc
Category: Music & DVDs,
Bookstore, Toy Store
Average price: Inexpensive
Area: Mount Pleasant
Address: 370 E Broadway
Vancouver, BC V5T 4G5
Phone: (604) 873-5277

#361
J76 Casual Wear
Category: Accessories, Women's Clothing
Average price: Modest
Area: West End
Address: 1188 Robson Street
Vancouver, BC V6E 1B2
Phone: (604) 685-8899

#362
Bestbuy99
Category: Electronics, Computers
Average price: Inexpensive
Area: Kensington-Cedar Cottage
Address: 1980 E39 Avenue
Vancouver, BC V5P 1H4
Phone: (604) 688-2366

#363
Planet Bingo
Category: Hobby Shop, Casino
Average price: Inexpensive
Area: Mount Pleasant
Address: 2655 Main St
Vancouver, BC V5T 3E7
Phone: (604) 879-8930

#364
Icebreaker TouchLab
Category: Sports Wear, Men's Clothing
Average price: Expensive
Area: Kitsilano
Address: 2089 W 4th Avenue
Vancouver, BC V6J 1N3
Phone: (778) 329-2710

#365
The Granville Island Toy Company
Category: Toy Store
Average price: Modest
Area: Riley Park
Address: 3298 Main Street
Vancouver, BC V5V 3M5
Phone: (604) 875-0065

#366
Joe Fresh Style
Category: Fashion
Average price: Inexpensive
Area: Downtown
Address: 540 Granville Street
Vancouver, BC V6C 1W6
Phone: (604) 681-4200

#367
Gallery of British Columbia Ceramics
Category: Arts & Crafts
Average price: Modest
Area: Granville Island/False Creek
Address: 1359 Cartwright St
Vancouver, BC V6H 3R7
Phone: (604) 669-3606

#368
Rexall
Category: Drugstore, Convenience Store
Average price: Modest
Area: Downtown
Address: 88 W Pender Street
Vancouver, BC V6B 6N9
Phone: (604) 683-4244

#369
Camelot Kids
Category: Toy Store
Average price: Modest
Area: Granville Island/False Creek
Address: 1496 Cartwright St
Vancouver, BC V6H 3Y5
Phone: (604) 688-9766

#370
West Elm
Category: Home Decor
Average price: Modest
Area: Fairview Slopes, South Granville
Address: 2947 Granville Street
Vancouver, BC V6H 1P1
Phone: (604) 733-6730

#371
Fast Frames
Category: Home Decor, Framing
Average price: Expensive
Area: West End
Address: 999 Denman St
Vancouver, BC V6G 2M3
Phone: (604) 688-7335

#372
Adrenaline Professional Body Piercing & Tattoos
Category: Tattoo, Piercing, Fashion
Average price: Modest
Area: Kitsilano
Address: 1926 4th Ave W
Vancouver, BC V6J 1M5
Phone: (604) 734-8282

#373
Northern Feather Dream Makers
Category: Furniture Store
Average price: Expensive
Area: Fairview Slopes
Address: 1750 Broadway W
Vancouver, BC V6J 1Y1
Phone: (604) 736-7233

#374
Showcase
Category: Outdoor Gear
Average price: Modest
Area: Fairview Slopes
Address: 1766 W 4th Ave
Vancouver, BC V6J 1M1
Phone: (604) 731-6449

#375
Vata Brasil
Category: Sports Wear
Average price: Modest
Area: Downtown
Address: 88 West Pender
Vancouver, BC V6B 6N9
Phone: (604) 689-7325

#376
Luksus Diamonds
Category: Jewelry
Average price: Expensive
Area: Downtown
Address: 719-602 W Hastings Street
Vancouver, BC V6B 1P2
Phone: (604) 569-3001

#377
Frocks Modern Bridesmaids
Category: Women's Clothing, Bridal
Average price: Expensive
Area: Riley Park
Address: 4814 Fraser Street
Vancouver, BC V5V 4H4
Phone: (604) 738-8622

#378
Oqoqo
Category: Sports Wear
Average price: Modest
Area: Kitsilano
Address: 2123 4th Ave W
Vancouver, BC V6K 1N7
Phone: (604) 732-6188

#379
Miz Mooz
Category: Shoe Store
Average price: Modest
Area: Kitsilano
Address: 2177 W 4th Ave
Vancouver, BC V6K 4S2
Phone: (604) 739-7430

#380
Applause Video
Category: Music & DVDs
Average price: Inexpensive
Area: Kensington-Cedar Cottage
Address: 2575 Commercial Dr
Vancouver, BC V5N
Phone: (604) 874-3133

#381
Norton Commons
Category: Flowers & Gifts, Convenience Store
Average price: Expensive
Area: Kitsilano
Address: 2501 W Broadway
Vancouver, BC V6K 2B4
Phone: (604) 732-8525

#382
Future Shop
Category: Electronics, Computers, IT Service& Computer Repair
Average price: Modest
Area: Downtown
Address: 796 Granville Street
Vancouver, BC V6Z 1E4
Phone: (604) 683-2502

#383
My Florist
Category: Florist
Average price: Modest
Area: West End
Address: 779 Denman St
Vancouver, BC V6G 2L6
Phone: (604) 688-1717

#384
The Drive Pharmacy
Category: Drugstore, Pharmacy
Average price: Modest
Area: Grandview-Woodlands, The Drive
Address: 1684 Commercial Drive
Vancouver, BC V5L 3Y4
Phone: (604) 254-0133

Shops, Restaurants, Attractions & Nightlife / Vancouver Travel Guide

---

#385
Penelope's
Category: Accessories,
Women's Clothing
Average price: Inexpensive
Area: Grandview-Woodlands, The Drive
Address: 1009 Commercial Dr
Vancouver, BC V5L 3X1
Phone: (604) 253-1010

#386
Rufus' Guitar Shop
Category: Musical Instruments
Average price: Modest
Area: Point Grey
Address: 2621 Alma St
Vancouver, BC V6R 3S1
Phone: (604) 222-1717

#387
Plush
Category: Home Decor, Flowers & Gifts
Average price: Inexpensive
Area: Riley Park
Address: 4296 Main St
Vancouver, BC V5V 3P9
Phone: (604) 708-5199

#388
Chinatown Flea Market
Category: Home Decor
Average price: Inexpensive
Area: Chinatown, Strathcona
Address: 268 Keefer st
Vancouver, BC V6A 1X4
Phone: (604) 688-0871

#389
Bath & Body Works
Category: Cosmetics & Beauty Supply
Average price: Modest
Area: Downtown
Address: 701 W Georgia St
Vancouver, BC V7Y 1G5
Phone: (604) 678-8745

#390
Your Dollar Store With More
Category: Discount Store
Average price: Inexpensive
Area: Downtown, Yaletown
Address: 1067 Hamilton Ave
Vancouver, BC V6B
Phone: (604) 669-6031

#391
Reckless the Bike Store
Category: Bikes, Bike Rental
Average price: Modest
Area: Fairview Slopes
Address: 1810 Fir Street
Vancouver, BC V6J 3B1
Phone: (604) 731-2420

#392
Banana Republic
Category: Accessories,
Women's Clothing, Men's Clothing
Average price: Expensive
Area: West End, Downtown
Address: 1098 Robson St
Vancouver, BC V6E 1A7
Phone: (604) 331-8285

#393
Homewares
Category: Kitchenware
Average price: Modest
Area: Sunset
Address: 6167 Fraser Street
Vancouver, BC V5W 2Z9
Phone: (604) 327-3212

#394
Hollywood Boutique
Category: Women's Clothing
Average price: Expensive
Area: Downtown, Yaletown
Address: 289 Davie Street
Vancouver, BC V6B 5P2
Phone: (604) 569-2887

#395
Rokko Sarees & Fabrics
Category: Fabric Store,
Women's Clothing
Average price: Modest
Area: Sunset
Address: 6201 Fraser St
Vancouver, BC V5W 3A2
Phone: (604) 327-3033

#396
Roberts & Brown Opticians
Category: Eyewear & Opticians,
Optometrists
Average price: Modest
Area: South Cambie
Address: 948 King Edward Avenue W
Vancouver, BC V5Z 2E2
Phone: (604) 731-5367

#397
Kali
Category: Women's Clothing
Average price: Modest
Area: Riley Park
Address: 3740 Main Street
Vancouver, BC V5V 3N7
Phone: (604) 709-9996

#398
Fantasy Factory
Category: Adult
Average price: Modest
Area: Downtown, Granville Entertainment District
Address: 1123 Granville Street
Vancouver, BC V6Z
Phone: (604) 684-3775

#399
Ray Rickburn Fine Men's Apparel
Category: Men's Clothing
Average price: Modest
Area: Kitsilano
Address: 2100 4th Ave W
Vancouver, BC V6K 1N6
Phone: (604) 738-9177

#400
The Helly Hansen Store
Category: Sports Wear
Average price: Expensive
Area: Downtown
Address: 766 Granville St
Vancouver, BC V6J 1N3
Phone: (604) 609-3932

#401
The Paper Hound
Category: Bookstore
Average price: Inexpensive
Area: Downtown
Address: 344 W Pender Street
Vancouver, BC V6B 1T1
Phone: (604) 428-1344

#402
Aruhndara
Category: Skin Care, Cosmetics & Beauty Supply
Average price: Expensive
Area: Downtown, Yaletown
Address: 1060 Hamilton Street
Vancouver, BC V6B 2R9
Phone: (604) 558-0979

#403
Used House Of Vintage
Category: Used, Vintage
Average price: Modest
Area: West End, Downtown
Address: 1008 Robson Street
Vancouver, BC V6E 1V9
Phone: (604) 683-6887

#404
CB2
Category: Home Decor, Furniture Store
Average price: Expensive
Area: West End
Address: 1277 Robson Street
Vancouver, BC V6E
Phone: (604) 669-9797

#405
Coach - Pacific Centre
Category: Accessories
Average price: Expensive
Area: Downtown
Address: 701 W Georgia St
Vancouver, BC V6C 2T4
Phone: (604) 681-9943

#406
Shoppers Drug Mart
Category: Drugstore
Average price: Modest
Area: Riley Park
Address: 4590 Fraser St
Vancouver, BC V5V 4H1
Phone: (604) 873-2681

#407
Dunbar Lumber Supply
Category: Hardware Store, Building Supplies
Average price: Modest
Area: Point Grey
Address: 3637 16th Avenue W
Vancouver, BC V6R 3C3
Phone: (604) 224-0434

#408
Gravity Pope Tailored Goods
Category: Women's Clothing, Men's Clothing, Accessories
Average price: Expensive
Area: Kitsilano
Address: 2203 W 4th Ave
Vancouver, BC V6K 1N9
Phone: (604) 731-7647

#409
Motherland
Category: Accessories
Average price: Modest
Area: Riley Park
Address: 3647 Main St
Vancouver, BC V5V 3N6
Phone: (604) 568-7530

#410
Hill's Native Art
Category: Jewelry, Art Gallery
Average price: Expensive
Area: Downtown, Gastown
Address: 165 Water St
Vancouver, BC V6B 1A7
Phone: (604) 685-4249

#411
Fullhouse Modern
Category: Home Decor, Furniture Store
Average price: Expensive
Area: Fairview Slopes
Address: 1545 W 4th Ave
Vancouver, BC V6J 1L6
Phone: (604) 733-7789

#412
Nine West
Category: Shoe Store
Average price: Modest
Area: Downtown
Address: 701 W Georgia St
Vancouver, BC V7Y 1K8
Phone: (604) 899-9406

#413
Sleep Country
Category: Furniture Store, Mattresses
Average price: Modest
Area: Downtown
Address: 756 Granville St
Vancouver, BC V6Z 1E4
Phone: (604) 684-3900

#414
m0851
Category: Accessories, Leather Goods
Average price: Expensive
Area: Downtown, Gastown
Address: 44 Water Street
Vancouver, BC V6B 1A4
Phone: (604) 682-7704

#415
Greenstems
Category: Florist, Wedding Planning
Average price: Modest
Area: Gastown, Downtown Eastside
Address: 315 Abbott St
Vancouver, BC V6B 1G8
Phone: (604) 568-1314

#416
Twist Fashions
Category: Accessories, Women's Clothing
Average price: Expensive
Area: Kitsilano
Address: 2952 W 4th Ave
Vancouver, BC V6K 1R4
Phone: (604) 732-0199

#417
The Garden Health Foods
Category: Health Food Store, Cosmetics & Beauty Supply
Average price: Modest
Area: West End
Address: 1204 Davie Street
Vancouver, BC V6E 1N3
Phone: (604) 688-4325

#418
Mark's Work Wearhouse
Category: Accessories, Women's Clothing, Sports Wear, Men's Clothing
Average price: Modest
Area: Kitsilano
Address: 1885 4th Ave W
Vancouver, BC V6J 1M4
Phone: (604) 736-2678

#419
T Room Bakery & Kitchenware
Category: Bakery, Kitchen & Bath
Average price: Modest
Area: Point Grey
Address: 4445 10th Ave W
Vancouver, BC V6R 2H9
Phone: (604) 677-2579

#420
Pharmasave on the Drive
Category: Drugstore
Average price: Modest
Area: Grandview-Woodlands, The Drive
Address: 1308 Commercial Dr
Vancouver, BC V5L 3X6
Phone: (604) 215-5500

#421
Browns Shoe B2
Category: Shoe Store
Average price: Expensive
Area: West End
Address: 1112 Robson Street
Vancouver, BC V6E 1B2
Phone: (604) 687-3383

#422
J.Crew
Category: Women's Clothing,
Men's Clothing, Accessories
Average price: Expensive
Area: West End, Downtown
Address: 1088 Robson Street
Vancouver, BC V6E 1A9
Phone: (604) 684-2367

#423
City Cigar Emporium
Category: Tobacco Shop
Average price: Modest
Area: Fairview Slopes
Address: 888 6th Ave W
Vancouver, BC V5Z 1A6
Phone: (604) 879-0208

#424
Deakin Equipment
Category: Outdoor Gear
Average price: Modest
Area: Grandview-Woodlands
Address: 1361 Powell St
Vancouver, BC V5L 1G8
Phone: (604) 253-2685

#425
Urbanity
Category: Fashion
Average price: Modest
Area: Fairview Slopes, South Granville
Address: 2412 Granville St
Vancouver, BC V6H 3G6
Phone: (604) 801-6262

#426
Tom Harris TELUS
Category: Mobile Phones,
Television Service Provider
Average price: Inexpensive
Area: Kitsilano
Address: 2163 4th Ave W
Vancouver, BC V6K 1N7
Phone: (604) 739-5886

#427
Pyrrha Design Inc
Category: Jewelry
Average price: Modest
Area: Mount Pleasant
Address: 2040 Columbia Street
Vancouver, BC V5Y 3E1
Phone: (604) 688-1834

#428
Call the Kettle Black
Category: Kitchen & Bath
Average price: Expensive
Area: Kitsilano
Address: 2294 W 4th Avenue
Vancouver, BC V6K 1N8
Phone: (604) 736-1412

#429
Wild Birds Unlimited
Category: Hobby Shop
Average price: Modest
Area: Fairview Slopes
Address: 1302 W Broadway
Vancouver, BC V6H 1H2
Phone: (604) 736-2676

#430
Gastown Photo
Category: Hobby Shop,
Photography Store
Average price: Inexpensive
Area: Downtown
Address: 200 Burrard Street
Vancouver, BC V6C 3L6
Phone: (604) 608-2728

#431
The Wood Co-op
Category: Art Gallery
Average price: Expensive
Area: Granville Island/False Creek
Address: 1592 Johnston St
Vancouver, BC V6H 3S2
Phone: (877) 966-3500

#432
Lüt Boutique
Category: Men's Clothing,
Women's Clothing
Average price: Inexpensive
Area: Riley Park
Address: 4219 Main St
Vancouver, BC V5V 3P8
Phone: (604) 568-1188

#433
Atomic Bike Shop
Category: Bikes
Average price: Modest
Area: Fairview Slopes, South Granville
Address: 1555 6th Ave W
Vancouver, BC V6J 1R1
Phone: (604) 714-0158

#434
Violet
Category: Women's Clothing
Average price: Modest
Area: Fairview Slopes, South Granville
Address: 1563 W 6th Avenue
Vancouver, BC V6J 1R1
Phone: (604) 569-1514

#435
Reckless Electric Bikes
Category: Bike Rental, Bikes
Average price: Expensive
Area: Downtown
Address: 1357 Hornby Street
Vancouver, BC V6Z 1W7
Phone: (604) 669-8311

#436
Oceandrive Leather
Category: Leather Goods
Average price: Exclusive
Area: Shaughnessy, Fairview Slopes
Address: 1560 16th Avenue W
Vancouver, BC V6J 2L6
Phone: (604) 647-2244

#437
KENT Picture Framing
Category: Home Decor
Average price: Expensive
Area: Fairview Slopes
Address: 1666 W 8th Avenue
Vancouver, BC V6J 1V4
Phone: (604) 558-3040

#438
Used House of Vintage
Category: Used, Vintage
Average price: Modest
Area: Downtown, Granville Entertainment District
Address: 831 Granville Street
Vancouver, BC V6B 2C9
Phone: (604) 694-0322

#439
Chapel Arts
Category: Music Venues, Art Gallery
Average price: Modest
Area: Downtown Eastside
Address: 304 Dunlevy St
Vancouver, BC V6A
Phone: (778) 371-9210

#440
High End Resale
Category: Accessories, Used, Vintage, Jewelry
Average price: Modest
Area: Downtown
Address: 813 Hornby Street
Vancouver, BC V6Z 2H7
Phone: (604) 682-8893

#441
Cinephile Video
Category: Videos, Video Game Rental
Average price: Modest
Area: Riley Park
Address: 4340 Main St
Vancouver, BC V5V 3P9
Phone: (604) 876-3456

#442
Clearly Contacts
Category: Eyewear & Opticians, Optometrists
Average price: Inexpensive
Area: Downtown
Address: 961 Robson Street
Vancouver, BC V6Z 2V7
Phone: (778) 372-3993

#443
They Live Video
Category: Videos, Video Game Rental
Average price: Inexpensive
Area: Riley Park
Address: 4340 Main Street
Vancouver, BC V5V 3P9
Phone: (604) 876-3456

#444
Flip Flop Shop
Category: Accessories, Shoe Store
Average price: Modest
Area: Kitsilano
Address: 1820 W 4th Avenue
Vancouver, BC V6J 1M3
Phone: (604) 568-5318

#445
The Pendulum Gallery
Category: Art Gallery
Average price: Inexpensive
Area: Downtown
Address: 885 Georgia St W
Vancouver, BC V6C 3E8
Phone: (604) 879-7714

#446
Lushuz Fashion Boutique
Category: Accessories,
Women's Clothing
Average price: Modest
Area: Kitsilano
Address: 2352 West 4th Avenue
Vancouver, BC V6K 1P1
Phone: (604) 738-9333

#447
Metropolitan Home
Category: Furniture Store, Antiques
Average price: Expensive
Area: Fairview Slopes
Address: 1626 W 2nd Ave
Vancouver, BC V6J 1H4
Phone: (604) 681-2313

#448
Even Design
Category: Jewelry
Average price: Expensive
Area: Downtown
Address: 31st Avenue
Vancouver, BC V6L 1Z9
Phone: (604) 732-7248

#449
Spank On The Drive
Category: Accessories,
Women's Clothing
Average price: Modest
Area: Grandview-Woodlands, The Drive
Address: 1027 Commercial Drive
Vancouver, BC V5L 3X1
Phone: (604) 255-1131

#450
Complex
Category: Accessories, Men's Clothing
Average price: Modest
Area: Downtown, Gastown
Address: 231 Abbott Street
Vancouver, BC V6B
Phone: (604) 602-1668

#451
Neighbour
Category: Men's Clothing,
Accessories, Shoe Store
Average price: Modest
Area: Downtown, Gastown
Address: 12 Water St
Vancouver, BC V6B 0B7
Phone: (604) 558-2555

#452
Granville Optical
Category: Eyewear & Opticians
Average price: Modest
Area: Downtown
Address: 670 Granville St
Vancouver, BC V6C 3J3
Phone: (604) 683-6419

#453
Action Liquidators
Category: Lingerie, Women's Clothing
Average price: Modest
Area: Hastings-Sunrise
Address: 1820 Renfrew St
Vancouver, BC V5M 3H9
Phone: (604) 255-4577

#454
Millennium
Category: Women's Clothing,
Men's Clothing
Average price: Expensive
Area: Downtown, Granville
Entertainment District
Address: 1109 Granville Street
Vancouver, BC V6Z 1K3
Phone: (604) 451-7500

#455
Loulou Luv
Category: Jewelry, Accessories
Average price: Modest
Area: Kitsilano
Address: 3071 W Broadway
Vancouver, BC V6K 2G9
Phone: (604) 677-0682

#456
Spectus Eyewear
Category: Eyewear & Opticians
Average price: Expensive
Area: Kitsilano
Address: 2209 4th Avenue W
Vancouver, BC V6K 1N9
Phone: (604) 730-0503

#457
The Urban Rack
Category: Accessories,
Women's Clothing
Average price: Modest
Area: Kitsilano
Address: 2207 4th Avenue W
Vancouver, BC V6K 1N9
Phone: (604) 733-6553

#458
Halo Boutique
Category: Women's Clothing
Average price: Modest
Area: Kitsilano
Address: 2693 W Broadway
Vancouver, BC V6K 2G2
Phone: (604) 568-4256

#459
Always Discount Boots & Shoes
Category: Shoe Store
Average price: Inexpensive
Area: Kensington-Cedar Cottage
Address: 1435 Kingsway
Vancouver, BC V5N 2R6
Phone: (604) 872-0319

#460
Eugene Choo
Category: Accessories,
Women's Clothing, Men's Clothing
Average price: Expensive
Area: Riley Park
Address: 3683 Main Street
Vancouver, BC V5V 3N6
Phone: (604) 873-8874

#461
R.J. Clarke Tobacconist
Category: Tobacco Shop
Average price: Modest
Area: Oakridge
Address: 5844 Cambie St
Vancouver, BC V5Z 3A8
Phone: (604) 687-4136

#462
Fun In The Sun
Category: Sporting Goods,
Accessories, Women's Clothing
Average price: Inexpensive
Area: Kitsilano
Address: 3518 4th Ave W
Vancouver, BC V6R 1N8
Phone: (604) 738-9798

#463
Sephora
Category: Cosmetics & Beauty Supply
Average price: Expensive
Area: Downtown
Address: 701 W Georgia St
Vancouver, BC V7Y 1E4
Phone: (778) 331-3942

#464
Little Miss Vintage
Category: Used, Vintage
Average price: Expensive
Area: Grandview-Woodlands, The Drive
Address: 941 Commercial Dr
Vancouver, BC V5L 3W8
Phone: (604) 255-3554

#465
Michelle's Import Plus
Category: Furniture Store
Average price: Modest
Area: Downtown, Gastown
Address: 73 Water St
Vancouver, BC V6B 1A1
Phone: (604) 687-5930

#466
Charlie & Lee
Category: Women's Clothing,
Accessories, Men's Clothing
Average price: Expensive
Area: Strathcona
Address: 223 Union Street
Vancouver, BC V6A 2B2
Phone: (604) 558-3030

#467
The Archetype
Category: Leather Goods,
Men's Clothing, Women's Clothing
Average price: Modest
Area: Mount Pleasant
Address: 2549 Main Street
Vancouver, BC V5T 3E5
Phone: (604) 872-1144

#468
Robinson Lighting & Bath Centre
Category: Lighting Fixtures & Equipment,
Kitchen & Bath
Average price: Modest
Area: Fairview Slopes
Address: 2285 Cambie Street
Vancouver, BC V5Z 2T5
Phone: (604) 879-2494

#469
Hager Books
Category: Bookstore
Average price: Modest
Area: Kerrisdale, Arbutus Ridge
Address: 2176 41st Ave W
Vancouver, BC V6M 1Z1
Phone: (604) 263-9412

#470
The Lip Lounge
Category: Women's Clothing
Average price: Modest
Area: Riley Park
Address: 3628 Main St
Vancouver, BC V5V 3N5
Phone: (778) 330-6952

#471
Esprit De Corporation (1980)Ltd
Category: Accessories, Women's Clothing
Average price: Modest
Area: West End
Address: 1160 Robson Street
Vancouver, BC V6E 1B2
Phone: (604) 632-0452

#472
Shoppers Drug Mart
Category: Drugstore
Average price: Modest
Area: Mount Pleasant
Address: 370 Broadway E
Vancouver, BC V5T 4G5
Phone: (604) 873-3558

#473
Staples Business Depot
Category: Office Equipment
Average price: Modest
Area: Downtown, Granville Entertainment District
Address: 901 Seymour St
Vancouver, BC V6B 3M1
Phone: (604) 602-5959

#474
New Balance
Category: Sporting Goods, Shoe Store
Average price: Modest
Area: West End
Address: 1158 Robson Street
Vancouver, BC V6Z 2E7
Phone: (604) 685-2281

#475
Second Suit For Men & Women
Category: Used, Vintage
Average price: Modest
Area: Kitsilano
Address: 2036 4th Avenue W
Vancouver, BC V6J 1M9
Phone: (604) 732-0338

#476
Cartier Jewellers
Category: Jewelry
Average price: Exclusive
Area: Downtown
Address: 456 Howe St
Vancouver, BC V6C 2X1
Phone: (604) 683-6878

#477
Kerrisdale Pharmacy
Category: Drugstore
Average price: Modest
Area: Kerrisdale, Arbutus Ridge
Address: 5591 W Boulevard
Vancouver, BC V6M 4H3
Phone: (604) 261-0333

#478
Mexx Robson
Category: Accessories, Women's Clothing
Average price: Modest
Area: West End
Address: 1119 Robson St
Vancouver, BC V6E 1B5
Phone: (604) 801-6399

#479
Spectacle Shoppe
Category: Eyewear & Opticians, Accessories, Optometrists
Average price: Modest
Area: Kerrisdale, Arbutus Ridge
Address: 5683 W Boulevard
Vancouver, BC V6M 3W7
Phone: (604) 263-2628

#480
Michael Kors
Category: Watches, Men's Clothing, Women's Clothing
Average price: Expensive
Area: Oakridge
Address: 650 W 41st Aveune
Vancouver, BC V5Z 2M9
Phone: (604) 629-0286

#481
Shoppers Drug Mart
Category: Drugstore
Average price: Modest
Area: Downtown
Address: 586 Granville St
Vancouver, BC V6C 1X5
Phone: (604) 683-4063

#482
Fido Store
Category: Mobile Phones
Average price: Expensive
Area: Downtown
Address: 481 Robson St
Vancouver, BC V6B 6L9
Phone: (604) 687-3291

#483
East Side Re-Rides
Category: Thrift Store,
Leather Goods, Used, Vintage
Average price: Expensive
Area: Fraserview
Address: 7105 Victoria Dr
Vancouver, BC V5P 3Y7
Phone: (604) 327-7433

#484
The Home Depot
Category: Department Store,
Home Improvement Retailer
Average price: Modest
Area: Strathcona
Address: 900 Terminal Avenue
Vancouver, BC V6A 4G4
Phone: (604) 608-1423

#485
Womyn's Ware
Category: Adult
Average price: Modest
Area: Grandview-Woodlands, The Drive
Address: 896 Commercial Drive
Vancouver, BC V5L 3Y5
Phone: (604) 254-2543

#486
Australian Boot Company
Category: Shoe Store
Average price: Modest
Area: Kitsilano
Address: 1968 4th Avenue W
Vancouver, BC V6J 1M5
Phone: (604) 738-2668

#487
Balconi Floral Design Studio
Category: Florist
Average price: Modest
Area: Mount Pleasant
Address: 422 2nd Avenue W
Vancouver, BC V5Y 1E2
Phone: (604) 709-0082

#488
West Point Cycle
Category: Bikes, Bike Rental
Average price: Expensive
Area: Kerrisdale
Address: 6069 W Boulevard
Vancouver, BC V6M 3X2
Phone: (604) 263-7587

#489
KJM Country Garden
Category: Gardening
Average price: Modest
Area: Dunbar-Southlands
Address: 7226 Blenheim Street
Vancouver, BC V6N 1S3
Phone: (604) 266-1397

#490
Bakers Dozen Antiques
Category: Toy Store, Antiques
Average price: Expensive
Area: Riley Park
Address: 3520 Main St
Vancouver, BC V5V 3N3
Phone: (604) 879-3348

#491
House of Knives
Category: Kitchen & Bath
Average price: Expensive
Area: Fairview Slopes, South Granville
Address: 2655 Granville Street
Vancouver, BC V6H
Phone: (604) 737-3663

#492
Rona Home Centre
Category: Hardware Store
Average price: Modest
Area: Kensington-Cedar Cottage
Address: 1503 Kingsway
Vancouver, BC V5N 2R8
Phone: (604) 877-1171

Shops, Restaurants, Attractions & Nightlife / Vancouver Travel Guide

#493
Le Petit Spa
Category: Day Spa, Cosmetics & Beauty Supply
Average price: Expensive
Area: Point Grey
Address: 3701 W Broadway
Vancouver, BC V6R 2B9
Phone: (604) 224-4314

#494
Apple Store
Category: Electronics, Computers, Mobile Phones
Average price: Expensive
Area: Oakridge
Address: 650 W 41st Ave
Vancouver, BC V5Z 2M9
Phone: (778) 373-4500

#495
Mac-Talla Cycles
Category: Bikes
Average price: Modest
Area: Hastings-Sunrise
Address: 2626 E Hastings
Vancouver, BC V5K 1Z5
Phone: (604) 707-0822

#496
Scott Landon Antiques
Category: Antiques
Average price: Expensive
Area: Fairview Slopes, South Granville
Address: 2227 Granville Street
Vancouver, BC V6H 3G1
Phone: (604) 731-2576

#497
Taraxca Jewellery
Category: Jewelry
Average price: Modest
Area: Granville Island/False Creek
Address: 1518 Duranleau St
Vancouver, BC V6H 3X4
Phone: (604) 732-8990

#498
Lush Handmade Cosmetics
Category: Cosmetics & Beauty Supply
Average price: Modest
Area: Kitsilano
Address: 2248 W 4th Ave
Vancouver, BC V6K 1N8
Phone: (604) 733-5874

#499
Country Furniture
Category: Furniture Store
Average price: Expensive
Area: Shaughnessy, Fairview Slopes, South Granville
Address: 3097 Granville Street
Vancouver, BC V6H 3J9
Phone: (604) 738-6411

#500
Granville Island Florist
Category: Florist
Average price: Modest
Area: Granville Island/False Creek
Address: 1689 Johnston St
Vancouver, BC V6H 3R9
Phone: (604) 669-1228

TOP 500 RESTAURANTS
The Most Recommended by Locals & Trevelers
(From #1 to #500)

#1
Fable
Cuisines: Canadian
Average price: $11-30
Area: Kitsilano
Address: 1944 W 4th Ave
Vancouver, BC V6J 1M7
Phone: (604) 732-1322

#2
Tuc Craft Kitchen
Cuisines: Canadian, Comfort Food
Average price: $11-30
Area: Gastown
Address: 60 Cordova Street
Vancouver, BC V6B 1C9
Phone: (604) 559-8999

#3
The Flying Pig
Cuisines: Canadian
Average price: $11-30
Area: Downtown, Yaletown
Address: 1168 Hamilton Street
Vancouver, BC V6B 2S2
Phone: (604) 568-1344

#4
Guu with Garlic
Cuisines: Japanese, Tapas Bar
Average price: $11-30
Area: West End
Address: 1698 Robson Street
Vancouver, BC V6G 1C7
Phone: (604) 685-8678

#5
Café Medina
Cuisines: Breakfast & Brunch
Average price: $11-30
Area: Downtown
Address: 556 Beatty Street
Vancouver, BC V6B 2L3
Phone: (604) 879-3114

#6
Twisted Fork
Cuisines: French, Breakfast & Brunch
Average price: $11-30
Area: Downtown, Granville
Entertainment District
Address: 1147 Granville Street
Vancouver, BC V6Z 1M1
Phone: (604) 568-0749

#7
Tavola
Cuisines: Italian
Average price: $31-60
Area: West End
Address: 1829 Robson Street
Vancouver, BC V6G 3E4
Phone: (604) 606-4680

#8
Ajisai Sushi Bar
Cuisines: Sushi Bar, Japanese
Average price: $11-30
Area: Kerrisdale
Address: 2081 W 42nd Avenue
Vancouver, BC V6M 2B4
Phone: (604) 266-1428

#9
Le Crocodile Restaurant
Cuisines: French
Average price: Above $61
Area: West End, Downtown
Address: 909 Burrard St
Vancouver, BC V6Z 2N2
Phone: (604) 669-4298

#10
La Taqueria Pinche Taco Shop
Cuisines: Mexican
Average price: Under $10
Area: Fairview Slopes
Address: 2549 Cambie Street
Vancouver, BC V5Z 3V6
Phone: (604) 558-2549

#11
The Flying Pig
Cuisines: Canadian
Average price: $11-30
Area: Downtown, Gastown
Address: 102 Water Street
Vancouver, BC V6B 2K8
Phone: (604) 559-7968

#12
The Oakwood Canadian Bistro
Cuisines: Gastropub,
Breakfast & Brunch, Canadian
Average price: $11-30
Area: Kitsilano
Address: 2741 W 4th Avenue
Vancouver, BC V6K 3V9
Phone: (604) 558-1965

#13
La Taqueria Pinche Taco Shop
Cuisines: Mexican, Caterer
Average price: Under $10
Area: Downtown
Address: 322 W Hastings Street
Vancouver, BC V8B 1K6
Phone: (604) 568-4406

#14
Chambar
Cuisines: Belgian, Moroccan
Average price: $31-60
Area: Downtown
Address: 562 Beatty Street
Vancouver, BC V6B 2L3
Phone: (604) 879-7119

#15
Guu Original Thurlow
Cuisines: Japanese, Tapas Bar
Average price: $11-30
Area: West End, Downtown
Address: 838 Thurlow Street
Vancouver, BC V6E 1W2
Phone: (604) 685-8817

#16
Kishimoto Japanese Kitchen
Cuisines: Japanese, Sushi Bar
Average price: $11-30
Area: Grandview-Woodlands, The Drive
Address: 2054 Commercial Drive
Vancouver, BC V5N 4A9
Phone: (604) 255-5550

#17
Lupo
Cuisines: Italian
Average price: $31-60
Area: Downtown, Yaletown
Address: 869 Hamilton St
Vancouver, BC V6B 2R7
Phone: (604) 569-2535

#18
Shizen Ya
Cuisines: Japanese
Average price: $11-30
Area: Downtown
Address: 985 Hornby Street
Vancouver, BC V6Z 1V3
Phone: (604) 568-0013

#19
Salt Tasting Room
Cuisines: Wine Bar, Tapas
Average price: $11-30
Area: Downtown, Gastown
Address: 45 Blood Alley Square
Vancouver, BC V6B 1A4
Phone: (604) 633-1912

#20
Trilussa Pizza and Pane
Cuisines: Pizza
Average price: Under $10
Area: Riley Park
Address: 4363 Main Street
Vancouver, BC V5V 3R1
Phone: (604) 558-3338

#21
Pourhouse Restaurant
Cuisines: Lounge, Canadian, Cocktail Bar
Average price: $31-60
Area: Downtown, Gastown
Address: 162 Water Street
Vancouver, BC V6B 1B2
Phone: (604) 568-7022

#22
Phnom Penh
Cuisines: Cambodian, Vietnamese
Average price: $11-30
Area: Strathcona
Address: 244 E Georgia Street
Vancouver, BC V6A 1Z7
Phone: (604) 682-5777

#23
Bishop's Restaurant
Cuisines: Canadian
Average price: $31-60
Area: Kitsilano
Address: 2183 W 4th Avenue
Vancouver, BC V6K 1N7
Phone: (604) 738-2025

#24
CHAU VeggiExpress
Cuisines: Vegan, Vegetarian, Vietnamese
Average price: $11-30
Area: Kensington-Cedar Cottage
Address: 5052 Victoria Drive
Vancouver, BC V5P 3T8
Phone: (604) 568-9508

#25
Forage
Cuisines: Canadian
Average price: $31-60
Area: West End
Address: 1300 Robson Street
Vancouver, BC V6E 1C5
Phone: (604) 661-1400

#26
La Quercia
Cuisines: Italian
Average price: $31-60
Area: Point Grey, Kitsilano
Address: 3689 W 4th Avenue
Vancouver, BC V6R 1P2
Phone: (604) 676-1007

#27
Nuba Gastown
Cuisines: Middle Eastern, Mediterranean, Vegetarian
Average price: $11-30
Area: Downtown
Address: 207 W Hastings Street
Vancouver, BC V6B 1H7
Phone: (604) 688-1655

#28
J N & Z Deli
Cuisines: Deli, Sandwiches
Average price: Under $10
Area: Grandview-Woodlands, The Drive
Address: 1729 Commercial Dr
Vancouver, BC V5N 4A4
Phone: (604) 251-4144

#29
Sushi Mart
Cuisines: Sushi Bar, Japanese
Average price: $11-30
Area: West End
Address: 1668 Robson Street
Vancouver, BC V6G 1C7
Phone: (604) 687-2422

#30
Nook
Cuisines: Italian, Pizza
Average price: $11-30
Area: West End
Address: 781 Denman Street
Vancouver, BC V6G
Phone: (604) 568-4554

#31
Scoozis
Cuisines: Breakfast & Brunch, Greek, Italian
Average price: $11-30
Area: Downtown
Address: 445 Howe Street
Vancouver, BC V6C 2X4
Phone: (604) 684-1009

#32
L'Abattoir
Cuisines: French, Canadian
Average price: $31-60
Area: Downtown, Gastown
Address: 217 Carrall Street
Vancouver, BC V6B 2J1
Phone: (604) 568-1701

#33
Yaletown L'Antipasto
Cuisines: Tapas, Italian, Wine Bar
Average price: $11-30
Area: Downtown, Yaletown
Address: 1127 Mainland Street
Vancouver, BC V6B 5P2
Phone: (604) 558-1174

#34
The Mexican Antojitos y Cantina
Cuisines: Mexican
Average price: $11-30
Area: Downtown, Granville Entertainment District
Address: 1049 Granville Street
Vancouver, BC V6Z 1L4
Phone: (604) 569-0955

#35
Toshi Sushi
Cuisines: Sushi Bar, Japanese
Average price: $11-30
Area: Mount Pleasant, Riley Park
Address: 181 E 16th Avenue
Vancouver, BC V5T 4R2
Phone: (604) 874-5173

#36
Go Fish Ocean Emporium
Cuisines: Seafood, Fish & Chips
Average price: $11-30
Area: Granville Island/False Creek
Address: 1505 W 1st Ave
Vancouver, BC V6J 1E8
Phone: (604) 730-5040

Shops, Restaurants, Attractions & Nightlife / Vancouver Travel Guide

#37
Kitsilano Daily Kitchen
Cuisines: French, Canadian
Average price: $31-60
Area: Kitsilano
Address: 1809 W 1st Avenue
Vancouver, BC V6J 5B8
Phone: (604) 569-2741

#38
Los Cuervos Taqueria y Cantina
Cuisines: Mexican, Latin American
Average price: $11-30
Area: Mount Pleasant
Address: 603 Kingsway
Vancouver, BC V5T 3K5
Phone: (604) 558-1518

#39
Pizzeria Farina
Cuisines: Pizza
Average price: $11-30
Area: Downtown, Strathcona
Address: 915 Main Street
Vancouver, BC V6A 2V8
Phone: (604) 681-9334

#40
La Brasserie
Cuisines: French, German, Breakfast & Brunch
Average price: $11-30
Area: West End
Address: 1091 Davie St
Vancouver, BC V6E 1M5
Phone: (604) 568-6499

#41
Harvest Deli
Cuisines: Deli, Sandwiches, Breakfast & Brunch
Average price: Under $10
Area: Kitsilano
Address: 2963 W Broadway
Vancouver, BC V6K 2G9
Phone: (604) 739-3354

#42
Miku
Cuisines: Japanese, Sushi Bar
Average price: $31-60
Area: Downtown
Address: 200 Granville Street
Vancouver, BC V6C 2R6
Phone: (604) 568-3900

#43
Oyster Express
Cuisines: Seafood, Bar
Average price: $11-30
Area: Chinatown, Strathcona
Address: 296 Keefer Street
Vancouver, BC V6A 1X5
Phone: (604) 684-3300

#44
Lost + Found Café
Cuisines: Cafe, Sandwiches
Average price: Under $10
Area: Downtown, Downtown Eastside
Address: 33 W Hastings Street
Vancouver, BC V6B 1G4
Phone: (604) 559-7444

#45
Ramen Santouka
Cuisines: Japanese
Average price: $11-30
Area: West End
Address: 1690 Robson Street
Vancouver, BC V6G 1C7
Phone: (604) 681-8121

#46
Les Faux Bourgeois
Cuisines: French, Cafe
Average price: $11-30
Area: Mount Pleasant
Address: 663 E 15th Avenue
Vancouver, BC V5T 2R6
Phone: (604) 873-9733

#47
The Re-Up BBQ
Cuisines: Barbeque, Sandwiches, Food Truck
Average price: Under $10
Area: Downtown
Address: 700 Hornby St
Vancouver, BC V6Z 2H7
Phone: (604) 724-0894

#48
Sal y Limón
Cuisines: Mexican
Average price: Under $10
Area: Mount Pleasant
Address: 701 Kingsway
Vancouver, BC V5T 2R7
Phone: (604) 677-4247

#49
Acacia Fillo Bar
Cuisines: Breakfast & Brunch, European
Average price: $11-30
Area: West End
Address: 1103 Denman Street
Vancouver, BC V6G 2M7
Phone: (604) 633-3884

#50
La Grotta Del Formaggio
Cuisines: Deli, Sandwiches, Cheese Shop
Average price: Under $10
Area: Grandview-Woodlands, The Drive
Address: 1791 Commercial Dr
Vancouver, BC V5N 4A4
Phone: (604) 255-3911

#51
Fritz European Fry House
Cuisines: Fast Food, Poutinerie
Average price: Under $10
Area: Downtown, Granville Entertainment District
Address: 718 Davie Street
Vancouver, BC V6Z 1B6
Phone: (604) 684-0811

#52
Peaceful Restaurant
Cuisines: Chinese
Average price: $11-30
Area: Fairview Slopes
Address: 532 W Broadway
Vancouver, BC V5Z 1E9
Phone: (604) 879-9878

#53
Bestie
Cuisines: German, Specialty Food
Average price: $11-30
Area: Chinatown
Address: 105 E Pender Street
Vancouver, BC V6A 1T5
Phone: (604) 620-1175

#54
Hawksworth
Cuisines: Canadian
Average price: $31-60
Area: Downtown
Address: 801 W Georgia St
Vancouver, BC V6C 3G1
Phone: (604) 673-7000

#55
The Refinery
Cuisines: Wine Bar, European
Average price: $11-30
Area: Downtown, Granville Entertainment District
Address: 1115 Granville Street
Vancouver, BC V6Z 1M1
Phone: (604) 687-8001

#56
Seasons In the Park
Cuisines: Seafood
Average price: $31-60
Area: Riley Park
Address: Cambie St W 33rd Ave
Vancouver, BC V5Y 2M5
Phone: (604) 874-8008

#57
Mirchi Restaurant
Cuisines: Indian
Average price: $11-30
Area: Marpole
Address: 7964 Granville Street
Vancouver, BC V6P 4Z2
Phone: (604) 266-7000

#58
Fat Duck Mobile Eatery
Cuisines: Food Truck, Sandwiches
Average price: Under $10
Area: Downtown
Address: 600 Hamilton
Vancouver, BC V6B 6A1
Phone: (604) 831-0453

#59
Zefferelli's
Cuisines: Italian
Average price: $11-30
Area: West End
Address: 1136 Robson Street
Vancouver, BC V6E 1B2
Phone: (604) 687-0655

#60
Kaide Sushi
Cuisines: Sushi Bar
Average price: $11-30
Area: Downtown
Address: 1375 Richards Street
Vancouver, BC V6B 3G7
Phone: (604) 681-5886

#61
Guu with Otokomae
Cuisines: Japanese, Tapas Bar
Average price: $11-30
Area: Downtown, Gastown
Address: 105-375 Water Street
Vancouver, BC V6B 5C6
Phone: (604) 685-8682

#62
España Restaurant
Cuisines: Spanish
Average price: $11-30
Area: West End
Address: 1118 Denman Street
Vancouver, BC V6G 2M8
Phone: (604) 558-4040

#63
The Teahouse Restaurant
Cuisines: Seafood
Average price: $31-60
Area: West End
Address: Ferguson Point
Vancouver, BC V6G 3E2
Phone: (604) 669-3281

#64
Kingyo
Cuisines: Japanese, Tapas Bar, Tapas
Average price: $11-30
Area: West End
Address: 871 Denman Street
Vancouver, BC V6G 2L9
Phone: (604) 608-1677

#65
Rodney's Oyster House
Cuisines: Seafood
Average price: $31-60
Area: Downtown, Yaletown
Address: 1228 Hamilton Street
Vancouver, BC V6B 6L2
Phone: (604) 609-0080

#66
Pink Peppercorn
Cuisines: Seafood
Average price: $31-60
Area: Kensington-Cedar Cottage
Address: 1485 Kingsway
Vancouver, BC V5N 2R6
Phone: (604) 569-3626

#67
Miura Waffle Milk Bar
Cuisines: Sandwiches
Average price: Under $10
Area: Mount Pleasant
Address: 2521 Main Street
Vancouver, BC V5T 3E5
Phone: (604) 687-2909

#68
Long's Noodle House
Cuisines: Chinese
Average price: $11-30
Area: Riley Park
Address: 4853 Main Street
Vancouver, BC V5V 3R9
Phone: (604) 879-7879

#69
Calabash Bistro
Cuisines: Caribbean
Average price: $11-30
Area: Downtown Eastside
Address: 428 Carrall Street
Vancouver, BC V6B 2J7
Phone: (604) 568-5882

#70
East Is East
Cuisines: Indian, Afghan
Average price: $11-30
Area: Kitsilano
Address: 3243 Broadway W
Vancouver, BC V6K 2H5
Phone: (604) 734-5881

#71
Tacofino Commissary
Cuisines: Mexican
Average price: $11-30
Area: Grandview-Woodlands
Address: 2327 E Hastings Street
Vancouver, BC V5L 1V6
Phone: (604) 253-8226

#72
La Belle Patate
Cuisines: Fast Food, Poutinerie
Average price: Under $10
Area: West End
Address: 1215 Davie St
Vancouver, BC V6E 1N4
Phone: (604) 569-1215

#73
Vij's Restaurant
Cuisines: Indian
Average price: $31-60
Area: Fairview Slopes, South Granville
Address: 1480 W 11th Avenue
Vancouver, BC V6H 1L1
Phone: (604) 736-6664

#74
The Acorn
Cuisines: Vegetarian, Gluten-Free
Average price: $11-30
Area: Riley Park
Address: 3995 Main Street
Vancouver, BC V5V 3P5
Phone: (604) 566-9001

#75
Bandidas Taqueria
Cuisines: Mexican, Vegetarian, Breakfast & Brunch
Average price: $11-30
Area: Kensington-Cedar Cottage
Address: 2781 Commercial Drive
Vancouver, BC V5N 4C5
Phone: (604) 568-8224

#76
The Patty Shop
Cuisines: Caribbean
Average price: Under $10
Area: Arbutus Ridge
Address: 4019 MacDonald St
Vancouver, BC V6L 2N8
Phone: (604) 738-2144

#77
Joe Fortes Seafood & Chop House
Cuisines: Seafood, Steakhouse, Bar
Average price: $31-60
Area: West End
Address: 777 Thurlow Street
Vancouver, BC V6E 3V5
Phone: (604) 669-1940

#78
East is East
Cuisines: Middle Eastern
Average price: $11-30
Area: Riley Park
Address: 4433 Main Street
Vancouver, BC V5V 3R2
Phone: (604) 565-4401

#79
Suika
Cuisines: Japanese, Tapas
Average price: $11-30
Area: Fairview Slopes
Address: 1626 W Broadway
Vancouver, BC V6J 1X6
Phone: (604) 730-1678

#80
Revel Room
Cuisines: Lounge, Southern
Average price: $11-30
Area: Downtown, Gastown
Address: 238 Abbott St
Vancouver, BC V6B 2K8
Phone: (604) 687-4088

#81
Cuchillo
Cuisines: Latin American
Average price: $31-60
Area: Downtown Eastside
Address: 261 Powell Street
Vancouver, BC V6A 2Z1
Phone: (604) 559-7585

#82
PiDGiN
Cuisines: Japanese, Korean, French
Average price: $31-60
Area: Downtown Eastside
Address: 350 Carrall Street
Vancouver, BC V6B 2J3
Phone: (604) 620-9400

#83
The Red Wagon
Cuisines: Cafe
Average price: $11-30
Area: Grandview-Woodlands
Address: 2296 E Hastings Street
Vancouver, BC V5L
Phone: (604) 568-4565

#84
The Fish Counter
Cuisines: Fish & Chips, Seafood
Average price: $11-30
Area: Riley Park
Address: 3825 Main Street
Vancouver, BC V5V 3P2
Phone: (604) 876-3474

#85
Cactus Club Cafe
Cuisines: Cafe
Average price: $11-30
Area: Coal Harbour, Downtown
Address: 1085 Place
Vancouver, BC V6C 0C3
Phone: (604) 620-7410

#86
The Parlour
Cuisines: Pizza, Gluten-Free, Champagne Bar
Average price: $11-30
Area: Downtown, Yaletown
Address: 1011 Hamilton Street
Vancouver, BC V6B 2W7
Phone: (604) 568-3322

#87
Absinthe Bistro
Cuisines: Cafe, French
Average price: $31-60
Area: Grandview-Woodlands, The Drive
Address: 1260 Commercial Drive
Vancouver, BC V5L 2T6
Phone: (604) 566-9053

#88
Pronto
Cuisines: Italian
Average price: $11-30
Area: South Cambie, Riley Park
Address: 3473 Cambie Street
Vancouver, BC V5Z 2W7
Phone: (604) 722-9331

#89
Café Salade de Fruits
Cuisines: French
Average price: $11-30
Area: Fairview Slopes, South Granville
Address: 1555 W 7th Avenue
Vancouver, BC V6J 1S1
Phone: (604) 714-5987

#90
Pied-à-Terre
Cuisines: French
Average price: $31-60
Area: South Cambie, Riley Park
Address: 3369 Cambie St
Vancouver, BC V5Z 2W6
Phone: (604) 873-3131

#91
Six Acres
Cuisines: Pub, Canadian, Cafe
Average price: $11-30
Area: Downtown, Gastown
Address: 203 Carrall Street
Vancouver, BC V6B 2J2
Phone: (604) 488-0110

#92
Café Kathmandu
Cuisines: Himalayan/Nepalese
Average price: $11-30
Area: Kensington-Cedar Cottage
Address: 2779 Commercial Dr
Vancouver, BC V5N 4C5
Phone: (604) 879-9909

#93
Motomachi Shokudo
Cuisines: Japanese
Average price: $11-30
Area: West End
Address: 740 Denman St
Vancouver, BC V6G 2L5
Phone: (604) 609-0310

#94
The Irish Heather
Cuisines: Irish, Gastropub
Average price: $11-30
Area: Downtown, Gastown
Address: 210 Carrall St
Vancouver, BC V6B 2J2
Phone: (604) 688-9779

#95
Au Petit Café
Cuisines: Vietnamese, Sandwiches
Average price: Under $10
Area: Riley Park
Address: 4851 Main Street
Vancouver, BC V5V 3R9
Phone: (604) 873-3328

#96
Bon Crepe
Cuisines: Creperie
Average price: Under $10
Area: West End
Address: 1238 Robson Street
Vancouver, BC V6E 3Z6
Phone: (604) 719-2060

#97
Hawkers Delight Deli
Cuisines: Malaysian, Singaporean
Average price: Under $10
Area: Riley Park
Address: 4127 Main Street
Vancouver, BC V5V 3P6
Phone: (604) 709-8188

#98
The Parker
Cuisines: Vegetarian, Gluten-Free
Average price: $31-60
Area: Strathcona
Address: 237 Union Street
Vancouver, BC V6A 3A1
Phone: (604) 779-3804

#99
Kintaro Ramen Noodle
Cuisines: Japanese
Average price: Under $10
Area: West End
Address: 788 Denman Street
Vancouver, BC V6G 2L5
Phone: (604) 682-7568

#100
Fassil Ethiopian Restaurant
Cuisines: Ethiopian
Average price: $11-30
Area: Mount Pleasant
Address: 736 Broadway E
Vancouver, BC V5T 1X9
Phone: (604) 879-2001

#101
The Cascade Room
Cuisines: Pub, Canadian
Average price: $11-30
Area: Mount Pleasant
Address: 2616 Main Street
Vancouver, BC V5T 3E6
Phone: (604) 709-8650

#102
The Templeton
Cuisines: Diner, Breakfast & Brunch
Average price: $11-30
Area: Downtown, Granville
Entertainment District
Address: 1087 Granville Street
Vancouver, BC V6Z 1L4
Phone: (604) 685-4612

#103
Banana Leaf
Cuisines: Malaysian
Average price: $11-30
Area: West End
Address: 1096 Denman Street
Vancouver, BC V6G 2M8
Phone: (604) 683-3333

#104
Bin 941 Tapas Parlour
Cuisines: Tapas Bar
Average price: $31-60
Area: Downtown
Address: 941 Davie Street
Vancouver, BC V6Z 1B9
Phone: (604) 683-1246

#105
Basho Cafe
Cuisines: Cafe, Bakery
Average price: Under $10
Area: Grandview-Woodlands
Address: 2007 E Hastings
Vancouver, BC V5L 1T9
Phone: (604) 428-6276

#106
The Fish House In Stanley Park
Cuisines: Seafood
Average price: $31-60
Area: West End
Address: 8901 Stanley Park Drive
Vancouver, BC V6G 3E2
Phone: (604) 681-7275

#107
The Kaboom Box
Cuisines: Seafood, Sandwiches,
Food Truck
Average price: Under $10
Area: Downtown
Address: 777 Granville Street
Vancouver, BC V6B 2C9
Phone: (604) 788-6367

#108
Marulilu Cafe
Cuisines: Japanese,
Breakfast & Brunch, Cafe
Average price: Under $10
Area: Mount Pleasant
Address: 451 W Broadway
Vancouver, BC V5Y 1R4
Phone: (604) 568-4211

#109
Baoqi Vietnamese Eateri
Cuisines: Vietnamese, Sandwiches
Average price: $11-30
Area: Downtown, Granville
Entertainment District
Address: 620 Davie Street
Vancouver, BC V6B 2J5
Phone: (604) 568-7980

#110
The Wallflower Modern Diner
Cuisines: Breakfast & Brunch
Average price: $11-30
Area: Mount Pleasant
Address: 2420 Main Street
Vancouver, BC V5T 3E2
Phone: (604) 568-7554

#111
Zero One Sushi
Cuisines: Sushi Bar, Japanese
Average price: Under $10
Area: Downtown
Address: 559 W Pender Street
Vancouver, BC V6B 1V5
Phone: (604) 605-1625

#112
Burgoo Bistro
Cuisines: Bar, Soup, Canadian
Average price: $11-30
Area: Kitsilano
Address: 2272 W 4th Avenue
Vancouver, BC V6K 1P2
Phone: (604) 734-3478

#113
The Locus
Cuisines: Lounge, Canadian
Average price: $11-30
Area: Riley Park
Address: 4121 Main Street
Vancouver, BC V5V 3P6
Phone: (604) 708-4121

#114
Basil Pasta Bar
Cuisines: Italian
Average price: Under $10
Area: Downtown, Granville
Entertainment District
Address: 636 Davie Street
Vancouver, BC V6B
Phone: (604) 568-3106

#115
YEW Seafood + Bar
Cuisines: Seafood, Wine Bar
Average price: $31-60
Area: Downtown
Address: 791 W Georgia Street
Vancouver, BC V6C 2T4
Phone: (604) 692-4939

#116
Hubbub Sandwiches
Cuisines: Sandwiches, Salad
Average price: Under $10
Area: Downtown
Address: 859 Hornby Street
Vancouver, BC V6Z 1T9
Phone: (604) 568-3398

#117
Hapa Izakaya - Robson
Cuisines: Japanese, Tapas Bar
Average price: $11-30
Area: West End
Address: 1479 Robson Street
Vancouver, BC V6G 1C1
Phone: (604) 689-4272

#118
La Mezcaleria
Cuisines: Mexican
Average price: $11-30
Area: Grandview-Woodlands, The Drive
Address: 1622 Commercial Drive
Vancouver, BC V5L 3Y4
Phone: (604) 559-8226

#119
Acme Café
Cuisines: American, Coffee & Tea
Average price: $11-30
Area: Gastown, Downtown Eastside
Address: 51 W Hastings Street
Vancouver, BC V6B 1G4
Phone: (604) 569-1022

#120
Shizen Ya
Cuisines: Japanese, Vegetarian
Average price: $11-30
Area: Fairview Slopes
Address: 1102 W Broadway
Vancouver, BC V6H
Phone: (604) 569-3721

#121
Einstein Wrap House
Cuisines: Middle Eastern, Mediterranean
Average price: Under $10
Area: Downtown
Address: 516 Abbott Street
Vancouver, BC V6B 6C1
Phone: (604) 558-2733

#122
JapaDog
Cuisines: Japanese, Hot Dogs
Average price: Under $10
Area: Downtown
Address: 530 Robson St
Vancouver, BC V6B 2B7
Phone: (604) 569-1158

#123
Tibisti Foods & Grill
Cuisines: Halal, Middle Eastern
Average price: $11-30
Area: Fraserview
Address: 6990 Victoria Dr
Vancouver, BC V5P 3Y8
Phone: (604) 737-1000

#124
Stock Market
Cuisines: Soup
Average price: Under $10
Area: Granville Island/False Creek
Address: 1689 Johnston St
Vancouver, BC V6H 3R9
Phone: (604) 687-2433

#125
Ask For Luigi
Cuisines: Italian
Average price: $11-30
Area: Downtown Eastside
Address: 305 Alexander Street
Vancouver, BC V6A 1C4
Phone: (604) 428-2544

#126
Nuba Yaletown
Cuisines: Middle Eastern, Mediterranean, Vegetarian
Average price: $11-30
Area: Downtown, Granville Entertainment District
Address: 1206 Seymour Street
Vancouver, BC V6B 3N9
Phone: (778) 371-3266

#127
Loving Hut Express
Cuisines: Vegan, Street Vendor
Average price: Under $10
Area: Downtown, Yaletown
Address: 1200 Pacific Boulevard
Vancouver, BC V6Z 2V4
Phone: (604) 780-1029

#128
Chewies Steam & Oyster Bar
Cuisines: Cajun/Creole
Average price: $11-30
Area: Kitsilano
Address: 2201 W 1st Avenue
Vancouver, BC V6K 1E9
Phone: (604) 558-4448

#129
Mangal Kiss Mid-East BBQ
Cuisines: Barbeque, Middle Eastern
Average price: Under $10
Area: Downtown
Address: Georgia & Howe
Vancouver, BC V6Z
Phone: (778) 868-4045

#130
Jules French Bistro
Cuisines: French
Average price: $11-30
Area: Downtown, Gastown
Address: 216 Abbott St
Vancouver, BC V6B 2K8
Phone: (604) 669-0033

#131
Cafe de l'Orangerie
Cuisines: French, Japanese
Average price: $11-30
Area: Marpole
Address: 1320 W 73rd Avenue
Vancouver, BC V6P 4R3
Phone: (604) 266-0066

#132
Cardero's Restaurant & Marine Pub
Cuisines: Cajun/Creole, Canadian
Average price: $31-60
Area: Coal Harbour, Downtown
Address: 1583 Coal Harbour Quay
Vancouver, BC V6G 3E7
Phone: (604) 669-7666

#133
The Union
Cuisines: Asian Fusion, Bar
Average price: $11-30
Area: Strathcona
Address: 219 Union Street
Vancouver, BC V6A 0B4
Phone: (604) 568-3230

#134
Raw Canvas
Cuisines: Wine Bar, Tapas,
Party & Event Planning
Average price: $11-30
Area: Downtown, Yaletown
Address: 1046 Hamilton St
Vancouver, BC V6B 2R9
Phone: (604) 687-1729

#135
Chongqing
Cuisines: Seafood, Chinese
Average price: $11-30
Area: West End
Address: 1260 Robson Street
Vancouver, BC V6E
Phone: (604) 568-0303

#136
Via Tevere
Cuisines: Italian, Pizza
Average price: $11-30
Area: Grandview-Woodlands, The Drive
Address: 1190 Victoria Drive
Vancouver, BC V5L 4G5
Phone: (604) 336-1803

#137
House of Dosas
Cuisines: Indian
Average price: $11-30
Area: Kensington-Cedar Cottage
Address: 1391 Kingsway
Vancouver, BC V5V 3E3
Phone: (604) 875-1283

#138
Score on Davie
Cuisines: Sports Bar
Average price: $11-30
Area: West End
Address: 1262 Davie St
Vancouver, BC V6J 5L1
Phone: (604) 632-1646

#139
Burgoo Bistro
Cuisines: American
Average price: $11-30
Area: Point Grey
Address: 4434 10th Avenue W
Vancouver, BC V6R 2H9
Phone: (604) 221-7839

#140
Pizzeria Barbarella
Cuisines: Pizza
Average price: $11-30
Area: Mount Pleasant
Address: 654 E Broadway
Vancouver, BC V5T 1X7
Phone: (604) 210-6111

#141
Mui Ngo Gai
Cuisines: Vietnamese
Average price: Under $10
Area: Kensington-Cedar Cottage
Address: 2052 Kingsway
Vancouver, BC V5N 2T3
Phone: (604) 876-8885

#142
Finch's Tea & Coffee House
Cuisines: Coffee & Tea, Sandwiches
Average price: $11-30
Area: Downtown
Address: 353 W Pender St
Vancouver, BC V6B 1T3
Phone: (604) 899-4040

#143
Mochikas Peruvian Cafe
Cuisines: Peruvian
Average price: $11-30
Area: Fairview Slopes
Address: 1696 West 5th Avenue
Vancouver, BC V6J 1N5
Phone: (604) 739-7378

#144
Goldies Pizza & Beer Lounge
Cuisines: Pizza
Average price: Under $10
Area: Downtown
Address: 605 W Pender St
Vancouver, BC V6B 1W7
Phone: (604) 681-0650

#145
Mango Thai
Cuisines: Thai
Average price: Under $10
Area: West End
Address: 1206 Davie Street
Vancouver, BC V6E 1N3
Phone: (604) 689-9980

#146
Heirloom Vegetarian
Cuisines: Breakfast & Brunch, Vegetarian, Vegan
Average price: $11-30
Area: Fairview Slopes, South Granville
Address: 1509 W 12th Avenue
Vancouver, BC V6J 2E1
Phone: (604) 733-2231

#147
Hitoe Sushi Japanese Restaurant
Cuisines: Japanese, Sushi Bar
Average price: $11-30
Area: Kitsilano
Address: 3347 W 4th Avenue
Vancouver, BC V6R 1N6
Phone: (778) 371-4619

#148
Moderne Burger
Cuisines: Burgers
Average price: $11-30
Area: Kitsilano
Address: 2507 Broadway W
Vancouver, BC V6K 2E9
Phone: (604) 739-0005

#149
Banana Leaf
Cuisines: Malaysian
Average price: $11-30
Area: West End
Address: 1043 Davie St
Vancouver, BC V6E 1N2
Phone: (604) 669-3389

#150
Memphis Blues Barbeque House
Cuisines: Barbeque
Average price: $11-30
Area: Fairview Slopes, South Granville
Address: 1465 W Broadway
Vancouver, BC V6H 1H6
Phone: (604) 738-6806

#151
Simba's Grill
Cuisines: African
Average price: $11-30
Area: West End
Address: 825 Denman Street
Vancouver, BC V6G 2L7
Phone: (604) 974-0649

#152
La Petite Cuillère
Cuisines: Sandwiches, Cafe
Average price: $11-30
Area: Mount Pleasant
Address: 55 Kingsway Street
Vancouver, BC V5T 3J1
Phone: (604) 298-0088

#153
Fire Pizza
Cuisines: Pizza
Average price: Under $10
Area: Grandview-Woodlands, The Drive
Address: 1918 Commercial Drive
Vancouver, BC V5N 4A7
Phone: (604) 253-5607

#154
Provence Marinaside
Cuisines: Seafood, French
Average price: $31-60
Area: Downtown, Yaletown
Address: 1177 Marinaside Crès
Vancouver, BC V6Z 2Y3
Phone: (604) 681-4144

#155
Campagnolo
Cuisines: Italian
Average price: $11-30
Area: Downtown, Strathcona
Address: 1020 Main Street
Vancouver, BC V6A
Phone: (604) 484-6018

#156
Gurkha Himalayan Kitchen
Cuisines: Himalayan/Nepalese
Average price: $11-30
Area: West End
Address: 1141 Davie Street
Vancouver, BC V6E 1N2
Phone: (604) 565-7965

Shops, Restaurants, Attractions & Nightlife / Vancouver Travel Guide

#157
Minami
Cuisines: Japanese, Sushi Bar
Average price: $31-60
Area: Downtown, Yaletown
Address: 1118 Mainland Street
Vancouver, BC V6B 2T9
Phone: (604) 685-8080

#158
Cactus Club Cafe
Cuisines: Canadian
Average price: $11-30
Area: Downtown
Address: 588 Burrard Street
Vancouver, BC V7X 1M9
Phone: (604) 682-0933

#159
Sushi Nanaimo
Cuisines: Sushi Bar, Japanese
Average price: $11-30
Area: Grandview-Woodlands
Address: 350 Nanaimo Street
Vancouver, BC V5L 4R7
Phone: (604) 876-9200

#160
Paul's Omelettery Restaurant
Cuisines: Breakfast & Brunch
Average price: $11-30
Area: Fairview Slopes, South Granville
Address: 2211 Granville Street
Vancouver, BC V6H 3G1
Phone: (604) 737-2857

#161
Madras Dosa House
Cuisines: Indian
Average price: Under $10
Area: Riley Park
Address: 5656 Fraser Street
Vancouver, BC V5W 2Z4
Phone: (604) 327-1233

#162
Save On Meats
Cuisines: Butcher, Diner
Average price: Under $10
Area: Downtown, Downtown Eastside
Address: 43 W Hastings St
Vancouver, BC V6B 1G4
Phone: (604) 569-3568

#163
Romer's Burger Bar
Cuisines: Burgers
Average price: $11-30
Area: Kitsilano
Address: 1873 W 4th Avenue
Vancouver, BC V6J 1M4
Phone: (604) 732-9545

#164
Kalvin's Szechuan Restaurant
Cuisines: Taiwanese, Chinese
Average price: $11-30
Area: Kensington-Cedar Cottage
Address: 5225 Victoria
Vancouver, BC V5P 3V4
Phone: (604) 321-2888

#165
**Gotham Steakhouse
& Cocktail Bar**
Cuisines: Steakhouse, Cocktail Bar
Average price: Above $61
Area: Downtown
Address: 615 Seymour Street
Vancouver, BC V6B 3K3
Phone: (604) 605-8282

#166
Ukrainian Village
Cuisines: Ukrainian
Average price: $11-30
Area: West End
Address: 815 Denman Street
Vancouver, BC V6G 2L7
Phone: (604) 687-7440

#167
Artisan Sake Maker
Cuisines: Winery, Japanese
Average price: $11-30
Area: Granville Island/False Creek
Address: 1339 Railspur Alley
Vancouver, BC V6H 4G9
Phone: (604) 685-7253

#168
Donair Dude
Cuisines: Middle Eastern,
Mediterranean, Donairs
Average price: Under $10
Area: West End
Address: 1172 Davie Street
Vancouver, BC V6E 1N1
Phone: (604) 681-1801

#169
Burgoo Bistro
Cuisines: American
Average price: $11-30
Area: Mount Pleasant
Address: 3096 Main Street
Vancouver, BC V5T 3G5
Phone: (604) 873-1441

#170
Baru Latino
Cuisines: Latin American
Average price: $31-60
Area: Point Grey
Address: 2535 Alma St
Vancouver, BC V6R 2C1
Phone: (604) 222-9171

#171
Bao Bei Chinese Brasserie
Cuisines: Chinese
Average price: $31-60
Area: Chinatown
Address: 163 Keefer St
Vancouver, BC V6A 1X3
Phone: (604) 688-0876

#172
ZAC.ZAC Japanese Curry House
Cuisines: Japanese
Average price: Under $10
Area: Downtown
Address: 590 Robson Street
Vancouver, BC V6B 2B7
Phone: (604) 608-2887

#173
Viet Sub
Cuisines: Vietnamese, Sandwiches
Average price: Under $10
Area: Downtown
Address: 520 Robson St
Vancouver, BC V6B
Phone: (604) 569-3340

#174
Bob Likes Thai Food
Cuisines: Thai
Average price: $11-30
Area: Fairview Slopes, South Granville
Address: 1521 W Broadway
Vancouver, BC V6J 1W6
Phone: (604) 558-3320

#175
The Sandbar Seafood Restaurant
Cuisines: Seafood, Sushi Bar
Average price: $31-60
Area: Granville Island/False Creek
Address: 1535 Johnston Street
Vancouver, BC V6H 3R9
Phone: (604) 669-9030

#176
Al Basha
Cuisines: Middle Eastern, Halal, Donairs
Average price: Under $10
Area: Kitsilano
Address: 3143 W Broadway
Vancouver, BC V6K 2H2
Phone: (604) 568-8841

#177
Hy's Encore
Cuisines: Steakhouse
Average price: Above $61
Area: Downtown
Address: 637 Hornby Street
Vancouver, BC V6C 2G3
Phone: (604) 683-7671

#178
Argo Café
Cuisines: American
Average price: Under $10
Area: Mount Pleasant
Address: 1836 Ontario St
Vancouver, BC V5T 2W6
Phone: (604) 876-3620

#179
Green Lemongrass
Cuisines: Vietnamese
Average price: Under $10
Area: Kensington-Cedar Cottage
Address: 1086 Kingsway
Vancouver, BC V5V
Phone: (604) 875-6638

#180
Green Leaf Sushi
Cuisines: Sushi Bar
Average price: $11-30
Area: Kitsilano
Address: 3416 W Broadway
Vancouver, BC V6R 2B3
Phone: (604) 568-9406

#181
BierCraft Bistro
Cuisines: Tapas Bar, Lounge
Average price: $11-30
Area: South Cambie, Riley Park
Address: 3305 Cambie Street
Vancouver, BC V5Z 2W6
Phone: (604) 874-6900

#182
JOEY Burrard
Cuisines: Canadian, Lounge
Average price: $11-30
Area: Downtown
Address: 820 Burrard Street
Vancouver, BC V6C 0B6
Phone: (604) 683-5639

#183
Baoguette Vietnamese Bistro
Cuisines: Vietnamese, Sandwiches
Average price: Under $10
Area: West End
Address: 1184 Denman Street
Vancouver, BC V6G 1Z1
Phone: (604) 563-2468

#184
Brix Restaurant
Cuisines: Wine Bar, French
Average price: $31-60
Area: Downtown, Yaletown
Address: 1138 Homer Street
Vancouver, BC V6B 2X6
Phone: (604) 915-9463

#185
Sushiholic
Cuisines: Sushi Bar, Japanese
Average price: $11-30
Area: Hastings-Sunrise
Address: 3311 E Broadway
Vancouver, BC V5M 2A1
Phone: (604) 879-4881

#186
Railtown Cafe & Catering
Cuisines: Cafe
Average price: $11-30
Area: Downtown Eastside
Address: 397 Railway Street
Vancouver, BC V6A 1A4
Phone: (604) 428-0800

#187
Thai Basil
Cuisines: Thai
Average price: Under $10
Area: West End
Address: 1215 Thurlow St
Vancouver, BC V6E 1X4
Phone: (604) 685-6754

#188
Ha Long Bay
Cuisines: Vietnamese
Average price: Under $10
Area: Downtown
Address: 430 W Pender Street
Vancouver, BC V6B 1T1
Phone: (604) 568-7976

#189
Shaolin Noodle House
Cuisines: Chinese
Average price: Under $10
Area: Fairview Slopes
Address: 656 W Broadway
Vancouver, BC V5Z 1E9
Phone: (604) 873-1618

#190
Gyoza King
Cuisines: Japanese
Average price: $11-30
Area: West End
Address: 1508 Robson Street
Vancouver, BC V6G 1C2
Phone: (604) 669-8278

#191
Yakinikuya Japanese BBQ
Cuisines: Japanese, Barbeque
Average price: $11-30
Area: West End
Address: 793 Jervis St
Vancouver, BC V6E 2B1
Phone: (604) 669-1222

#192
Jitlada
Cuisines: Thai
Average price: $11-30
Area: Fairview Slopes, South Granville
Address: 1459 W Broadway
Vancouver, BC V6H 1H6
Phone: (604) 738-9888

#193
Canra Srilankan Cuisine
Cuisines: Indian, Ethnic Food
Average price: Under $10
Area: Downtown
Address: 88 W Pender Street
Vancouver, BC V6B 6N9
Phone: (604) 568-3545

#194
La Cigale French Bistro
Cuisines: French
Average price: $31-60
Area: Kitsilano
Address: 1961 W 4th Avenue
Vancouver, BC V6J 1M7
Phone: (604) 732-0004

#195
Kaya Malay Bistro
Cuisines: Malaysian, Singaporean
Average price: $11-30
Area: Fairview Slopes
Address: 1063 W Broadway
Vancouver, BC V6H 1E5
Phone: (604) 730-9963

#196
Kessel&March
Cuisines: European
Average price: $11-30
Area: Grandview-Woodlands
Address: 1701 Powell Street
Vancouver, BC V5L 5C9
Phone: (604) 874-1196

#197
**The Tipper Restaurant
& Review Room**
Cuisines: Burgers, Canadian
Average price: $11-30
Area: Kensington-Cedar Cottage
Address: 2066 Kingsway
Vancouver, BC V5N 2T3
Phone: (604) 873-1010

#198
Jethro's Fine Grub
Cuisines: Breakfast & Brunch
Average price: $11-30
Area: Dunbar-Southlands
Address: 3420 Dunbar St
Vancouver, BC V6S
Phone: (604) 569-3441

#199
Tacofino
Cuisines: Mexican
Average price: Under $10
Area: Downtown
Address: Robson St & Howe St
Vancouver, BC V6Z 2H7
Phone: (604) 253-8226

#200
Le Marché St.George
Cuisines: Coffee & Tea, Cafe, Convenience Store
Average price: $11-30
Area: Riley Park
Address: 4393 St. George Street
Vancouver, BC V5V 2K6
Phone: (604) 565-5107

#201
Heidi's Cafe
Cuisines: Diner
Average price: Under $10
Area: Sunset
Address: 5943 Fraser Street
Vancouver, BC V5W 2Z6
Phone: (604) 639-6317

#202
East of Main
Cuisines: Mediterranean, Tapas Bar
Average price: $11-30
Area: Chinatown, Strathcona
Address: 223 E Georgia Street
Vancouver, BC V6A 2Z9
Phone: (604) 899-2777

#203
Budgies Burritos
Cuisines: Vegetarian, Mexican, Vegan
Average price: Under $10
Area: Mount Pleasant
Address: 44 Kingsway
Vancouver, BC V5T 3H9
Phone: (604) 874-5408

#204
Nicli Antica Pizzeria
Cuisines: Pizza
Average price: $11-30
Area: Downtown, Gastown
Address: 62 E Cordova St
Vancouver, BC V6A 1K3
Phone: (604) 669-6985

#205
Back Forty
Cuisines: Pub, Barbeque
Average price: $11-30
Area: Downtown
Address: 118 Robson Street
Vancouver, BC V6B 2M1
Phone: (604) 688-5840

#206
Le Petit Saigon
Cuisines: Vietnamese
Average price: Under $10
Area: Hastings-Sunrise
Address: 2783 Hastings Street E
Vancouver, BC V5K 1Z8
Phone: (604) 251-6340

#207
Afghan Horsemen Restaurant
Cuisines: Afghan
Average price: $11-30
Area: Granville Island/False Creek
Address: 1833 Anderson Street
Vancouver, BC V6H 4E5
Phone: (604) 873-5923

#208
Donburiya
Cuisines: Japanese
Average price: Under $10
Area: West End
Address: 1329 Robson Street
Vancouver, BC V6E 1C6
Phone: (604) 568-6066

#209
Bistro 101
Cuisines: French, European
Average price: $11-30
Area: Granville Island/False Creek
Address: 1505 W 2nd Avenue
Vancouver, BC V6J 1H2
Phone: (604) 734-0101

#210
Ho Yuen Kee
Cuisines: Chinese
Average price: $11-30
Area: Sunset
Address: 6236 Fraser Street
Vancouver, BC V5W 3A1
Phone: (604) 324-8855

#211
Shanti's Curries
Cuisines: Indian
Average price: $11-30
Area: Riley Park
Address: 4191 Main Street
Vancouver, BC V5V 3P6
Phone: (604) 568-7699

#212
Carthage Café
Cuisines: Mediterranean, African
Average price: $11-30
Area: Grandview-Woodlands, The Drive
Address: 1851 Commercial Drive
Vancouver, BC V5N 4A6
Phone: (604) 215-0661

#213
Union Food Market
Cuisines: Deli, Sandwiches, Grocery
Average price: Under $10
Area: Strathcona
Address: 810 Union St
Vancouver, BC V6A 2C4
Phone: (604) 255-5025

#214
Landmark Hotpot House
Cuisines: Chinese, Hot Pot
Average price: $31-60
Area: South Cambie
Address: 4023 Cambie St
Vancouver, BC V5Z 2X9
Phone: (604) 872-2868

#215
The Keg Steakhouse + Bar
Cuisines: Seafood, Steakhouse, Bar
Average price: $11-30
Area: Downtown
Address: 688 Dunsmuir Street
Vancouver, BC V6B 1N3
Phone: (604) 685-7502

#216
The Firewood Café
Cuisines: Pizza
Average price: $11-30
Area: Fairview Slopes
Address: 3004 Cambie Street
Vancouver, BC V5Z 2V9
Phone: (604) 873-0001

Shops, Restaurants, Attractions & Nightlife / Vancouver Travel Guide

#217
Raincity Grill
Cuisines: Seafood, Canadian
Average price: $31-60
Area: West End
Address: 1193 Denman Street
Vancouver, BC V6G 2N1
Phone: (604) 685-7337

#218
Cannibal Cafe
Cuisines: Diner, Burgers
Average price: $11-30
Area: Grandview-Woodlands, The Drive
Address: 1818 Commercial Drive
Vancouver, BC V5N 4A5
Phone: (604) 558-4199

#219
Penang Delight Cafe
Cuisines: Malaysian
Average price: $11-30
Area: Marpole
Address: 1316 W 73rd Avenue
Vancouver, BC V6P 4M9
Phone: (604) 559-9898

#220
Tung Hing Bakery
Cuisines: Bakery, Vietnamese, Sandwiches
Average price: Under $10
Area: Kensington-Cedar Cottage
Address: 1196 Kingsway
Vancouver, BC V5V 3C8
Phone: (604) 875-3394

#221
Marutama Ramen
Cuisines: Japanese
Average price: $11-30
Area: West End
Address: 780 Bidwell Street
Vancouver, BC V6G 1C8
Phone: (604) 688-8837

#222
Hai Phong Vietnamese Restaurant
Cuisines: Vietnamese
Average price: Under $10
Area: Kensington-Cedar Cottage
Address: 1242 Kingsway
Vancouver, BC V5V
Phone: (604) 872-3828

#223
Sawasdee Thai Restaurant
Cuisines: Thai
Average price: $11-30
Area: Riley Park
Address: 4250 Main St
Vancouver, BC V5V 3P9
Phone: (604) 876-4030

#224
StackHouse Burger Bar
Cuisines: Burgers, Canadian, Cocktail Bar
Average price: $11-30
Area: Downtown, Granville Entertainment District
Address: 1224 Granville Street
Vancouver, BC V6B 2G6
Phone: (604) 558-3499

#225
LOCAL Public Eatery
Cuisines: Canadian
Average price: $11-30
Area: Kitsilano
Address: 2210 Cornwall Ave
Vancouver, BC V6K 1B5
Phone: (604) 734-3589

#226
Banana Leaf
Cuisines: Malaysian, Singaporean
Average price: $11-30
Area: Fairview Slopes
Address: 820 W Broadway
Vancouver, BC V5Z 1J8
Phone: (604) 731-6333

#227
Kinemi's Kitchen
Cuisines: Pizza, Italian, Asian Fusion
Average price: $11-30
Area: Killarney, Champlain Heights
Address: 7751 Champlain Crescent
Vancouver, BC V5S 4J6
Phone: (604) 434-2868

#228
Magda's Restaurant
Cuisines: Venezuelan, Colombian, Salvadoran
Average price: $11-30
Area: Sunset
Address: 6345 Fraser Street
Vancouver, BC V5W 3A3
Phone: (604) 322-1001

#229
Chicha
Cuisines: Peruvian, Tapas
Average price: $11-30
Area: Mount Pleasant
Address: 136 E Broadway
Vancouver, BC V5T 1W1
Phone: (604) 620-3963

#230
IK2GO
Cuisines: Italian
Average price: Under $10
Area: West End, Downtown
Address: 1037 Alberni St
Vancouver, BC V6E 1A1
Phone: (604) 629-3436

#231
My Chau Restaurant
Cuisines: Vietnamese
Average price: Under $10
Area: Kensington-Cedar Cottage
Address: 1715 Kingsway
Vancouver, BC V5N 2S4
Phone: (604) 874-6880

#232
Cardero Bottega
Cuisines: Specialty Food, Deli
Average price: Under $10
Area: West End
Address: 1016 Cardero St
Vancouver, BC V6G 2H1
Phone: (604) 689-0450

#233
Lobsters Only Seafood
Cuisines: Seafood
Average price: $11-30
Area: Mount Pleasant
Address: 416 Broadway E
Vancouver, BC V5T 1X2
Phone: (604) 873-6820

#234
Tsuki Sushi Bar
Cuisines: Sushi Bar, Japanese
Average price: $11-30
Area: Downtown
Address: 509 Abbott Street
Vancouver, BC V6B 6N7
Phone: (604) 558-3805

#235
Spoon Kitchen
Cuisines: Thai, Malaysian
Average price: $11-30
Area: Kitsilano
Address: 1909 W 4th Avenue
Vancouver, BC V6J 1M7
Phone: (604) 428-6369

#236
Gyu-Kaku Japanese BBQ
Cuisines: Japanese, Barbeque
Average price: $11-30
Area: Downtown
Address: G3-888 Nelson Street
Vancouver, BC V6Z 2H1
Phone: (604) 558-3885

#237
Biercraft Tap and Tapas Bar
Cuisines: Belgian, Brewerie
Average price: $11-30
Area: Grandview-Woodlands, The Drive
Address: 1191 Commercial Drive
Vancouver, BC V5L 3X2
Phone: (604) 254-2437

#238
Pacifico Pizzeria & Restaurant
Cuisines: Pizza, Italian
Average price: $11-30
Area: Downtown
Address: 970 Smithe Street
Vancouver, BC V6Z 0A4
Phone: (604) 408-0808

#239
Chiffon Patisserie
Cuisines: Sandwiches, Bakery
Average price: $11-30
Area: Fairview Slopes
Address: 1073 W Broadway
Vancouver, BC V6H 1E2
Phone: (604) 732-1232

#240
Deer Garden Signatures
Cuisines: Seafood
Average price: Under $10
Area: Sunset
Address: 6270 Fraser Street
Vancouver, BC V5W 3A3
Phone: (604) 322-6116

#241
Stepho's Souvlaki Greek Taverna
Cuisines: Greek
Average price: $11-30
Area: West End
Address: 1124 Davie St
Vancouver, BC V6E 1N1
Phone: (604) 683-2555

#242
Balilicious Modern Indonesian
Cuisines: Indonesian
Average price: $11-30
Area: South Cambie, Riley Park
Address: 3488 Cambie St
Vancouver, BC V5Z 2W8
Phone: (604) 709-8150

#243
Mamie Taylor's
Cuisines: American
Average price: $11-30
Area: Chinatown, Strathcona
Address: 251 E Georgia Street
Vancouver, BC V6A 1Z6
Phone: (604) 620-8818

#244
Mr. Red Cafe
Cuisines: Vietnamese
Average price: Under $10
Area: Grandview-Woodlands
Address: 2234 E Hasting Street
Vancouver, BC V5L 1V4
Phone: (604) 710-9515

#245
Kam Gok Yuen
Cuisines: Chinese, Barbeque
Average price: Under $10
Area: Chinatown
Address: 142 E Pender St
Vancouver, BC V6A 1T3
Phone: (604) 683-3822

#246
Bay Sushi Express Cafe
Cuisines: Japanese, Sushi Bar
Average price: $11-30
Area: Downtown
Address: 678 Seymour St
Vancouver, BC V6B 1Z5
Phone: (604) 806-0363

#247
Mitra Canteen
Cuisines: Mediterranean, Halal
Average price: Under $10
Area: Mount Pleasant
Address: 3034 Main St
Vancouver, BC V5T 3G5
Phone: (604) 874-9820

#248
Merchant's Oyster Bar
Cuisines: Canadian, Seafood
Average price: $11-30
Area: Grandview-Woodlands, The Drive
Address: 1590 Commercial Drive
Vancouver, BC V5L 3Y2
Phone: (604) 258-0005

#249
Johnnie Fox's Irish Snug
Cuisines: Irish, Pub
Average price: $11-30
Area: Downtown, Granville
Entertainment District
Address: 1033 Granville Street
Vancouver, BC V6Z 1L4
Phone: (604) 685-4946

#250
Shiro
Cuisines: Japanese, Sushi Bar
Average price: $11-30
Area: Mount Pleasant
Address: 3096 Cambie Street
Vancouver, BC V5Z 2V9
Phone: (604) 874-0027

#251
Mean Poutine
Cuisines: Hot Dogs, Fast Food, Poutinerie
Average price: Under $10
Area: Downtown, Granville
Entertainment District
Address: 718 Nelson Street
Vancouver, BC V6Z 1A8
Phone: (604) 568-4351

#252
Curry Zone
Cuisines: Indian
Average price: $11-30
Area: Hastings-Sunrise
Address: 2671 E Hastings Street
Vancouver, BC V5K 1Z9
Phone: (604) 215-2207

#253
Summer In Greece
Cuisines: Greek
Average price: $11-30
Area: Kitsilano, Fairview Slopes
Address: 2351 Burrard St
Vancouver, BC V6J
Phone: (604) 558-1223

#254
Caffè Artigiano
Cuisines: Coffee & Tea, Sandwiches
Average price: Under $10
Area: Downtown
Address: 763 Hornby Street
Vancouver, BC V6Z 1S2
Phone: (604) 694-7737

#255
Havana
Cuisines: Latin American, Cuban
Average price: $11-30
Area: Grandview-Woodlands, The Drive
Address: 1212 Commercial Dr
Vancouver, BC V5L 3X4
Phone: (604) 253-9119

#256
Earls
Cuisines: Bar, Canadian
Average price: $11-30
Area: West End
Address: 1185 Robson Street
Vancouver, BC V6E 1B5
Phone: (604) 669-0020

#257
Number e food
Cuisines: Sandwiches, Juice Bar
Average price: $11-30
Area: Downtown
Address: 1308 Burrard Street
Vancouver, BC V6Z 2B7
Phone: (604) 559-6863

#258
Sushi Mania
Cuisines: Japanese, Sushi Bar
Average price: $11-30
Area: Riley Park
Address: 3851 Main Street
Vancouver, BC V5V 3P1
Phone: (604) 568-3363

#259
Sushi Bay
Cuisines: Japanese, Sushi Bar
Average price: $11-30
Area: Kensington-Cedar Cottage
Address: 1284 Kingsway
Vancouver, BC V5V 3E1
Phone: (604) 874-8028

#260
Zakkushi
Cuisines: Japanese
Average price: $31-60
Area: West End
Address: 823 Denman St
Vancouver, BC V6G 2L7
Phone: (604) 685-1136

#261
Sushi Bella
Cuisines: Sushi Bar, Japanese
Average price: $11-30
Area: West End
Address: 1175 Davie Street
Vancouver, BC V6E 1N1
Phone: (604) 559-7707

#262
Campagnolo Roma
Cuisines: Italian, Pizza
Average price: $11-30
Area: Grandview-Woodlands
Address: 2297 Hastings Street E
Vancouver, BC V5L 1V2
Phone: (604) 569-0456

#263
Fliptop Filipino Fusion
Cuisines: Food Truck, Filipino
Average price: Under $10
Area: Fairview Slopes, South Granville
Address: Granville St and W 10th Ave
Vancouver, BC V6H
Phone: (604) 306-7841

#264
Black Frog Eatery
Cuisines: Pub, American
Average price: $11-30
Area: Downtown, Gastown
Address: 108 Cambie Street
Vancouver, BC V6B 2M8
Phone: (604) 602-0527

#265
Thailicious
Cuisines: Thai, Food Delivery Service
Average price: $11-30
Area: Strathcona
Address: 1428 Vernon Drive
Vancouver, BC V5L 3K9
Phone: (604) 254-2000

#266
Blaq Sheep Coffee House & Bistro
Cuisines: Coffee & Tea, Breakfast & Brunch
Average price: $11-30
Area: Dunbar-Southlands
Address: 5601 Dunbar Street
Vancouver, BC V6N
Phone: (604) 261-8188

#267
Fujiya
Cuisines: Japanese
Average price: Under $10
Area: Coal Harbour, Downtown
Address: 115-1050 W Pender St
Vancouver, BC V6E 3S7
Phone: (604) 608-1050

#268
Caffé Rustico
Cuisines: Italian, Sandwiches
Average price: Under $10
Area: Mount Pleasant
Address: 3136 Main St
Vancouver, BC V5T 3G7
Phone: (604) 872-3444

#269
U & I Thai Fine Cuisine
Cuisines: Thai
Average price: $11-30
Area: South Cambie, Riley Park
Address: 3364 Cambie Street
Vancouver, BC V5Y 2A1
Phone: (604) 875-6999

#270
The Keg Steakhouse + Bar
Cuisines: Steakhouse, Bar, Seafood
Average price: $31-60
Area: Downtown, Yaletown
Address: 1011 Mainland Street
Vancouver, BC V6B 5P9
Phone: (604) 633-2534

#271
Dockside Restaurant
Cuisines: Seafood
Average price: $31-60
Area: Granville Island/False Creek
Address: 1253 Johnston St
Vancouver, BC V6H 3R9
Phone: (604) 685-7070

#272
La Buca Restaurant
Cuisines: Italian
Average price: $31-60
Area: Arbutus Ridge
Address: 4025 MacDonald St
Vancouver, BC V6L 2N8
Phone: (604) 730-6988

#273
The Whip Restaurant Gallery
Cuisines: Bar, American
Average price: $11-30
Area: Mount Pleasant
Address: 209 6th Avenue E
Vancouver, BC V5T 1J7
Phone: (604) 874-4687

#274
New Town Bakery & Restaurant
Cuisines: Bakery, Dim Sum
Average price: Under $10
Area: Chinatown
Address: 148 Pender Street E
Vancouver, BC V6A 2V2
Phone: (604) 681-1828

#275
Fujiya Japanese Foods
Cuisines: Caterer, Japanese, Grocery
Average price: Under $10
Area: Strathcona, Grandview-Woodlands
Address: 912 Clark Dr
Vancouver, BC V5L 3J8
Phone: (604) 251-3711

#276
Rocky Mountain Flatbread
Cuisines: Pizza, Breakfast & Brunch
Average price: $11-30
Area: Kitsilano
Address: 1876 1st Avenue W
Vancouver, BC V6J 1G5
Phone: (604) 730-0321

#277
Mom's Grilled Cheese Truck
Cuisines: Sandwiches, Food Truck
Average price: Under $10
Area: Downtown
Address: 800 W Georgia St
Vancouver, BC V5N 3P3
Phone: (604) 767-9768

#278
Rogue Kitchen & Wetbar
Cuisines: American, Gastropub
Average price: $11-30
Area: Downtown
Address: 601 W Cordova St
Vancouver, BC V6B 1G1
Phone: (604) 678-8000

#279
Roaming Dragon
Cuisines: Asian Fusion, Food Truck
Average price: Under $10
Area: Downtown
Address: Burrard & Robson
Vancouver, BC V6Z
Phone: (604) 639-3335

#280
Yagger's Downtown Restaurant & Sports Bar
Cuisines: American, Gastropub
Average price: $11-30
Area: Downtown
Address: 433 W Pender St
Vancouver, BC V6B 1V2
Phone: (604) 602-7030

#281
NOVO Pizzeria and Wine Bar
Cuisines: Wine Bar, Pizza, Italian
Average price: $11-30
Area: Fairview Slopes
Address: 2118 Burrard Street
Vancouver, BC V6J 3H6
Phone: (604) 736-2220

#282
Nando's Chicken
Cuisines: Barbeque, Portuguese
Average price: $11-30
Area: Downtown
Address: 828 Davie Street
Vancouver, BC V6Z 1B7
Phone: (604) 678-1217

#283
Maenam
Cuisines: Thai
Average price: $31-60
Area: Kitsilano
Address: 1938 4th Ave W
Vancouver, BC V6J 1M5
Phone: (604) 730-5579

#284
Wildebeest
Cuisines: Gastropub,
Wine Bar, Canadian
Average price: $31-60
Area: Downtown, Downtown Eastside
Address: 120 W Hastings Street
Vancouver, BC V6B 1G8
Phone: (604) 687-6880

#285
Juno Vancouver Sushi Bistro
Cuisines: Japanese, Sushi Bar
Average price: $11-30
Area: Downtown
Address: 572 Davie St
Vancouver, BC V6B 2G4
Phone: (604) 568-8805

#286
La Casita Tacos
Cuisines: Mexican
Average price: Under $10
Area: West End
Address: 1773 Robson Street
Vancouver, BC V6G 1C9
Phone: (604) 685-8550

#287
Rodney's Oyster House Gastown
Cuisines: Seafood
Average price: $31-60
Area: Downtown, Gastown
Address: 52 Powell Street
Vancouver, BC V6A 1E7
Phone: (604) 685-2005

#288
The Stable House
Cuisines: Tapas Bar, Wine Bar
Average price: $11-30
Area: Fairview Slopes, South Granville
Address: 1520 W 13th Avenue
Vancouver, BC V6J 2G4
Phone: (604) 736-1520

#289
The Sardine Can
Cuisines: Tapas Bar, Spanish
Average price: $11-30
Area: Downtown, Gastown
Address: 26 Powell Street
Vancouver, BC V6A 1E7
Phone: (604) 568-1350

#290
The Black Lodge
Cuisines: Vegetarian
Average price: $11-30
Area: Mount Pleasant, Riley Park, Kensington-Cedar Cottage
Address: 630 Kingsway
Vancouver, BC V5T 3K4
Phone: (604) 620-7070

#291
Café Zen On Yew
Cuisines: Breakfast & Brunch
Average price: $11-30
Area: Kitsilano
Address: 1631 Yew St
Vancouver, BC V6K 3E6
Phone: (604) 731-4018

#292
Donair Dude
Cuisines: Mediterranean, Middle Eastern
Average price: Under $10
Area: Downtown, Granville Entertainment District
Address: 1145 Granville Street
Vancouver, BC V6B 2G6
Phone: (604) 428-6699

#293
Bambo Café
Cuisines: Coffee & Tea, Sandwiches, Bagels
Average price: Under $10
Area: Downtown, Gastown
Address: 301 W Cordova St
Vancouver, BC V6B 1E5
Phone: (604) 681-4323

#294
Joyeaux Cafe & Restaurant
Cuisines: Vietnamese, Sandwiches, Breakfast & Brunch
Average price: Under $10
Area: Downtown
Address: 551 Howe Street
Vancouver, BC V6C 2C2
Phone: (604) 681-9168

#295
L & G Bubble Tea
Cuisines: Taiwanese, Coffee & Tea
Average price: Under $10
Area: Sunset
Address: 5816 Fraser Street
Vancouver, BC V5W 2Z5
Phone: (604) 568-7686

#296
DD Mau
Cuisines: Vietnamese, Sandwiches
Average price: Under $10
Area: Downtown, Yaletown
Address: 1239 Pacific Boulvard
Vancouver, BC V6Z 2R6
Phone: (604) 684-4446

#297
Tera V Burger
Cuisines: Vegetarian, Burgers
Average price: Under $10
Area: Kitsilano
Address: 2961 W Broadway
Vancouver, BC V6K 2G9
Phone: (604) 336-3575

#298
Yolk's Restaurant & Commissary
Cuisines: Breakfast & Brunch
Average price: $11-30
Area: Strathcona, Downtown Eastside
Address: 1298 E Hastings St
Vancouver, BC V6A 1S6
Phone: (604) 428-9655

#299
Dark Table
Cuisines: Canadian
Average price: $31-60
Area: Kitsilano
Address: 2611 W 4th Avenue
Vancouver, BC V6K 3V9
Phone: (604) 739-3275

#300
Babylon Café
Cuisines: Middle Eastern
Average price: Under $10
Area: West End
Address: 1156 Denman St
Vancouver, BC V6G 2M9
Phone: (604) 568-7010

#301
Ramen Jinya
Cuisines: Japanese
Average price: $11-30
Area: Downtown
Address: 270 Robson Street
Vancouver, BC V6B 0E7
Phone: (604) 568-9711

#302
La Bodega Restaurante & Tapas Bar
Cuisines: Spanish, Tapas Bar
Average price: $11-30
Area: Downtown
Address: 1277 Howe Street
Vancouver, BC V6Z 1R3
Phone: (604) 684-8814

#303
Momo Sushi House
Cuisines: Sushi Bar
Average price: Under $10
Area: West End
Address: 833 Bidwell Street
Vancouver, BC V6G 2J7
Phone: (604) 569-2001

#304
Portland Craft
Cuisines: Pub, Gastropub
Average price: $11-30
Area: Riley Park
Address: 3835 Main Street
Vancouver, BC V5V 3N9
Phone: (604) 569-2494

#305
Bangkok City Cafe
Cuisines: Thai
Average price: $11-30
Area: Kitsilano
Address: 2953 W 4th Avenue
Vancouver, BC V6K 1R3
Phone: (604) 736-5474

#306
The Morrissey Pub
Cuisines: Pub, Irish
Average price: $11-30
Area: Downtown, Granville Entertainment District
Address: 1227 Granville Street
Vancouver, BC V6Z 1M5
Phone: (604) 682-0909

#307
Donair King Restaurant
Cuisines: Mediterranean, Middle Eastern, Donairs
Average price: Under $10
Area: West End
Address: 1028 Davie Street
Vancouver, BC V6E 1M3
Phone: (604) 685-8723

#308
Laksa King
Cuisines: Burmese, Malaysian
Average price: Under $10
Area: Hastings-Sunrise
Address: 2546 E Hastings Street
Vancouver, BC V5K 1Z3
Phone: (604) 428-0155

#309
Salmon n' Bannock
Cuisines: Canadian
Average price: $11-30
Area: Fairview Slopes
Address: 1128 W Broadway
Vancouver, BC V6H 1G5
Phone: (604) 568-8971

#310
Cafe Xu Hue
Cuisines: Vietnamese
Average price: Under $10
Area: Kensington-Cedar Cottage
Address: 2226 Kingsway
Vancouver, BC V5N 2T7
Phone: (604) 454-9940

#311
Tamam
Cuisines: Middle Eastern
Average price: $11-30
Area: Hastings-Sunrise
Address: 2616 E Hastings Street
Vancouver, BC V5K 1Z6
Phone: (604) 620-7078

#312
Cactus Club Cafe
Cuisines: Canadian
Average price: $11-30
Area: West End
Address: 1790 Beach Avenue
Vancouver, BC V6E 1V3
Phone: (604) 681-2582

#313
Pho Linh Vietnamese Restaurant
Cuisines: Vietnamese
Average price: Under $10
Area: Mount Pleasant
Address: 325 Broadway E
Vancouver, BC V5T 1W5
Phone: (604) 875-6443

#314
Don't Argue! Pizzeria
Cuisines: Pizza
Average price: $11-30
Area: Riley Park
Address: 3240 Main Street
Vancouver, BC V5V 3M5
Phone: (604) 876-5408

#315
Ba Le Sandwich Shop
Cuisines: Sandwiches, Vietnamese
Average price: Under $10
Area: Chinatown, Strathcona
Address: 638 Main Street
Vancouver, BC V6A 2V4
Phone: (604) 662-8108

#316
Healthy Noodle House
Cuisines: Ethnic Food, Chinese
Average price: Under $10
Area: Kitsilano
Address: 2716 W 4th Avenue
Vancouver, BC V6K 3V9
Phone: (778) 371-8371

#317
Hyoga Japanese Cuisine
Cuisines: Japanese
Average price: $11-30
Area: Killarney, Renfrew-Collingwood
Address: 2-3343 Kingsway
Vancouver, BC V5R 5K6
Phone: (604) 438-0066

#318
The Ouisi Bistro
Cuisines: Cajun/Creole, Breakfast & Brunch
Average price: $11-30
Area: Fairview Slopes, South Granville
Address: 3014 Granville St
Vancouver, BC V6H 3J8
Phone: (604) 732-7550

#319
Bob Likes Thai Food
Cuisines: Thai
Average price: $11-30
Area: Riley Park
Address: 3755 Main St
Vancouver, BC V5V
Phone: (604) 568-8538

#320
Ba Le Sandwich Shop
Cuisines: Sandwiches, Vietnamese
Average price: Under $10
Area: Mount Pleasant
Address: 701 Kingsway
Vancouver, BC V5T 3K6
Phone: (604) 875-0088

#321
Tony's Fish & Oyster Café
Cuisines: Seafood
Average price: $11-30
Area: Granville Island/False Creek
Address: 1511 Anderson St
Vancouver, BC V6H 3R5
Phone: (604) 683-7127

#322
The August Jack
Cuisines: Tapas Bar
Average price: $11-30
Area: Kitsilano
Address: 2042 W 4th Avenue
Vancouver, BC V6J 1N3
Phone: (604) 428-0075

#323
Thyme To Indulge
Cuisines: Caterer, Brasserie, Cafe
Average price: $11-30
Area: Mount Pleasant
Address: 2858 Main Street
Vancouver, BC V5T 3G2
Phone: (604) 877-1760

#324
Indian Oven Restaurant
Cuisines: Indian
Average price: $11-30
Area: Kitsilano
Address: 2006 4th Avenue W
Vancouver, BC V6J 1M9
Phone: (604) 730-5069

#325
Eternal Abundance
Cuisines: Vegan, Juice Bar
Average price: $11-30
Area: Grandview-Woodlands, The Drive
Address: 1025 Commercial Drive
Vancouver, BC V5L 3X1
Phone: (604) 707-0088

#326
Cascades Lounge
Cuisines: Lounge, Canadian
Average price: $31-60
Area: Downtown
Address: 999 Place
Vancouver, BC V6C 3B5
Phone: (604) 662-8111

#327
Tokyo Thyme
Cuisines: Japanese, Sushi Bar
Average price: $11-30
Area: Kerrisdale, Arbutus Ridge
Address: 5405 W Boulevard
Vancouver, BC V6M 3W5
Phone: (604) 263-3262

#328
The Elbow Room Café
Cuisines: Diner, Breakfast & Brunch
Average price: $11-30
Area: Downtown
Address: 560 Davie St
Vancouver, BC V6B 2G4
Phone: (604) 685-3628

#329
Guu Garden
Cuisines: Japanese, Tapas
Average price: $11-30
Area: Downtown
Address: 888 Nelson St
Vancouver, BC V6Z
Phone: (604) 899-0855

#330
Breka Bakery & Cafe
Cuisines: Cafe, Bakery
Average price: Under $10
Area: West End
Address: 812 Bute Street
Vancouver, BC V6E 1Y4
Phone: (604) 620-8200

#331
Eight 1/2 Restaurant Lounge
Cuisines: Tapas, Pizza, Canadian
Average price: $11-30
Area: Mount Pleasant
Address: 151 E 8th Ave
Vancouver, BC V5T 1R8
Phone: (604) 568-2703

#332
Jambo Grill
Cuisines: African, Indian
Average price: $11-30
Area: Renfrew-Collingwood
Address: 3219 Kingsway
Vancouver, BC V5R 5K3
Phone: (604) 433-5060

#333
Red Pagoda
Cuisines: Vietnamese
Average price: $11-30
Area: Grandview-Woodlands, The Drive
Address: 1408 Commercial Dr
Vancouver, BC V5L 3X9
Phone: (604) 569-1919

#334
LanaLou's
Cuisines: Music Venues, Canadian
Average price: Under $10
Area: Downtown Eastside
Address: 362 Powell Street
Vancouver, BC V6A 1G4
Phone: (604) 563-5055

#335
Axum Restaurant
Cuisines: Ethiopian
Average price: $11-30
Area: Downtown Eastside
Address: 1279 E Hastings St
Vancouver, BC V6A 1S4
Phone: (604) 253-2986

#336
The Storm Crow Tavern
Cuisines: Pub, Canadian
Average price: Under $10
Area: Grandview-Woodlands, The Drive
Address: 1305 Commercial Drive
Vancouver, BC V5L 3X5
Phone: (604) 566-9669

#337
Sushi California
Cuisines: Japanese, Sushi Bar
Average price: Under $10
Area: Mount Pleasant
Address: 388 W Broadway
Vancouver, BC V5Y 4A8
Phone: (604) 873-8284

#338
Cafe Phin
Cuisines: Vietnamese, Sandwiches
Average price: Under $10
Area: West End
Address: 976 Denman Street
Vancouver, BC V6G 2M1
Phone: (604) 620-5595

#339
Tap and Barrel
Cuisines: Comfort Food
Average price: $11-30
Area: Coal Harbour, Downtown
Address: 1055 Place
Vancouver, BC V6C 0C3
Phone: (604) 235-9827

#340
Blue Moon Cafe
Cuisines: Cafe, Breakfast & Brunch
Average price: Under $10
Area: Fairview Slopes
Address: 1724 4th Avenue W
Vancouver, BC V6J 1M1
Phone: (604) 738-2656

#341
Nuba Mount Pleasant
Cuisines: Mediterranean, Lebanese
Average price: $11-30
Area: Mount Pleasant
Address: 146 E 3rd Avenue
Vancouver, BC V5T 1C8
Phone: (604) 568-6727

#342
Graze
Cuisines: Vegan, Vegetarian,
Breakfast & Brunch
Average price: $11-30
Area: Riley Park
Address: 3980 Fraser Street
Vancouver, BC V5V 4E4
Phone: (604) 620-8822

#343
**Lolita's South of
the Border Cantina**
Cuisines: Mexican
Average price: $11-30
Area: West End
Address: 1326 Davie Street
Vancouver, BC V6E 1N6
Phone: (604) 696-9996

#344
Scandilicious
Cuisines: Scandinavian
Average price: Under $10
Area: Grandview-Woodlands, The Drive
Address: 1340 Commercial Drive
Vancouver, BC V5L 2T6
Phone: (604) 879-7226

#345
The Greedy Pig
Cuisines: Gastropub
Average price: $11-30
Area: Downtown, Gastown
Address: 307 W Cordova Street
Vancouver, BC V6B 1E5
Phone: (604) 669-4991

#346
Sula Indian Restaurant
Cuisines: Indian, Vegetarian,
Gluten-Free
Average price: $11-30
Area: Grandview-Woodlands, The Drive
Address: 1128 Commercial Drive
Vancouver, BC V5L 2N1
Phone: (604) 215-1130

#347
Café Régalade
Cuisines: French
Average price: $11-30
Area: Kitsilano
Address: 2836 W 4th Avenue
Vancouver, BC V6K 1R2
Phone: (604) 733-2213

#348
Steamworks Brewing Company
Cuisines: Pub, Canadian, Brewerie
Average price: $11-30
Area: Downtown, Gastown
Address: 375 Water Street
Vancouver, BC V6B 5C6
Phone: (604) 689-2739

#349
Notturno
Cuisines: Italian, Wine Bar
Average price: $11-30
Area: Downtown, Gastown
Address: 280 Carrall Street
Vancouver, BC V6B 2J2
Phone: (604) 720-3145

#350
Damso
Cuisines: Korean
Average price: $11-30
Area: West End
Address: 867 Denman Street
Vancouver, BC V6G 2L9
Phone: (604) 632-0022

#351
The American Cheesesteak
Cuisines: Cheesesteaks, Sandwiches
Average price: $11-30
Area: Downtown, Granville Entertainment District
Address: 781 Davie Street
Vancouver, BC V6Z 2S7
Phone: (604) 681-0130

#352
Song Huong
Cuisines: Vietnamese, Chinese
Average price: Under $10
Area: Grandview-Woodlands
Address: 1613 Nanaimo Street
Vancouver, BC V5L 4T9
Phone: (604) 568-1196

#353
Emelle's Catering
Cuisines: Caterer, Cafe, Breakfast & Brunch
Average price: Under $10
Area: Mount Pleasant
Address: 177 W 7th Avenue
Vancouver, BC V5Y 1L8
Phone: (604) 875-6551

#354
Banana Leaf
Cuisines: Malaysian, Singaporean
Average price: $11-30
Area: Kitsilano
Address: 3005 W Broadway
Vancouver, BC V6K 2G9
Phone: (604) 734-3005

#355
Unforgettable Pizza & Pasta
Cuisines: Pizza, Italian
Average price: Under $10
Area: Mount Pleasant
Address: 450 8th Ave W
Vancouver, BC V5Y 1N9
Phone: (604) 739-7389

#356
Pizza Carano
Cuisines: Pizza, Italian
Average price: $11-30
Area: Riley Park
Address: 4241 Fraser Street
Vancouver, BC V5V 4G1
Phone: (604) 877-1270

#357
LIFT Bar Grill View
Cuisines: Seafood, Bar
Average price: $31-60
Area: Coal Harbour
Address: 333 Menchions Mews
Vancouver, BC V6G 3H5
Phone: (604) 689-5438

#358
The Reef
Cuisines: Caterer, Caribbean, Breakfast & Brunch
Average price: $11-30
Area: Riley Park
Address: 4172 Main Street
Vancouver, BC V5V 3P7
Phone: (604) 874-5375

#359
Trafiq Cafe & Bakery
Cuisines: Cafe, Bakery
Average price: $11-30
Area: Riley Park
Address: 4216 Main Street
Vancouver, BC V5V 3R1
Phone: (604) 648-2244

#360
The Noodle Box
Cuisines: Asian Fusion
Average price: $11-30
Area: Kitsilano
Address: 1867 W 4th Ave
Vancouver, BC V6J 1M3
Phone: (604) 734-1310

#361
Fresh Take-Out Japanese
Cuisines: Japanese, Sushi Bar
Average price: $11-30
Area: Downtown, Yaletown
Address: 909 Expo Boulevard
Vancouver, BC V6Z
Phone: (604) 568-6112

#362
The Farmer's Apprentice
Cuisines: French, Asian Fusion
Average price: $11-30
Area: Fairview Slopes, South Granville
Address: 1535 W 6th Avenue
Vancouver, BC V6H 3G1
Phone: (604) 620-2070

#363
Bambudda
Cuisines: Chinese
Average price: $11-30
Area: Downtown, Gastown
Address: 99 Powell Street
Vancouver, BC V6A 1E9
Phone: (604) 428-0301

#364
Caffè Artigiano
Cuisines: Coffee & Tea, Sandwiches
Average price: Under $10
Area: Downtown
Address: 740 W Hastings St
Vancouver, BC V6C 1A3
Phone: (604) 915-7200

#365
Babylon Cafe
Cuisines: Middle Eastern
Average price: Under $10
Area: West End
Address: 1610 Robson St
Vancouver, BC V6G
Phone: (604) 568-6324

#366
Nuba in Kitsilano
Cuisines: Middle Eastern, Vegetarian
Average price: $11-30
Area: Kitsilano
Address: 3116 West Broadway
Vancouver, BC V6K 2G9
Phone: (604) 336-1797

#367
Provence Mediterranean Grill
Cuisines: Mediterranean, French
Average price: $31-60
Area: Point Grey
Address: 4473 10th Ave W
Vancouver, BC V6R 2H8
Phone: (604) 222-1980

#368
Corduroy
Cuisines: Pizza, Lounge
Average price: $11-30
Area: Kitsilano
Address: 1943 Cornwall Ave
Vancouver, BC V6J
Phone: (604) 733-0162

#369
Cactus Club Cafe
Cuisines: Canadian
Average price: $11-30
Area: West End
Address: 1136 Robson St
Vancouver, BC V6E 1B2
Phone: (604) 687-3278

#370
Flamingo Restaurant
Cuisines: Chinese
Average price: $11-30
Area: Marpole
Address: 7510 Cambie Street
Vancouver, BC V5P 3H7
Phone: (604) 325-4511

#371
Slickity Jim's Chat 'N' Chew
Cuisines: Diner, Breakfast & Brunch
Average price: $11-30
Area: Riley Park
Address: 3475 Main Street
Vancouver, BC V5V 3M9
Phone: (604) 873-6760

#372
Aphrodite's Organic Café and Pie Shop
Cuisines: American, Gluten-Free
Average price: $11-30
Area: Kitsilano
Address: 3598 4th Ave W
Vancouver, BC V6R 1N8
Phone: (604) 733-8308

#373
Burdock & Co
Cuisines: Tapas Bar, French
Average price: $31-60
Area: Mount Pleasant
Address: 2702 Main Street
Vancouver, BC V5T 3E8
Phone: (604) 879-0077

#374
Trattoria Kitchen
Cuisines: Italian
Average price: $11-30
Area: Kitsilano
Address: 1850 W 4th Ave
Vancouver, BC V6J 1M3
Phone: (604) 732-1441

#375
Lucy's Eastside Diner
Cuisines: Diner, American
Average price: Under $10
Area: Mount Pleasant
Address: 2708 Main Street
Vancouver, BC V5T
Phone: (604) 568-1550

#376
Biiru-Bin
Cuisines: Japanese, Sushi Bar
Average price: $11-30
Area: Shaughnessy, Fairview Slopes
Address: 3098 Oak Street
Vancouver, BC V6H 2K8
Phone: (604) 568-8215

#377
La Terrazza
Cuisines: Italian
Average price: $31-60
Area: Downtown, Yaletown
Address: 1088 Cambie Street
Vancouver, BC V6B 6J5
Phone: (604) 899-4449

#378
Black & Blue
Cuisines: Steakhouse
Average price: $31-60
Area: West End, Downtown
Address: 1032 Alberni Street
Vancouver, BC V6E 1A3
Phone: (604) 637-0777

#379
Reflections
Cuisines: Canadian, Lounge
Average price: $31-60
Area: Downtown
Address: 801 W Georgia Street
Vancouver, BC V6C 1P7
Phone: (604) 682-5566

#380
Feastro
Cuisines: Food Stands
Average price: $11-30
Area: Coal Harbour, Downtown
Address: 200 Thurlow Street
Vancouver, BC V6Z 3T1
Phone: (604) 868-9339

#381
Chill Winston Restaurant & Lounge
Cuisines: Lounge, Canadian
Average price: $11-30
Area: Downtown, Gastown
Address: 3 Alexander Street
Vancouver, BC V6A
Phone: (604) 288-9575

#382
Memphis Blues Barbeque House
Cuisines: Barbeque
Average price: $11-30
Area: Downtown
Address: 430 Robson Street
Vancouver, BC V6B 2B7
Phone: (604) 682-6220

#383
Purple Olive Grill
Cuisines: Canadian, Seafood
Average price: Under $10
Area: West End, Downtown
Address: 850 Thurlow Street
Vancouver, BC V6E 1W2
Phone: (604) 558-2103

#384
2001 Flavours
Cuisines: Pizza
Average price: Under $10
Area: Downtown
Address: 595 W Pender Street
Vancouver, BC V6B 1V5
Phone: (604) 689-8847

#385
Famoso Neapolitan Pizzeria
Cuisines: Pizza, Italian
Average price: $11-30
Area: Grandview-Woodlands, The Drive
Address: 1380 Commercial Drive
Vancouver, BC V5L 3X6
Phone: (604) 251-2292

#386
Seoul Doogbaegi
Cuisines: Korean
Average price: $11-30
Area: Kensington-Cedar Cottage
Address: 1033 Kingsway
Vancouver, BC V5V
Phone: (604) 879-1515

#387
El Camino's
Cuisines: Latin American
Average price: $11-30
Area: Riley Park
Address: 3250 Main Street
Vancouver, BC V5V 3M5
Phone: (604) 875-6246

#388
Zakkushi Charcoal Grill
Cuisines: Japanese
Average price: $11-30
Area: Riley Park
Address: 4075 Main Street
Vancouver, BC V5V 3P5
Phone: (604) 874-9455

#389
Tatsu Japanese Bistro
Cuisines: Japanese
Average price: $11-30
Area: Grandview-Woodlands, The Drive
Address: 1441 Commercial Drive
Vancouver, BC V5L 3X8
Phone: (604) 558-2285

#390
Seventeen89
Cuisines: Seafood, Steakhouse, Lounge
Average price: $31-60
Area: West End
Address: 1789 Comox Street
Vancouver, BC V6G 2M5
Phone: (604) 428-0705

#391
Vij's Railway Express
Cuisines: Indian, Food Truck
Average price: $11-30
Area: West End, Downtown
Address: 1075 W Georgia Street
Vancouver, BC V6E 0B6
Phone: (604) 639-3335

#392
Joe's Grill
Cuisines: Breakfast & Brunch
Average price: Under $10
Area: West End
Address: 1031 Davie Street
Vancouver, BC V6E 1M5
Phone: (604) 682-3683

#393
Alpha Sushi Bar
Cuisines: Japanese, Sushi Ba
Average price: $11-30
Area: Downtown, Granville
Entertainment District
Address: 1265 Granville Street
Vancouver, BC V6Z 1M5
Phone: (604) 633-0355

#394
The Diner
Cuisines: Diner, Seafood, British
Average price: Under $10
Area: Point Grey
Address: 4556 10th Ave W
Vancouver, BC V6R 2J1
Phone: (604) 224-1912

#395
El Pulgarcito
Cuisines: Mexican, Salvadoran
Average price: Under $10
Area: Hastings-Sunrise
Address: 2522 E Hastings Street
Vancouver, BC V5K 1Z3
Phone: (604) 568-8591

#396
The Fish Shack
Cuisines: Seafood, Fish & Chips
Average price: $11-30
Area: Downtown, Granville
Entertainment District
Address: 1026 Granville Street
Vancouver, BC V6Z 1L2
Phone: (604) 678-1049

#397
Khunnai Chang Thai Cuisine
Cuisines: Thai
Average price: $11-30
Area: West End
Address: 835 Denman Street
Vancouver, BC V6G 2L7
Phone: (604) 801-6093

#398
Clough Club
Cuisines: Lounge, Tapas
Average price: $11-30
Area: Downtown, Gastown
Address: 212 Abbott Street
Vancouver, BC V6B 1B2
Phone: (604) 558-1581

#399
Shuraku Restaurant
Cuisines: Japanese, Sushi Bar
Average price: $11-30
Area: Downtown, Granville
Entertainment District
Address: 833 Granville Street
Vancouver, BC V6Z
Phone: (604) 687-6622

#400
Soho Road Naan Kebab
Cuisines: Indian, Food Truck
Average price: Under $10
Area: Downtown
Address: 700 W Georgia Street
Vancouver, BC V6Z 2H7
Phone: (778) 558-7272

#401
Yek O Yek
Cuisines: Deli, Sandwiches
Average price: Under $10
Area: Mount Pleasant
Address: 3046 Main Street
Vancouver, BC V5T 3G5
Phone: (604) 877-0139

#402
The Deli - Family Gourmet
Cuisines: Deli, Sandwiches
Average price: Under $10
Area: Downtown
Address: 1055 W Georgia St, Ste 242
Vancouver, BC V6E 3P1
Phone: (604) 605-3354

#403
Moose's Down Under
Cuisines: Pub, Australian
Average price: $11-30
Area: Downtown
Address: 830 Pender Street W
Vancouver, BC V6C 1J8
Phone: (604) 683-3300

#404
The Naam
Cuisines: Vegetarian, Burgers, Mexican
Average price: $11-30
Area: Kitsilano
Address: 2724 4th Avenue W
Vancouver, BC V6K 1R1
Phone: (604) 738-7151

#405
Le Parisien
Cuisines: French
Average price: $31-60
Area: West End
Address: 751 Denman Street
Vancouver, BC V6G 2L6
Phone: (604) 687-1418

#406
Liquids and Solids
Cuisines: Soup, Cafe, Canadian
Average price: Under $10
Area: Grandview-Woodlands, The Drive
Address: 1530 Venables Street
Vancouver, BC V5L 2G8
Phone: (604) 568-8343

#407
Romer's Burger Bar
Cuisines: Burgers
Average price: $11-30
Area: Killarney
Address: 8683 Kerr St
Vancouver, BC V5S 4V7
Phone: (604) 566-9545

#408
Zest Japanese Cuisine
Cuisines: Japanese
Average price: $31-60
Area: Kitsilano
Address: 2775 W 16th Avenue
Vancouver, BC V6K 3C3
Phone: (604) 731-9378

#409
Siegel's Bagels
Cuisines: Bagels, Bakery, Sandwiches
Average price: Under $10
Area: Kitsilano
Address: 1883 Cornwall Avenue
Vancouver, BC V6J 1C6
Phone: (604) 737-8151

#410
Symphonie Restaurant
Cuisines: Filipino
Average price: Under $10
Area: Coal Harbour, Downtown
Address: 1140 Pender Street W
Vancouver, BC V6E 4G1
Phone: (604) 662-3365

#411
**Lobby Lounge
at Shangri-La Hotel**
Cuisines: Canadian
Average price: Above $61
Area: West End, Downtown
Address: 1128 W Georgia Street
Vancouver, BC V6E 0A8
Phone: (604) 689-1120

#412
Rogue Kitchen & Wetbar
Cuisines: American, Gastropub
Average price: $11-30
Area: Fairview Slopes
Address: 602 West Broadway Avenue
Vancouver, BC V5Z 3J2
Phone: (604) 568-9400

#413
Finch's Market
Cuisines: Cafe, Grocery
Average price: $11-30
Area: Strathcona
Address: 501 E Georgia Street
Vancouver, BC V6A 1X8
Phone: (604) 558-1644

#414
Bistro Wagon Rouge
Cuisines: French
Average price: $11-30
Area: Grandview-Woodlands
Address: 1869 Powell Street
Vancouver, BC V5L 1H9
Phone: (604) 251-4070

#415
Rocky Mountain Flatbread
Cuisines: Breakfast & Brunch,
Pizza, Gluten-Free
Average price: $11-30
Area: Riley Park
Address: 4186 Main Street
Vancouver, BC V5V 3P6
Phone: (604) 566-9779

#416
Tap and Barrel
Cuisines: Comfort Food, Bar
Average price: $11-30
Area: Granville Island/False Creek
Address: 1 Athletes Way
Vancouver, BC V5Y 0B1
Phone: (604) 685-2223

#417
Peckinpah
Cuisines: Barbeque
Average price: $11-30
Area: Downtown, Gastown
Address: 2 Water Street
Vancouver, BC V6B 1B2
Phone: (604) 681-5411

#418
The Fountainhead Pub
Cuisines: Pub, Gastropub, Gay Bar
Average price: $11-30
Area: West End
Address: 1025 Davie Street
Vancouver, BC V6E 1M5
Phone: (604) 687-2222

#419
Applause Japanese Restaurant
Cuisines: Japanese, Sushi Bar
Average price: $11-30
Area: Marpole
Address: 8269 Oak Street
Vancouver, BC V6P 4A8
Phone: (604) 263-8968

#420
Sweetery Cafe + Dessert
Cuisines: Cafe, Coffee & Tea, Desserts
Average price: $11-30
Area: Mount Pleasant
Address: 340 W 2nd Avenue
Vancouver, BC V5Y 3W3
Phone: (604) 568-5486

#421
Pho Xe Lua 24
Cuisines: Vietnamese
Average price: Under $10
Area: South Cambie, Riley Park
Address: 3346 Cambie Street
Vancouver, BC V5Y 2A1
Phone: (604) 876-6618

#422
Indian Roti Kitchen
Cuisines: Indian, Vegetarian
Average price: $11-30
Area: Fairview Slopes
Address: 2961 Cambie Street
Vancouver, BC V5Z 2V7
Phone: (604) 876-3767

#423
Sandwich Plus
Cuisines: Sandwiches
Average price: Under $10
Area: Downtown
Address: 530 Hornby Street
Vancouver, BC V6C 2E7
Phone: (604) 682-7565

#424
Salsa & Agave Mexican Grill
Cuisines: Mexican
Average price: $11-30
Area: Downtown, Yaletown
Address: 1205 Pacific Boulevard
Vancouver, BC V6Z 2R6
Phone: (604) 408-4228

#425
Yamato Sushi Restaurant
Cuisines: Sushi Bar
Average price: Under $10
Area: Downtown, Granville Entertainment District
Address: 616 Davie Street
Vancouver, BC V6B 2G5
Phone: (604) 682-5494

#426
Green Lettuce Indian Style Chinese Restaurant
Cuisines: Chinese, Indian
Average price: $11-30
Area: Kensington-Cedar Cottage
Address: 1949 Kingsway
Vancouver, BC V5N 2T1
Phone: (604) 876-9883

#427
Tableau Bar Bistro
Cuisines: French, Wine Bar
Average price: $31-60
Area: Downtown
Address: 1181 Melville St
Vancouver, BC V6E 2S8
Phone: (604) 639-8692

#428
Market by Jean Georges
Cuisines: Diner
Average price: $31-60
Area: West End, Downtown
Address: 1115 Alberni Street
Vancouver, BC V6Z 2V6
Phone: (604) 695-1115

#429
Temaki Sushi
Cuisines: Sushi Bar, Japanese
Average price: $11-30
Area: Kitsilano
Address: 2156 Broadway W
Vancouver, BC V6K 2C8
Phone: (604) 738-4321

#430
Jamaican Pizza Jerk
Cuisines: Pizza, Caribbean
Average price: $11-30
Area: Kensington-Cedar Cottage
Address: 2707 Commercial Dr
Vancouver, BC V5N 4C5
Phone: (604) 876-3343

#431
Rice 'N Spice
Cuisines: Asian Fusion, Mediterranean
Average price: Under $10
Area: Downtown, Yaletown
Address: 883 Hamilton Street
Vancouver, BC V6B 2R7
Phone: (604) 568-4446

#432
Vera's Burger Shack
Cuisines: Burgers
Average price: $11-30
Area: West End
Address: 1030 Davie St
Vancouver, BC V6E 1M3
Phone: (604) 893-8372

#433
Sylvia's Restaurant & Lounge
Cuisines: Hotel, Lounge
Average price: $11-30
Area: West End
Address: 1154 Gilford St
Vancouver, BC V6G
Phone: (604) 681-9321

#434
The Pie Shoppe
Cuisines: Desserts, Cafe
Average price: $11-30
Area: Strathcona
Address: 721 Gore Avenue
Vancouver, BC V6A 2Z9
Phone: (604) 338-6646

#435
Scandilicious
Cuisines: Bakery, Scandinavian
Average price: Under $10
Area: Grandview-Woodlands
Address: 25 Victoria Drive
Vancouver, BC V5L 4C1
Phone: (604) 877-2277

#436
Cafe Mai-Mai
Cuisines: Vietnamese
Average price: Under $10
Area: Marpole
Address: 8636 Granville Street
Vancouver, BC V6P 5A1
Phone: (604) 428-4191

#437
La Notte Restaurant
Cuisines: Italian
Average price: $11-30
Area: Dunbar-Southlands
Address: 3307 Dunbar St
Vancouver, BC V6S 2B9
Phone: (604) 222-4033

#438
Mahony & Sons Burrard Landing
Cuisines: Irish, Pub, Burgers
Average price: $11-30
Area: Coal Harbour, Downtown
Address: 1055 Pl
Vancouver, BC V6C 0C3
Phone: (604) 647-7513

#439
Chipotle
Cuisines: Mexican, Fast Food
Average price: $11-30
Area: Downtown, Granville Entertainment District
Address: 818 Howe St
Vancouver, BC V6Z 2S9
Phone: (604) 683-6394

#440
Wick's Café
Cuisines: Cafe
Average price: Under $10
Area: Marpole
Address: 1300 W 73rd Ave
Vancouver, BC V6P 3E7
Phone: (604) 677-6396

#441
Splitz Grill
Cuisines: American, Burgers
Average price: $11-30
Area: Riley Park
Address: 4242 Main Street
Vancouver, BC V5V 3P9
Phone: (604) 875-9711

#442
Martini's
Cuisines: Pizza, Italian, Greek
Average price: $11-30
Area: Mount Pleasant
Address: 151 W Broadway St
Vancouver, BC V5Y
Phone: (604) 873-0021

#443
The Moose Vancouver
Cuisines: Tapas Bar
Average price: Under $10
Area: Downtown, Granville Entertainment District
Address: 724 Nelson Street
Vancouver, BC V6Z 1A8
Phone: (604) 633-1002

#444
Dream Sushi
Cuisines: Japanese, Sushi Bar
Average price: $11-30
Area: Riley Park
Address: 4401 Main Street
Vancouver, BC V5V 3R2
Phone: (604) 708-1768

#445
Chewies Steam & Oyster Bar
Cuisines: Cajun/Creole
Average price: $11-30
Area: Coal Harbour, Downtown
Address: 1055 West Hastings
Vancouver, BC V6E 2E9
Phone: (604) 620-7634

#446
Lin Chinese Cuisine and Tea House
Cuisines: Chinese
Average price: $11-30
Area: Fairview Slopes, South Granville
Address: 1537 West Broadway
Vancouver, BC V6J 1W6
Phone: (604) 733-9696

#447
Ki-Isu Japanese Restaurant
Cuisines: Japanese, Sushi Bar
Average price: $11-30
Area: Downtown, Yaletown
Address: 1275 Pacific Boulevard
Vancouver, BC V6Z 2R6
Phone: (604) 899-0366

#448
Huang's Beef Noodles
Cuisines: Taiwanese
Average price: Under $10
Area: Fraserview
Address: 6940 Victoria Dr
Vancouver, BC V5P 3Y8
Phone: (604) 324-8884

#449
Lily Mae's
Cuisines: Comfort Food, French, Breakfast & Brunch
Average price: $11-30
Area: Downtown, Gastown
Address: 12 Powell Street
Vancouver, BC V6A 1E7
Phone: (604) 558-2599

#450
Catch 122
Cuisines: Breakfast & Brunch, Canadian
Average price: $11-30
Area: Downtown, Downtown Eastside
Address: 122 W Hastings Street
Vancouver, BC V6B 1G8
Phone: (604) 731-3474

#451
Kimura
Cuisines: Sushi Bar, Japanese
Average price: $11-30
Area: Renfrew-Collingwood
Address: 3883 Rupert Street
Vancouver, BC V5R
Phone: (604) 569-2198

#452
Lions Den Cafe
Cuisines: Breakfast & Brunch, Cafe
Average price: Under $10
Area: Mount Pleasant
Address: 651 15th Avenue E
Vancouver, BC V5T 2R6
Phone: (604) 873-4555

#453
Red Ginger Asian Cuisine
Cuisines: Asian Fusion
Average price: $11-30
Area: Fairview Slopes
Address: 967 West Broadway
Vancouver, BC V5Z 1K3
Phone: (604) 558-0888

#454
Caffe Barney
Cuisines: Bar, Breakfast & Brunch
Average price: $11-30
Area: Fairview Slopes, South Granville
Address: 2975 Granville Street
Vancouver, BC V6H 3J6
Phone: (604) 731-6446

#455
Chaise Lounge Restaurant
Cuisines: Lounge, American
Average price: $11-30
Area: Riley Park
Address: 4444 Main St
Vancouver, BC V5V 3R3
Phone: (604) 874-7114

#456
La Pentola della Quercia
Cuisines: Italian
Average price: $31-60
Area: Downtown, Yaletown
Address: 350 Davie Street
Vancouver, BC V6B 1R2
Phone: (604) 642-0557

#457
Baguette & Co
Cuisines: Desserts, Cafe, Bakery
Average price: Under $10
Area: West End
Address: 1102 Davie Street
Vancouver, BC V6E 1N1
Phone: (604) 684-8003

#458
Pho Central
Cuisines: Vietnamese
Average price: Under $10
Area: West End
Address: 1118 Davie St
Vancouver, BC V6E
Phone: (604) 669-8638

#459
Kranky Cafe
Cuisines: Coffee & Tea, Bakery, Cafe
Average price: Under $10
Area: Mount Pleasant
Address: 228-216 E 4th Avenue
Vancouver, BC V5T 1G5
Phone: (604) 568-4272

#460
Kobob Burger
Cuisines: Burgers, Asian Fusion
Average price: Under $10
Area: Downtown, Strathcona
Address: 1019 Main Street
Vancouver, BC V6A 2V8
Phone: (604) 569-3939

#461
The Dime Road House
Cuisines: Canadian
Average price: Under $10
Area: Grandview-Woodlands, The Drive
Address: 1565 Commercial Drive
Vancouver, BC V6Z 1P5
Phone: (604) 340-3706

#462
Trafalgars Bistro
Cuisines: Desserts, French,
Breakfast & Brunch
Average price: $11-30
Area: Kitsilano
Address: 2603 16th Avenue W
Vancouver, BC V6K 3C2
Phone: (604) 739-0555

#463
Harvest Community Foods
Cuisines: Grocery, Cafe
Average price: $11-30
Area: Strathcona
Address: 243 Union Street
Vancouver, BC V6A 2B2
Phone: (604) 682-8851

#464
Taser Grilled Cheese Sandwiches
Cuisines: Street Vendor, Sandwiches
Average price: Under $10
Area: Strathcona
Address: Main St & Terminal Ave
Vancouver, BC V6A
Phone: (604) 448-2121

#465
Commercial Street Cafe
Cuisines: Cafe
Average price: Under $10
Area: Kensington-Cedar Cottage
Address: 3599 Commercial Street
Vancouver, BC V5N 4E8
Phone: (604) 877-8669

#466
Café Deux Soleils
Cuisines: Coffee & Tea, Vegetarian,
Breakfast & Brunch
Average price: $11-30
Area: Grandview-Woodlands, The Drive
Address: 2096 Commercial Dr
Vancouver, BC V5N 4B2
Phone: (604) 254-1195

#467
Chongqing Restaurant
Cuisines: Chinese
Average price: $11-30
Area: Kensington-Cedar Cottage
Address: 2808 Commercial Dr
Vancouver, BC V5N 4C6
Phone: (604) 254-7434

#468
Mui Garden Restaurant
Cuisines: Chinese
Average price: Under $10
Area: Riley Park
Address: 4265 Main St
Vancouver, BC V5V
Phone: (604) 872-8232

#469
The Eatery
Cuisines: Japanese, Sushi Bar, Asian Fusion
Average price: $11-30
Area: Kitsilano
Address: 3431 W Broadway
Vancouver, BC V6R 2B4
Phone: (604) 738-5298

#470
Guanaco Food Truck
Cuisines: Food Truck, Salvadoran
Average price: Under $10
Area: Downtown
Address: Granville Street & W Broadway
Vancouver, BC V6B
Phone: (604) 442-2374

#471
The Wolf & Hound
Cuisines: Pub, Irish
Average price: $11-30
Area: Kitsilano
Address: 3617 W Broadway
Vancouver, BC V6R 2B8
Phone: (604) 738-8909

#472
Maple Leaf Delicatessen
Cuisines: Deli
Average price: Under $10
Area: West End, Downtown
Address: 1233 Burrard St
Vancouver, BC V6Z 1Z5
Phone: (604) 689-3411

#473
Las Tortas
Cuisines: Mexican, Sandwiches, Delicatessen
Average price: $11-30
Area: South Cambie, Riley Park
Address: 3353 Cambie St
Vancouver, BC V5Z 2W6
Phone: (604) 569-1402

#474
Ebisu
Cuisines: Japanese, Sushi Bar
Average price: $11-30
Area: Fairview Slopes
Address: 601 W Broadway
Vancouver, BC V5Z 4C2
Phone: (604) 876-3388

#475
Roundel Cafe
Cuisines: Vegetarian, Breakfast & Brunch, Burgers
Average price: $11-30
Area: Hastings-Sunrise
Address: 2465 E Hastings Street
Vancouver, BC V5K 1Y8
Phone: (604) 253-2522

#476
Master Chef Café
Cuisines: American, Diner
Average price: Under $10
Area: Hastings-Sunrise
Address: 2481 Hastings St E
Vancouver, BC V5K 1Y8
Phone: (604) 254-6352

#477
Five Guys Burgers and Fries
Cuisines: Burgers, Fast Food
Average price: Under $10
Area: Downtown
Address: 635 Robson Street
Vancouver, BC V6B 5J3
Phone: (604) 685-1585

#478
Chili Pepper House
Cuisines: Chinese, Asian Fusion
Average price: $11-30
Area: Renfrew-Collingwood
Address: 3003 Kingsway
Vancouver, BC V5R 5J6
Phone: (604) 431-8633

#479
Co-Zi Cafe
Cuisines: Cafe
Average price: $11-30
Area: Riley Park
Address: 4376 Fraser Street
Vancouver, BC V5V 4G3
Phone: (604) 558-2694

#480
Fresh Bowl
Cuisines: Malaysian, Vegetarian
Average price: Under $10
Area: Downtown, Gastown
Address: 360 Cambie St
Vancouver, BC V6B 1H7
Phone: (604) 248-5070

#481
Pho Goodness
Cuisines: Vietnamese
Average price: Under $10
Area: West End
Address: 1183 Davie Street
Vancouver, BC V6E 4L7
Phone: (604) 568-3253

#482
Irori Sushi
Cuisines: Sushi Bar
Average price: $11-30
Area: Point Grey
Address: 3692 W 4th Avenue
Vancouver, BC V6R 1P1
Phone: (604) 558-0885

#483
BT Cafe
Cuisines: Breakfast & Brunch, Chinese
Average price: Under $10
Area: Kensington-Cedar Cottage
Address: 920 Kingsway
Vancouver, BC V5V 3C4
Phone: (604) 872-3368

#484
Nook
Cuisines: Italian
Average price: $11-30
Area: Kitsilano
Address: 1524-1546 Yew Street
Vancouver, BC V6K 3E4
Phone: (604) 734-0099

#485
Gorilla Food
Cuisines: Vegan
Average price: $11-30
Area: Downtown
Address: 101 - 436 Richards Street
Vancouver, BC V6B 2Z4
Phone: (604) 684-3663

#486
Tandoori Raj
Cuisines: Indian
Average price: $11-30
Area: Sunset
Address: 689 E 65th Avenue
Vancouver, BC V5X 2P7
Phone: (604) 325-1301

#487
Joe's Grill
Cuisines: Diner, Breakfast & Brunch
Average price: Under $10
Area: Mount Pleasant
Address: 3048 Main Street
Vancouver, BC V5T 3G5
Phone: (604) 879-6586

#488
Tractor
Cuisines: Salad
Average price: $11-30
Area: Kitsilano
Address: 1903 W 4th Avenue
Vancouver, BC V6J 1M7
Phone: (604) 222-2557

#489
Amay's House
Cuisines: Burmese
Average price: $11-30
Area: Kensington-Cedar Cottage
Address: 5076 Victoria Drive
Vancouver, BC V5P 3V1
Phone: (604) 327-2629

#490
Foundation
Cuisines: Vegetarian
Average price: $11-30
Area: Mount Pleasant
Address: 2301 Main St
Vancouver, BC V5T 3C9
Phone: (604) 708-0881

#491
Big Lou's Butcher Shop
Cuisines: Meat Shop, Sandwiches
Average price: $11-30
Area: Downtown Eastside
Address: 269 Powell Street
Vancouver, BC V6A 0B6
Phone: (604) 566-9229

#492
Raga Restaurant
Cuisines: Caterer, Middle Eastern, Indian, Pakistani
Average price: $11-30
Area: Fairview Slopes
Address: 1177 Broadway W
Vancouver, BC V6H 1G3
Phone: (604) 733-1127

#493
Satori Factory
Cuisines: Cafe
Average price: Under $10
Area: Kensington-Cedar Cottage
Address: 5054 Victoria Drive
Vancouver, BC V5P 3T8
Phone: (604) 569-0420

#494
Jun Sushi Japanese Restaurant
Cuisines: Japanese, Sushi Bar
Average price: Under $10
Area: Kitsilano
Address: 3309 Broadway W
Vancouver, BC V6R 2B1
Phone: (604) 739-7181

#495
Ebi-Ten
Cuisines: Japanese, Fast Food
Average price: Under $10
Area: Downtown
Address: 388 Robson St
Vancouver, BC V6B 2B2
Phone: (604) 689-9938

#496
James on Hastings Chinese Restaurant
Cuisines: Chinese
Average price: $11-30
Area: Hastings-Sunrise
Address: 2683 Hastings Street E
Vancouver, BC V5K 3W8
Phone: (604) 255-3188

#497
Belgian Fries
Cuisines: Belgian, Fast Food, Poutinerie
Average price: Under $10
Area: Grandview-Woodlands, The Drive
Address: 1885 Commercial Drive
Vancouver, BC V5N 4A6
Phone: (604) 253-4220

#498
Tokiwa Sushi
Cuisines: Sushi Bar, Japanese
Average price: $11-30
Area: Shaughnessy, South Cambie
Address: 3720 Oak Street
Vancouver, BC V6H 2M3
Phone: (604) 737-7728

#499
Truong Thanh Vietnamese Restaurant
Cuisines: Vietnamese
Average price: Under $10
Area: Kensington-Cedar Cottage
Address: 2096 Kingsway
Vancouver, BC V5N 2T3
Phone: (604) 876-9288

#500
Beefy Beef Noodle House
Cuisines: Taiwanese
Average price: Under $10
Area: Riley Park
Address: 4063 Main Street
Vancouver, BC V5V 3P5
Phone: (604) 568-6821

TOP 500
ARTS & ENTERTAINMENT
The Most Recommended by Locals & Trevelers
(From #1 to #500)

#1
Rio Theatre
Category: Cinema, Performing Arts
Area: Grandview-Woodlands, The Drive, Kensington-Cedar Cottage
Address: 1660 Broadway E
Vancouver, BC V5N 1W1
Phone: (604) 879-3456

#2
VanDusen Botanical Garden
Category: Parks, Botanical Garden
Area: Shaughnessy
Address: 5251 Oak Street
Vancouver, BC V6M 4H1
Phone: (604) 257-8677

#3
Orpheum
Category: Music Venues, Performing Arts
Average price: Modest
Area: Downtown, Granville Entertainment District
Address: 884 Granville St
Vancouver, BC V6Z 1K3
Phone: (604) 665-3050

#4
Zombie Walk
Category: Festival
Area: Downtown
Address: 750 Hornby St
Vancouver, BC V6Z 2H7
Phone: (604) 662-4700

#5
Sun Yat-Sen Chinese Garden
Category: Botanical Garden
Area: Chinatown
Address: 578 Carrall Street
Vancouver, BC V6B 5K2
Phone: (604) 662-3207

#6
Guilt & Co
Category: Music Venues, Lounge
Average price: Modest
Area: Downtown, Gastown
Address: 1 Alexander Street
Vancouver, BC V6A 1B2
Phone: (604) 288-1704

#7
The Biltmore Cabaret
Category: Music Venues, Bar
Average price: Inexpensive
Area: Mount Pleasant
Address: 2755 Prince Edward Street
Vancouver, BC V5T 3J7
Phone: (604) 676-0541

#8
Fifth Avenue Cinemas
Category: Cinema
Area: Kitsilano, Fairview Slopes
Address: 2110 Burrard St
Vancouver, BC V6J 3H6
Phone: (604) 734-8700

#9
Revel Room
Category: Lounge, Southern, Music Venues
Average price: Modest
Area: Downtown, Gastown
Address: 238 Abbott St
Vancouver, BC V6B 2K8
Phone: (604) 687-4088

#10
Pacific Cinematheque
Category: Cinema
Area: Downtown
Address: 1131 Howe Street
Vancouver, BC V6Z 2L7
Phone: (604) 688-8202

#11
Railway Club
Category: Bar, Music Venues
Average price: Modest
Area: Downtown
Address: 579 Dunsmuir Street
Vancouver, BC V6B 1Y4
Phone: (604) 681-1625

#12
Cineplex Odeon International Village Cinemas
Category: Cinema
Area: Downtown
Address: 88 W Pender Street
Vancouver, BC V6B 6N9
Phone: (604) 806-0799

#13
The Improv Centre
Category: Performing Arts, Comedy Club
Average price: Modest
Area: Granville Island/False Creek
Address: 1502 Duranleau St
Vancouver, BC V6H
Phone: (604) 738-7013

#14
Vancity Theatre
Category: Cinema
Area: Downtown, Granville Entertainment District
Address: 1181 Seymour St
Vancouver, BC V6B 3M7
Phone: (604) 683-3456

#15
Army Navy & Airforce Veterans Unit 298 Canteen
Category: Bar, Social Club
Average price: Inexpensive
Area: Riley Park
Address: 3917 Main St
Vancouver, BC V5V
Phone: (604) 879-1020

#16
The Cultch
Category: Performing Arts, Venues & Event Space
Area: Grandview-Woodlands, The Drive
Address: 1895 Venables St
Vancouver, BC V5L 2H6
Phone: (604) 251-1363

#17
Arts Club Theatre Company
Category: Performing Arts
Area: Granville Island/False Creek
Address: 1585 Johnston Street
Vancouver, BC V6H 3R9
Phone: (604) 687-5315

#18
Vancouver Art Gallery
Category: Museum, Art Gallery
Average price: Modest
Area: Downtown
Address: 750 Hornby Street
Vancouver, BC V6Z 2H7
Phone: (604) 662-4700

#19
Dunbar Theatre
Category: Cinema
Area: Dunbar-Southlands
Address: 4555 Dunbar St
Vancouver, BC V6S 2G7
Phone: (604) 222-2991

#20
Park Theatre
Category: Cinema
Area: South Cambie, Riley Park
Address: 3440 Cambie Street
Vancouver, BC V5Z 2W8
Phone: (604) 709-3456

#21
Rogers Arena
Category: Arena
Area: Downtown
Address: 800 Griffiths Way
Vancouver, BC V6B 6G1
Phone: (604) 899-7400

#22
The Cobalt
Category: Bar, Music Venues
Average price: Modest
Area: Downtown, Strathcona
Address: 917 Main Street
Vancouver, BC V6A
Phone: (778) 918-3671

#23
Roundhouse Arts & Recreation Centre
Category: Performing Arts, Leisure Center
Area: Downtown, Yaletown
Address: 181 Roundhouse Mews
Vancouver, BC V6Z 2W3
Phone: (604) 713-1800

#24
The Rickshaw Theatre
Category: Music Venues, Venues & Event Space
Average price: Inexpensive
Area: Downtown Eastside
Address: 254 E Hastings St
Vancouver, BC V6A 1A1
Phone: (604) 681-8915

#25
Kino Café
Category: Performing Arts, Tapas Bar
Average price: Modest
Area: South Cambie, Riley Park
Address: 3456 Cambie Street
Vancouver, BC V5Z 2W8
Phone: (604) 875-1998

#26
LanaLou's
Category: Music Venues, Canadian
Average price: Inexpensive
Area: Downtown Eastside
Address: 362 Powell Street
Vancouver, BC V6A 1G4
Phone: (604) 563-5055

#27
Commodore Lanes & Billiards
Category: Pool Hall, Bowling, Casino
Average price: Modest
Area: Downtown, Granville Entertainment District
Address: 838 Granville St
Vancouver, BC V6Z 1K3
Phone: (604) 681-1531

#28
Vancouver Police Museum
Category: Museum
Area: Downtown Eastside
Address: 240 Cordova Street E
Vancouver, BC V6A 1L3
Phone: (604) 665-3346

#29
Theatre Under the Stars
Category: Performing Arts
Area: Coal Harbour
Address: 610 Pipeline Road
Vancouver, BC V6G 1Z4
Phone: (604) 734-1917

#30
The Media Club
Category: Lounge, Music Venues
Average price: Modest
Area: Downtown
Address: 695 Cambie St
Vancouver, BC V6B 2P1
Phone: (604) 608-2871

#31
Blarney Stone
Category: Dance Club, Pub, Music Venues
Average price: Modest
Area: Downtown, Gastown
Address: 216 Carrall St
Vancouver, BC V6B 2J1
Phone: (604) 687-4322

#32
Vancouver Opera
Category: Performing Arts
Area: Grandview-Woodlands
Address: 1945 McLean Drive
Vancouver, BC V5N 3J7
Phone: (604) 683-0222

#33
The Roxy
Category: Bar, Music Venues, Dance Club
Average price: Modest
Area: Downtown, Granville Entertainment District
Address: 932 Granville Street
Vancouver, BC V6Z 1L2
Phone: (604) 331-7999

#34
Gam Gallery
Category: Art Gallery, Music Venues
Average price: Inexpensive
Area: Downtown Eastside
Address: 110 E Hastings Street
Vancouver, BC V6A 1N4
Phone: (778) 235-6928

#35
Red Room Ultra Bar
Category: Dance Club, Music Venues
Average price: Expensive
Area: Downtown
Address: 398 Richards Street
Vancouver, BC V6B 4Y2
Phone: (604) 687-5007

#36
Firehall Arts Centre
Category: Performing Arts
Area: Downtown Eastside
Address: 280 Cordova St E
Vancouver, BC V6A 1L3
Phone: (604) 689-0926

#37
Arts Club Theatre Company
Category: Cinema, Performing Arts
Area: Fairview Slopes, South Granville
Address: 2750 Granville St
Vancouver, BC V6H 3J3
Phone: (604) 687-1644

#38
Crafthouse
Category: Art Gallery
Area: Granville Island/False Creek
Address: 1386 Cartwright Street
Vancouver, BC V6H 3R8
Phone: (604) 687-7270

#39
Pat's Pub & Brewhouse
Category: Music Venues, Pub
Average price: Modest
Area: Downtown Eastside
Address: 403 E Hastings Street
Vancouver, BC V6A 1P6
Phone: (604) 255-4301

#40
The Mod Club
Category: Music Venues
Average price: Expensive
Area: Downtown Eastside
Address: 455 Abbott St
Vancouver, BC V6B 2N3
Phone: (604) 685-7777

#41
Wise Hall
Category: Venues & Event Space, Performing Arts, Music Venues
Average price: Inexpensive
Area: Grandview-Woodlands, The Drive
Address: 1882 Adanac Street
Vancouver, BC V5L 2E2
Phone: (604) 254-5858

#42
Spectral Theatre Society
Category: Performing Arts
Area: Downtown Eastside
Address: 350 Powell St
Vancouver, BC V6A
Phone: (604) 569-2013

#43
Fringe Festival
Category: Performing Arts, Cinema
Area: Granville Island/False Creek
Address: 1398 Cartwright St
Vancouver, BC V6H 3R8
Phone: (604) 257-0350

#44
Venue Nightclub
Category: Music Venues, Dance Club
Average price: Modest
Area: Downtown, Granville Entertainment District
Address: 881 Granville St
Vancouver, BC V6Z 1K7
Phone: (604) 646-0064

#45
Hastings Racecourse
Category: Stadium
Area: Hastings-Sunrise
Address: 188 N Renfrew St
Vancouver, BC V5K 3N8
Phone: (604) 254-1631

#46
Roedde House Museum
Category: Museum
Area: West End
Address: 1415 Barclay Street
Vancouver, BC V6G 1J6
Phone: (604) 684-7040

#47
Vancouver Pride Parade
Category: Festival
Area: West End
Address: Denman St
Vancouver, BC V6G
Phone: (604) 687-0955

#48
BC Place
Category: Stadium, Music Venues
Average price: Modest
Area: Downtown
Address: 777 Pacific Blvd.
Vancouver, BC V6B 4Y8
Phone: (604) 669-2300

#49
Bar None Nightclub
Category: Bar, Music Venues
Average price: Expensive
Area: Downtown, Yaletown
Address: 1222 Hamilton St
Vancouver, BC V6B 2S8
Phone: (604) 689-7000

#50
Vancouver Christmas Market
Category: Festival
Area: Downtown
Address: 650 Hamilton Street
Vancouver, BC V6B 6G5
Phone: (604) 561-7597

#51
Stanley Industrial Alliance Stage
Category: Performing Arts
Area: Fairview Slopes, South Granville
Address: 2750 Granville St
Vancouver, BC V6J 5L1
Phone: (604) 731-4687

#52
Pole Dance Studio
Category: Dance Studio, Performing Arts
Area: West End
Address: 1026 Davie St
Vancouver, BC V6E 1M3
Phone: (604) 765-5034

#53
Movieland Arcade
Category: Arcade
Area: Downtown, Granville Entertainment District
Address: 906 Granville St
Vancouver, BC V6Z 1L2
Phone: (604) 681-6915

#54
Eat! Vancouver
Category: Festival, Food
Average price: Modest
Area: Downtown
Address: 777 Pacific Boulevard
Vancouver, BC V6B 4Y8
Phone: (866) 688-0504

#55
Edgewater Casino
Category: Casino
Area: Downtown
Address: 750 Pacific Boulevard
Vancouver, BC V6B 5E7
Phone: (604) 687-3343

#56
Studio 58 Theatre
Category: Performing Arts
Area: Oakridge
Address: 100 49th Ave W
Vancouver, BC V5Y 2Z6
Phone: (604) 323-5227

#57
Under the Piano
Category: Performing Arts
Area: West End
Address: 1350 Broughton Street
Vancouver, BC V6G 2X3
Phone: (604) 662-3053

#58
Performance Works
Category: Performing Arts
Area: Granville Island/False Creek
Address: 1218 Cartwright St
Vancouver, BC V6H 3R8
Phone: (604) 687-3020

#59
Ayden Gallery
Category: Art Gallery
Average price: Modest
Area: Downtown
Address: 88 W Pender Street
Vancouver, BC V6B 6N9
Phone: (604) 376-6947

#60
Pacific Coliseum
Category: Arena
Area: Hastings-Sunrise
Address: 100 N Renfrew Street
Vancouver, BC V5K 3N7
Phone: (604) 253-2311

#61
Intersections Film Club
Category: Cinema
Area: Downtown Eastside
Address: 319 Main St
Vancouver, BC V6A 2S9
Phone: (604) 899-1077

#62
Scotiabank Theatre Vancouver
Category: Cinema
Area: Downtown
Address: 900 Burrard Street
Vancouver, BC V6Z 3G5
Phone: (604) 630-1407

#63
Playhouse Winefest Vancouver
Category: Festival
Area: Coal Harbour, Downtown
Address: 1055 Pl
Vancouver, BC V6C
Phone: (604) 872-6622

#64
Backstage Lounge
Category: Music Venues, Lounge
Average price: Modest
Area: Granville Island/False Creek
Address: 1585 Johnston St
Vancouver, BC V6H 3R9
Phone: (604) 687-1354

#65
Croatian Cultural Centre
Category: Venues & Event Space
Area: Kensington-Cedar Cottage
Address: 3250 Commercial Dr
Vancouver, BC V5N 4E4
Phone: (604) 879-0154

#66
ArtStarts Gallery
Category: Art Gallery, Music Venues
Area: Downtown
Address: 808 Richards Street
Vancouver, BC V6B 3A7
Phone: (604) 336-0626

#67
Vinci's Caffe & Gallery
Category: Art Gallery
Area: Mount Pleasant
Address: 194 West 3rd Avenue
Vancouver, BC V5Y 1E9
Phone: (604) 681-5883

#68
The Yale Hotel
Category: Music Venues
Average price: Expensive
Area: Downtown
Address: 1300 Granville St
Vancouver, BC V6Z 1M7
Phone: (604) 681-9253

#69
Urban Wasp
Category: Cinema
Area: Fairview Slopes
Address: 1535 W 4th Avenue
Vancouver, BC V6J 1L6
Phone: (604) 708-0455

#70
Planet Bingo
Category: Hobby Shops, Casino
Average price: Inexpensive
Area: Mount Pleasant
Address: 2655 Main St
Vancouver, BC V5T 3E7
Phone: (604) 879-8930

#71
Okanagan Cider Company
Category: Winery
Average price: Modest
Area: Mount Pleasant, Strathcona
Address: 887 Great Northern Way
Vancouver, BC V5T 1E1
Phone: (604) 263-9994

#72
Commodore Ballroom
Category: Music Venues
Average price: Modest
Area: Downtown, Granville Entertainment District
Address: 868 Granville Street
Vancouver, BC V6Z 1K3
Phone: (604) 739-4550

#73
Library Square Public House
Category: Pub, Sports Bar, Music Venues
Average price: Modest
Area: Downtown
Address: 300 W Georgia St
Vancouver, BC V6B 6B4
Phone: (604) 633-9644

#74
Jericho Arts Centre
Category: Performing Arts
Area: Point Grey
Address: 1675 Discovery St
Vancouver, BC V6R 4K5
Phone: (604) 224-8007

#75
Regal Beagle
Category: Gastropub, Music Venues
Average price: Modest
Area: Kitsilano
Address: 2283 Broadway W
Vancouver, BC V6K 2E4
Phone: (604) 739-0677

#76
Janet's Custom Framing
Category: Home Decor, Art Gallery
Average price: Modest
Area: Kitsilano
Address: 3659 4th Avenue W
Vancouver, BC V6R 1P2
Phone: (604) 222-1622

#77
Taboo Naughty but Nice Show
Category: Festival, Adult
Average price: Expensive
Area: Coal Harbour, Downtown
Address: 1055 Pl
Vancouver, BC V6C 3T4
Phone: (403) 242-0859

#78
Bau-Xi Gallery
Category: Art Gallery
Average price: Expensive
Area: Fairview Slopes, South Granville
Address: 3045 Granville St
Vancouver, BC V6H 3J9
Phone: (604) 733-7011

#79
**Bill Reid Gallery
of Northwest Coast Art**
Category: Museum, Art Gallery
Average price: Modest
Area: Downtown
Address: 639 Hornby St
Vancouver, BC V6C 2G3
Phone: (604) 682-3455

#80
The Centre
Category: Performing Arts
Area: Downtown
Address: 777 Homer St
Vancouver, BC V6B 2W1
Phone: (604) 602-0616

#81
Powell Street Festival Society
Category: Local Flavor, Festival
Area: Downtown, Downtown Eastside
Address: West Hastings Street
Vancouver, BC V6B 1H4
Phone: (604) 739-9388

#82
Lickerish Restaurant & Lounge
Category: Tapas Bar, Music Venues
Average price: Modest
Area: Downtown
Address: 903 Davie Street
Vancouver, BC V6Z 2E9
Phone: (604) 696-0725

#83
**Vancouver International
Writers Festival**
Category: Festival
Area: Granville Island/False Creek
Address: 1398 Cartwright Street
Vancouver, BC V6H 3R8
Phone: (604) 681-6330

#84
**Jacana Contemporary
Art Gallery**
Category: Art Gallery
Area: Fairview Slopes, South Granville
Address: 2435 Granville St
Vancouver, BC V6H 3G5
Phone: (604) 879-9306

#85
Ballet BC
Category: Opera & Ballet
Area: Downtown, Granville
Entertainment District
Address: 677 Davie Street
Vancouver, BC V6B 2G6
Phone: (604) 732-5003

#86
Revue Stage
Category: Performing Arts
Area: Granville Island/False Creek
Address: 1601 Johnston St
Vancouver, BC V6H 3R9
Phone: (604) 738-7013

#87
Ian Tan Gallery
Category: Art Gallery
Average price: Modest
Area: Fairview Slopes, South Granville
Address: 2202 Granville St
Vancouver, BC V6H 4H7
Phone: (604) 738-1077

#88
Fibre Arts Studio
Category: Art Gallery
Average price: Modest
Area: Granville Island/False Creek
Address: 1610 Johnston St
Vancouver, BC V6H 3S2
Phone: (604) 688-3047

#89
Creative Framing Company
Category: Home Decor,
Art Gallery, Framing
Average price: Modest
Area: Riley Park
Address: 3332 Main St
Vancouver, BC V5V 3M7
Phone: (604) 432-6777

#90
Gallery Jones
Category: Art Gallery
Average price: Expensive
Area: Fairview Slopes
Address: 1725 W 3rd Ave
Vancouver, BC V6J 1K7
Phone: (604) 714-2216

#91
The Window
Category: Jewelry, Art Gallery
Average price: Modest
Area: Downtown, Downtown Eastside
Address: 9 West Hastings St
Vancouver, BC V6B 1G8
Phone: (604) 629-8396

#92
The Pendulum Gallery
Category: Art Gallery
Average price: Inexpensive
Area: Downtown
Address: 885 Georgia St W
Vancouver, BC V6C 3E8
Phone: (604) 879-7714

#93
Ironwork Studio Productions
Category: Art Gallery, Music Venues
Area: Downtown Eastside
Address: 235 Alexander St
Vancouver, BC V6A 1C2
Phone: (604) 681-5033

#94
Fan Expo Vancouver
Category: Festival
Area: Downtown
Address: 999 Pl
Vancouver, BC V6C 3C1
Phone: (604) 689-8232

#95
Vancouver Symphony Orchestra
Category: Performing Arts
Area: Downtown, Granville
Entertainment District
Address: 500-843 Seymour Street
Vancouver, BC V6B 3L4
Phone: (604) 876-3434

#96
Oh Brothers
Category: Home Decor, Art Gallery
Area: Kitsilano
Address: 2575 W Broadway
Vancouver, BC V6K 2E9
Phone: (604) 738-6695

#97
PNE Forum
Category: Music Venues
Average price: Modest
Area: Hastings-Sunrise
Address: 100 N. Renfrew St.
Vancouver, BC V5K 4W3
Phone: (604) 253-2311

#98
Vancouver Recital Society
Category: Performing Arts
Area: Downtown, Yaletown
Address: 873 Beatty Street
Vancouver, BC V6B 2M6
Phone: (604) 602-0363

#99
Pacific Theatre
Category: Performing Arts
Area: Fairview Slopes, South Granville
Address: 1440 12th Avenue W
Vancouver, BC V6H 1M8
Phone: (604) 731-5518

#100
H R MacMillan Space Centre
Category: Museum
Area: Kitsilano
Address: 1100 Chestnut St
Vancouver, BC V6J 3J9
Phone: (604) 738-7827

#101
Museum of Vancouver
Category: Museum
Area: Kitsilano
Address: 1100 Chestnut St
Vancouver, BC V6J 3J9
Phone: (604) 736-4431

#102
Italian Cultural Centre Society
Category: Venues & Event Space, Social Club, Caterers
Area: Renfrew-Collingwood
Address: 3075 Slocan St
Vancouver, BC V5M 3E4
Phone: (604) 430-3337

#103
FanClub
Category: Dance Club, Music Venues
Average price: Modest
Area: Downtown, Granville Entertainment District
Address: 1050 Granville Street
Vancouver, BC V6Z 1L5
Phone: (604) 689-7720

#104
Artspeak Gallery
Category: Art Gallery
Average price: Modest
Area: Downtown, Gastown
Address: 233 Carrall St
Vancouver, BC V6B 2J2
Phone: (604) 688-0051

#105
Van East Cinema
Category: Cinema
Area: Grandview-Woodlands, The Drive
Address: 2290 Commercial Drive
Vancouver, BC V5N
Phone: (604) 251-1313

#106
University Women's Club of Vancouver at Hycroft
Category: Social Club, Venues & Event Space, Party & Event Planning
Area: Shaughnessy
Address: 1489 McRae Ave
Vancouver, BC V6H 1V1
Phone: (604) 731-4661

#107
Arthur Murray Dance Studio
Category: Performing Arts
Area: Downtown, Granville Entertainment District
Address: 929 Granville St
Vancouver, BC V6Z 1L3
Phone: (604) 684-2477

#108
The FALL
Category: Tattoo, Art Gallery, Piercing
Average price: Modest
Area: Downtown
Address: 644 Seymour Street
Vancouver, BC V6B 3K4
Phone: (604) 676-3066

#109
Hilary Morris
Category: Art Gallery
Average price: Inexpensive
Area: Granville Island/False Creek
Address: 1381 Railspur Alley
Vancouver, BC V6H 4G9
Phone: (604) 682-1993

#110
Newsmall & Sterling Studio Glass
Category: Art Gallery, Art School
Average price: Expensive
Area: Granville Island/False Creek
Address: 1440 Old Bridge Street
Vancouver, BC V6H 3S6
Phone: (604) 681-6730

#111
Petley-Jones Gallery
Category: Home Decor, Art Gallery
Average price: Expensive
Area: Fairview Slopes, South Granville
Address: 1554 W 6th Avenue
Vancouver, BC V6J 1R2
Phone: (604) 732-5353

#112
Wickaninnish Gallery
Category: Jewelry, Art Gallery
Average price: Inexpensive
Area: Granville Island/False Creek
Address: 1666 Johnston St
Vancouver, BC V6H 3S2
Phone: (604) 681-1057

#113
Jean Lyons School of Music
Category: Performing Arts
Area: Mount Pleasant
Address: 77 E 7th Avenue
Vancouver, BC V5T 1M6
Phone: (604) 734-4019

#114
Vin de Garde Cellar Systems
Category: Winery
Area: Mount Pleasant
Address: 112 W 2nd Avenue
Vancouver, BC V5Y 1C2
Phone: (604) 568-8460

#115
Hot Art Wet City Gallery
Category: Art Gallery
Average price: Modest
Area: Mount Pleasant
Address: 2206 Main Street
Vancouver, BC V5T 3C7
Phone: (604) 764-2266

#116
Early Music Vancouver
Category: Performing Arts
Area: Fairview Slopes
Address: 1254 West 7th Avenue
Vancouver, BC V6H 1B6
Phone: (604) 732-1610

#117
Catriona Jeffries Gallery
Category: Art Gallery
Average price: Expensive
Area: Mount Pleasant, Strathcona
Address: 274 1st Ave E
Vancouver, BC V5T 1A6
Phone: (604) 736-1554

#118
Mosaic Arts Academy
Category: Performing Arts, Yoga
Area: Point Grey
Address: 4511 W 10th Ave
Vancouver, BC V6R 2J2
Phone: (604) 568-9840

#119
Chali Rosso Art Gallery
Category: Art Gallery
Area: Fairview Slopes, South Granville
Address: 2250 Granville Street
Vancouver, BC V6H 4H7
Phone: (604) 733-3594

#120
Douglas Reynolds Gallery
Category: Jewelry, Art Gallery
Area: Fairview Slopes, South Granville
Address: 2335 Granville St
Vancouver, BC V6H 3G4
Phone: (604) 731-9292

#121
Armoury Studio
Category: Music Venues, Recording Studio
Area: Fairview Slopes
Address: 1688 W 1st Avenue
Vancouver, BC V6J 1G1
Phone: (604) 737-1687

#122
White Ocean Gallery
Category: Art Gallery, Jewelry
Area: Granville Island/False Creek
Address: 1620 Duranleau Street
Vancouver, BC V6H 3S4
Phone: (604) 669-8880

#123
Eagle Spirit Gallery
Category: Art Gallery
Area: Granville Island/False Creek
Address: 1803 Maritime Mews
Vancouver, BC V6J 5L1
Phone: (604) 801-5205

#124
Kimoto Gallery
Category: Art Gallery
Area: Fairview Slopes, South Granville
Address: 1525 W 6th Avenue
Vancouver, BC V6J 1R1
Phone: (604) 428-0903

#125
Bryant and Tuck Studio
Category: Performing Arts
Area: Downtown
Address: 480 Smithe
Vancouver, BC V6B 5E4
Phone: (604) 837-5416

#126
Ten Ten Tapas
Category: Jazz & Blues
Average price: Modest
Area: Downtown
Address: 1010 Beach Avenue
Vancouver, BC V6E 1T7
Phone: (604) 689-7800

#127
Portuguese Club of Vancouver
Category: Social Club, Portuguese
Area: Grandview-Woodlands, The Drive
Address: 1144 Commercial Drive
Vancouver, BC V5L 3X2
Phone: (604) 251-2042

#128
Lattimer Gallery
Category: Jewelry, Art Gallery
Average price: Modest
Area: Fairview Slopes
Address: 1590 2nd Ave W
Vancouver, BC V6J 1H2
Phone: (604) 732-4556

#129
Northern Tickets
Category: Music Venues
Area: Downtown, Granville Entertainment District
Address: 918 Granville Street
Vancouver, BC V6B 2C9
Phone: (604) 569-1144

#130
The Herb Museum
Category: Art Gallery, Museum
Average price: Inexpensive
Area: Downtown
Address: 303 W Hastings Street
Vancouver, BC V6B 1H6
Phone: (778) 987-8349

#131
Japantown Multicultural Neighbourhood Celebration
Category: Performing Arts
Area: Downtown Eastside
Address: 487 Alexander Street
Vancouver, BC V6A
Phone: (604) 628-5672

#132
Coastal Peoples Fine Arts Gallery
Category: Art Gallery
Average price: Expensive
Area: Downtown, Gastown
Address: 312 Water Street
Vancouver, BC V6B 1B6
Phone: (604) 684-9222

#133
Dorian Rae Collection
Category: Antiques, Art Gallery
Average price: Exclusive
Area: Downtown
Address: 410 Howe St
Vancouver, BC V6C 2X1
Phone: (604) 874-6100

#134
EWMA Store
Category: Arts & Crafts, Art Gallery
Area: Downtown Eastside
Address: 802 E Hastings
Vancouver, BC V6A 1R8
Phone: (604) 253-2512

#135
LES Gallery
Category: Art Gallery
Area: Grandview-Woodlands
Address: 1879 Powell St
Vancouver, BC V5L 1H8
Phone: (778) 370-1999

#136
Folkart
Category: Antiques, Art Gallery, Furniture Store
Average price: Exclusive
Area: Point Grey
Address: 3720 10th Ave W
Vancouver, BC V6R 2G4
Phone: (604) 731-7576

#137
Hastings Mill Museum
Category: Museum
Area: Point Grey
Address: 1575 Alma St
Vancouver, BC V6R 3P3
Phone: (604) 734-1212

#138
Coastal Peoples Fine Arts Gallery
Category: Art Gallery
Average price: Expensive
Area: Downtown, Yaletown
Address: 1024 Mainland St
Vancouver, BC V6B 2T4
Phone: (604) 685-9298

#139
Vancouver International Bhangra Celebration
Category: Performing Arts
Area: West End
Address: 1755 Robson St
Vancouver, BC V6G
Phone: (604) 628-6406

#140
Vaneast Theatre
Category: Cinema
Area: Grandview-Woodlands, The Drive
Address: 2290 Commercial Dr
Vancouver, BC V5N 4B5
Phone: (604) 251-1313

#141
Vancouver Playhouse Theatre
Category: Performing Arts
Area: Downtown
Address: Dunsmuir St & Hamilton St
Vancouver, BC V6B 2P1
Phone: (604) 665-3035

#142
United Players of Vancouver
Category: Cinema, Performing Arts
Area: Point Grey
Address: 1675 Discovery St
Vancouver, BC V6R 4K5
Phone: (604) 224-8007

#143
Contemporary Art Gallery
Category: Art Gallery
Average price: Inexpensive
Area: Downtown
Address: 555 Nelson Street
Vancouver, BC V6B 6R5
Phone: (604) 681-2700

#144
Funky Winker Beans
Category: Music Venues, Karaoke
Average price: Inexpensive
Area: Downtown, Downtown Eastside
Address: 37 W Hastings Street
Vancouver, BC V6B 1G4
Phone: (604) 569-3515

#145
West End Fest
Category: Festival
Area: West End
Address: Davie Street from Burrard and Denman Vancouver, BC V6E 1M7
Phone: (604) 696-0144

#146
Coppertank Grill
Category: Sports Bar, Music Venues
Average price: Modest
Area: Kitsilano
Address: 3135 W Broadway
Vancouver, BC V6K 2H2
Phone: (604) 731-6565

#147
the JEM gallery
Category: Music Venues, Art Gallery
Area: Mount Pleasant
Address: 225 Broadway E
Vancouver, BC V5T 1W4
Phone: (604) 879-5366

#148
Rennie Collection at Wing Sang
Category: Art Gallery
Area: Chinatown
Address: 51 E Pender
Vancouver, BC V6A
Phone: (604) 682-2088

#149
Vancouver Theatre Sports League
Category: Performing Arts
Area: Granville Island/False Creek
Address: 1502 Duranleau Street
Vancouver, BC V6H 3S4
Phone: (604) 738-7013

#150
Heavens Door Lounge
Category: Music Venues, Lounge, Comfort Food
Area: West End
Address: 1216 Bute Street
Vancouver, BC V6E 1Z8
Phone: (604) 428-0602

#151
BC Sports Hall of Fame and Museum
Category: Museum
Area: Downtown
Address: 777 Pacific Blvd
Vancouver, BC V6B 4Y8
Phone: (604) 687-5520

#152
Guys & Dolls Billiards
Category: Pool Hall, Casino
Average price: Expensive
Area: Mount Pleasant
Address: 2434 Main St
Vancouver, BC V5T 3E2
Phone: (604) 879-4433

#153
Jade Mine
Category: Jewelry, Art Gallery
Average price: Expensive
Area: Downtown, Gastown
Address: 375 Water Street
Vancouver, BC V6B 5C6
Phone: (604) 687-5233

#154
Rio Tinto Alcan Dragon Boat Festival
Category: Festival
Area: Downtown Eastside
Address: 418 Main St
Vancouver, BC V6A 2T4
Phone: (604) 732-7035

#155
Vancouver Maritime Museum
Category: Museum
Area: Kitsilano
Address: 1905 Ogden Avenue
Vancouver, BC V6J 1A3
Phone: (604) 257-8300

#156
Art Works Gallery
Category: Home Decor, Art Gallery
Area: Downtown, Yaletown
Address: 225 Smithe St
Vancouver, BC V6B 4X7
Phone: (604) 688-3301

#157
Vancouver Holocaust Education Centre
Category: Museum
Address: 950 41st Ave W
Vancouver, BC V5Z 2N7
Phone: (604) 264-0499

#158
Southlands Country Fair
Category: Festival
Area: Kerrisdale
Address: 7025 Macdonald Street
Vancouver, BC V6N 1G2
Phone: (604) 263-4817

#159
Art of Compassion Gallery
Category: Art Gallery
Area: Downtown
Address: 438 Richards St
Vancouver, BC V6B 2Z3
Phone: (604) 779-4040

#160
Vancouver Tap Dance Society
Category: Performing Arts, Dance School
Area: Hastings-Sunrise
Address: 2775 Hastings St E
Vancouver, BC V5K 1Z8
Phone: (604) 253-0293

#161
Inuit Gallery of Vancouver
Category: Art Gallery
Average price: Expensive
Area: Downtown, Gastown
Address: 206 Cambie St
Vancouver, BC V6B 2M9
Phone: (604) 688-7323

Shops, Restaurants, Attractions & Nightlife / Vancouver Travel Guide

#162
La Casa del Artista
Category: Music Venues
Average price: Inexpensive
Area: Mount Pleasant
Address: 150 E 3rd Ave
Vancouver, BC V5T 1C8
Phone: (604) 709-4300

#163
Vivo Media Arts Centre
Category: Venues & Event Space, Art Gallery, Vocational School
Area: Mount Pleasant
Address: 1965 Main Street
Vancouver, BC V5T 3B9
Phone: (604) 872-8337

#164
Art of Life Gallery
Category: Art Gallery
Area: Kitsilano
Address: 3325 4th Ave W
Vancouver, BC V6R 1N6
Phone: (604) 737-2588

#165
Grace Gallery
Category: Art Gallery
Area: Mount Pleasant
Address: 1898 Main St
Vancouver, BC V5T 3B7
Phone: (604) 839-5780

#166
Liberty Wine Merchants
Category: Winery
Area: Mount Pleasant, Strathcona
Address: 291 2nd Ave E
Vancouver, BC V5T 1B8
Phone: (604) 739-7801

#167
Plaza of Nations
Category: Performing Arts, Music Venues
Average price: Modest
Area: Downtown
Address: 750 Pacific Blvd
Vancouver, BC V6B 5E7
Phone: (604) 682-0777

#168
Winsor Gallery
Category: Art Gallery
Average price: Expensive
Area: Mount Pleasant, Strathcona
Address: 258 East 1st Avenue
Vancouver, BC V5T 1A6
Phone: (604) 681-4870

#169
Grunt Gallery
Category: Art Gallery
Average price: Modest
Area: Mount Pleasant, Strathcona
Address: 350 2nd Avenue E
Vancouver, BC V5T 4R8
Phone: (604) 875-9516

#170
Omnimax Theatre
Category: Cinema
Area: Granville Island/False Creek
Address: 1455 Quebec St
Vancouver, BC V6A 3Z7
Phone: (604) 443-7443

#171
Jennifer Kostuik Gallery
Category: Art Gallery
Average price: Expensive
Area: Downtown, Yaletown
Address: 1070 Homer St
Vancouver, BC V6B 2W9
Phone: (604) 737-3969

#172
Peter Kiss Gallery
Category: Art Gallery
Average price: Expensive
Area: Granville Island/False Creek
Address: 1327 Railspur Alley
Vancouver, BC V6H 4G9
Phone: (604) 696-0433

#173
Textile Context Studio
Category: Art Gallery
Area: Granville Island/False Creek
Address: 1420 Old Bridge St
Vancouver, BC V6H 3S6
Phone: (604) 684-6661

#174
Atelier Gallery
Category: Art Gallery
Average price: Expensive
Area: Fairview Slopes, South Granville
Address: 2421 Granville St
Vancouver, BC V6H 3G5
Phone: (604) 732-3021

#175
Equinox Gallery
Category: Art Gallery
Average price: Expensive
Area: Fairview Slopes, South Granville
Address: 2321 Granville St
Vancouver, BC V6H 3G4
Phone: (604) 736-2405

#176
False Creek Yacht Club
Category: Boating, Social Club
Area: Downtown
Address: 1661 Granville Street
Vancouver, BC V6Z 1N3
Phone: (604) 682-3292

#177
Fragrant Wood Gallery
Category: Art Gallery
Area: Fairview Slopes, South Granville
Address: 2233 Granville Street
Vancouver, BC V6H 3G1
Phone: (604) 558-2889

#178
Dundarave Print Workshop
Category: Art Gallery
Area: Granville Island/False Creek
Address: 1640 Johnston St
Vancouver, BC V6H 3S2
Phone: (604) 689-1650

#179
The Raven & the Bear Arts
Category: Art Gallery
Area: Granville Island/False Creek
Address: 1528 Duranleau St
Vancouver, BC V6H 3S4
Phone: (604) 669-3990

#180
Pacific Wave Glass Art
Category: Home Decor, Art Gallery
Area: Fairview Slopes, South Granville
Address: 1560 W 6th Avenue
Vancouver, BC V6J 1R2
Phone: (604) 566-9889

#181
Diane Farris Gallery
Category: Home Decor, Art Gallery
Average price: Expensive
Area: Fairview Slopes, South Granville
Address: 1590 7th Ave W
Vancouver, BC V6J 1S2
Phone: (604) 737-2629

#182
Edzerza Gallery
Category: Art Gallery
Area: Granville Island/False Creek, Fairview Slopes
Address: 1536 W 2nd Ave
Vancouver, BC V6J 1H2
Phone: (604) 731-4874

#183
Centre For Performing Arts
Category: Performing Arts
Area: Downtown
Address: 777 Homer St
Vancouver, BC V6B 2W1
Phone: (604) 684-1361

#184
Talking Stick Festival
Category: Festival
Area: Mount Pleasant, Strathcona
Address: 555 Great Northern Way
Vancouver, BC V5T 1E2
Phone: (604) 683-0497

#185
Republic Gallery
Category: Art Gallery
Area: Downtown
Address: 732 Richards Street
Vancouver, BC V6B 3A4
Phone: (604) 632-1590

#186
City of Bhangra
Category: Festival
Area: Downtown, Downtown Eastside
Address: 210 - 111 West Hastings Street
Vancouver, BC V6B 1H4
Phone: (604) 315-2599

#187
Pera Art Gallery
Category: Art Gallery
Area: Downtown
Address: 413 Hastings St W
Vancouver, BC V6B 1L4
Phone: (604) 689-7370

#188
Gallery Gachet
Category: Art Gallery
Area: Gastown, Downtown Eastside
Address: 88 Cordova St E
Vancouver, BC V6A 1K2
Phone: (604) 687-2468

#189
Vancouver Guitar Show
Category: Festival, Performing Arts
Area: Kitsilano
Address: 1808 Whyte Avenue
Vancouver, BC V6J 1B1
Phone: (604) 785-5795

#190
Tom's Eastvin Winemaking
Category: Winery
Area: Downtown Eastside
Address: 825 E Hastings Street
Vancouver, BC V6A 1R8
Phone: (604) 558-3846

#191
Blanket Art Gallery & Consulting
Category: Art Gallery
Average price: Expensive
Area: Downtown Eastside
Address: 758 Alexander St
Vancouver, BC V6A 1E3
Phone: (604) 709-6100

#192
PAL Theatre
Category: Performing Arts
Area: Coal Harbour, Downtown
Address: 581 Cardero St
Vancouver, BC V6G 3L3
Phone: (604) 255-4312

#193
Havana Theatre
Category: Performing Arts
Area: Grandview-Woodlands, The Drive
Address: 1212 Commercial Dr
Vancouver, BC V5L 3X4
Phone: (604) 253-9119

#194
Goh Ballet Academy
Category: Performing Arts, Dance School
Area: Mount Pleasant
Address: 2345 Main St
Vancouver, BC V5T 3C9
Phone: (604) 872-4014

#195
The Wine Castle on Premise Wine Making
Category: Winery
Average price: Modest
Area: Sunset, Punjabi Market
Address: 6428 Main Street
Vancouver, BC V5V 4E8
Phone: (604) 877-1177

#196
Beyond the Grape Beer & Wine Making
Category: Kitchen & Bath, Winery
Area: Renfrew-Collingwood
Address: 2603 Kingsway
Vancouver, BC V5R 5H4
Phone: (604) 437-7100

#197
Broadway Brewing Company
Category: Winery
Area: Kitsilano
Address: 2-2801 W 16th Avenue
Vancouver, BC V6K 3C5
Phone: (604) 736-4801

#198
Electric Owl Social Club
Category: Music Venues, Bar
Average price: Modest
Area: Strathcona
Address: 928 Main Street
Vancouver, BC V6A 2W1
Phone: (604) 558-0928

#199
CircusWest
Category: Performing Arts
Area: Hastings-Sunrise
Address: 2901 East Hastings Street
Vancouver, BC V5K
Phone: (604) 252-3679

#200
Elissa Cristall Gallery
Category: Art Gallery
Average price: Modest
Area: Fairview Slopes, South Granville
Address: 2245 Granville St
Vancouver, BC V6H 3G1
Phone: (604) 730-9611

#201
The Art Emporium
Category: Art Gallery
Average price: Expensive
Area: Fairview Slopes, South Granville
Address: 2928 Granville St
Vancouver, BC V6H 3J7
Phone: (604) 738-3510

#202
Brass Fan Entertainment
Category: Performing Arts
Area: Fairview Slopes
Address: 1755 W Broadway
Vancouver, BC V6J 1Y2
Phone: (604) 720-1008

#203
Trunk Gallery
Category: Art Gallery
Average price: Expensive
Area: Fairview Slopes
Address: 1755 3rd Ave W
Vancouver, BC V6J 1K7
Phone: (604) 739-0800

#204
Audain Gallery at SFU
Category: Art Gallery
Area: Downtown, Downtown Eastside
Address: 149 West Hastings Street
Vancouver, BC V6B 1H4
Phone: (778) 782-9102

#205
Teck Gallery
Category: Art Gallery
Area: Downtown
Address: 515 W Hastings St
Vancouver, BC V6B 5K3
Phone: (778) 782-4266

#206
Empire Theatres
Category: Cinema
Area: Oakridge
Address: 650 41st Avenue W
Vancouver, BC V5Z 2M9
Phone: (604) 263-1944

#207
Beckwoman's Too
Category: Fabric Store, Art Gallery
Area: Hastings-Sunrise
Address: 2651 E Hastings St
Vancouver, BC V5K
Phone: (778) 889-4430

#208
Raja Cinema
Category: Cinema
Area: Renfrew-Collingwood
Address: 3215 Kingsway
Vancouver, BC V5R 5K3
Phone: (604) 436-1545

#209
Chinese Cultural Centre of Greater Vancouver
Category: Museum
Area: Chinatown
Address: 50 Pender St E
Vancouver, BC V6A 1T1
Phone: (604) 708-9807

#210
Framing & Art Centre
Category: Framing, Art Gallery
Area: Kitsilano
Address: 2065 W 4th Street
Vancouver, BC V6J 1N3
Phone: (604) 732-3097

#211
The Wood Co-op
Category: Art Gallery
Average price: Expensive
Area: Granville Island/False Creek
Address: 1592 Johnston St
Vancouver, BC V6H 3S2
Phone: (877) 966-3500

#212
Serotonin Afterhours
Category: Music Venues
Area: Downtown, Granville Entertainment District
Address: 1058 Granville Street
Vancouver, BC V6Z 1L2
Phone: (604) 688-8151

#213
Justice Rocks Festival
Category: Festival
Area: Strathcona
Address: 700 Malkin Ave
Vancouver, BC V6A 2K5
Phone: (604) 713-1838

#214
Vogue Theatre
Category: Performing Arts, Music Venues, Venues & Event Space
Average price: Modest
Area: Downtown, Granville Entertainment District
Address: 918 Granville St
Vancouver, BC V6Z 1L2
Phone: (604) 569-1144

#215
Metro Theatre Centre
Category: Performing Arts
Area: Marpole
Address: 1370 Marine Drive Southwest
Vancouver, BC V6P 5Z9
Phone: (604) 266-7191

#216
Allstar Tickets
Category: Theatre, Concert and Sports Tickets
Area: Downtown
Address: 110 W Georgia Street
Vancouver, BC V6B 4P4
Phone: (604) 255-7827

#217
Divino Wine Shop
Category: Winery
Area: West End
Address: 1610 Robson St
Vancouver, BC V6G 1C7
Phone: (604) 683-8466

#218
School of Remix
Category: Musical Instruments, Arts & Entertainment, DJs
Average price: Modest
Area: Downtown Eastside
Address: 49 Dunlevy
Vancouver, BC V6A 3A3
Phone: (604) 681-5586

#219
Western Front
Category: Museum, Art Gallery, Venues & Event Space
Average price: Modest
Area: Mount Pleasant
Address: 303 E 8th Avenue
Vancouver, BC V5T 1S1
Phone: (604) 876-9343

#220
Sephine Jewelry & Art
Category: Jewelry, Framing, Art Gallery
Area: Downtown, Yaletown
Address: 1241 Hamilton St
Vancouver, BC V6B 6K3
Phone: (604) 688-6903

#221
Cabana Lounge
Category: Lounge, Music Venues
Average price: Exclusive
Area: Downtown, Granville Entertainment District
Address: 1159 Granville Street
Vancouver, BC V6Z 1L8
Phone: (778) 251-3335

#222
Vancouver Mysteries
Category: Tours, Party & Event Planning, Arts & Entertainment
Area: Downtown
Address: 930 Seymour Street
Vancouver, BC V6B 1B4
Phone: (604) 728-7179

#223
Jewish Museum and Archives of British Columbia
Category: Museum
Area: Oakridge
Address: 6184 Ash St
Vancouver, BC V5Z 3G9
Phone: (604) 257-5199

#224
JPeachy Gallery Office
Category: Performing Arts, Art Gallery
Average price: Exclusive
Area: Downtown, Granville Entertainment District
Address: 1067 Granville Street
Vancouver, BC V6Z 1L4
Phone: (778) 708-4701

#225
Crystalworks Gallery
Category: Jewelry, Art Gallery
Area: Fairview Slopes
Address: 1760 W 3rd Avenue
Vancouver, BC V6J 1K4
Phone: (604) 732-3870

#226
Or Gallery
Category: Art Gallery
Area: Downtown
Address: 555 Hamilton St
Vancouver, BC V6B 2R1
Phone: (604) 683-7395

#227
Howe Street Gallery of Fine Art
Category: Art Gallery
Area: Downtown
Address: 555 Howe Street
Vancouver, BC V6C 2C2
Phone: (604) 681-5777

#228
The Brush and Wand Studio
Category: Art School, Performing Arts
Area: Point Grey
Address: 4333 W 10th Avenue
Vancouver, BC V6R 2H6
Phone: (604) 655-6703

#229
Norman Rothstein Theatre
Category: Performing Arts
Area: Oakridge
Address: 950 W 41st Ave
Vancouver, BC V5Z 2N7
Phone: (604) 257-5111

#230
Fazakas Gallery
Category: Art Gallery
Area: Mount Pleasant
Address: 145 W 6th Avenue
Vancouver, BC V5Y 1K3
Phone: (604) 876-2729

#231
RENEW Period Lighting and Decorative Arts
Category: Antiques, Art Gallery
Average price: Expensive
Area: Mount Pleasant
Address: 5 E 5th Avenue
Vancouver, BC V5T 1G7
Phone: (604) 872-3131

#232
Read Books
Category: Art Gallery, Bookstore
Area: Granville Island/False Creek
Address: 1399 Johnston Street
Vancouver, BC V6H 3R9
Phone: (604) 630-7411

#233
Dance Vancouver
Category: Performing Arts, Dance Studio
Area: Mount Pleasant
Address: 395 Kingsway
Vancouver, BC V5T 3J7
Phone: (778) 229-3002

#234
Mark Igonia Ticket Broker
Category: Music Venues
Area: Downtown, Yaletown
Address: 1133 Homer Street
Vancouver, BC V6B 0B1
Phone: (604) 782-9961

#235
Granville Fine Art
Category: Art Gallery
Area: Fairview Slopes, South Granville
Address: 2447 Granville St
Vancouver, BC V6H 3G5
Phone: (604) 266-6010

#236
Pousette Gallery
Category: Art Gallery
Area: Fairview Slopes, South Granville
Address: 529 W 6th Avenue
Vancouver, BC V6J 1R1
Phone: (604) 563-2717

#237
Monte Clark Gallery
Category: Art Gallery
Area: Strathcona
Address: 525 Great Northern Way
Vancouver, BC V5E 1E1
Phone: (604) 730-5000

#238
Picture Listen Art
Category: Art Gallery
Average price: Inexpensive
Area: Mount Pleasant
Address: 418 E Broadway
Vancouver, BC V5T 1X2
Phone: (604) 762-1854

#239
Vancouver Latin Fever
Category: Music Venues, Dance Club
Area: Downtown
Address: 398 Richards Street
Vancouver, BC V5R 3T9
Phone: (604) 722-1559

#240
Levykh Academy
Category: Performing Arts
Area: Sunset
Address: 480 45th Avenue E
Vancouver, BC V5W 1X4
Phone: (604) 322-1019

#241
Stewart Stephenson Modern Art Gallery
Category: Art Gallery
Area: West End
Address: 1300 Robson Street
Vancouver, BC V6E 1C5
Phone: (877) 278-7100

#242
Creative Arts & Crafts
Category: Art Gallery
Area: Fraserview
Address: 6404 Victoria Dr
Vancouver, BC V5P 3X7
Phone: (604) 325-2196

#243
The Afrika Shrine
Category: Music Venues, Ethnic Food
Area: Grandview-Woodlands, The Drive
Address: 2205 Commercial Drive
Vancouver, BC V5N 4B6
Phone: (778) 552-8238

#244
Visual Space
Category: Art Gallery
Area: Mount Pleasant
Address: 2075 Alberta Street
Vancouver, BC V5Y 1C4
Phone: (604) 739-0429

#245
Michel Blais Art Gallery
Category: Art Gallery
Area: Hastings-Sunrise
Address: 2546 Hastings St E
Vancouver, BC V5K 1Z3
Phone: (604) 688-4520

#246
John's Jukes
Category: Arcade
Area: Mount Pleasant
Address: 2343 Main Street
Vancouver, BC V5T 3C9
Phone: (604) 872-5757

#247
Queen Bijoux
Category: Art Gallery, Jewelry
Average price: Expensive
Area: Granville Island/False Creek
Address: 1351 Railspur Alley
Vancouver, BC V6H 3S5
Phone: (778) 858-8959

#248
Kurbatoff Art Gallery
Category: Art Gallery
Area: Fairview Slopes, South Granville
Address: 2427 Granville St
Vancouver, BC V6H 3G5
Phone: (604) 736-5444

#249
Vancouver Online Gallery
Category: Art Gallery
Area: Downtown
Address: 1702 - 969 Richards Street
Vancouver, BC V6B 1A8
Phone: (604) 620-5095

#250
The Lido
Category: Music Venues
Area: Mount Pleasant
Address: 518 E Broadway
Vancouver, BC V5T 1X5
Phone: (604) 879-5436

#251
Blue Seas Gallery
Category: Art Gallery, Jewelry
Area: Granville Island/False Creek
Address: 1535 Johnston St
Vancouver, BC V6H 3R9
Phone: (604) 568-3488

#252
C+C Music and Video Factory
Category: Performing Arts, Cinema
Area: Downtown, Granville Entertainment District
Address: 1065 Granville Street
Vancouver, BC V6Z 1P6
Phone: (778) 708-4701

Shops, Restaurants, Attractions & Nightlife / Vancouver Travel Guide

#253
Frame of Mind
Fine Art & Framing
Category: Home Decor, Art Gallery
Area: Mount Pleasant, Strathcona
Address: 350 2nd Ave E
Vancouver, BC V5T 4R8
Phone: (604) 871-1175

#254
Vancouver International
Children's Festival
Category: Festival
Area: Granville Island/False Creek
Address: Granville Island
Vancouver, BC V6H 3R8
Phone: (604) 708-5655

#255
Vancouver Academy
of Dramatic Arts
Category: Specialty School,
Performing Arts
Area: Downtown
Address: 900 Helmcken Street
Vancouver, BC V6Z 1B3
Phone: (604) 633-1525

#256
Department of W.O'W.
Category: Fashion, Art Gallery, Jewelry
Average price: Modest
Area: Strathcona
Address: 110-243 Union Street
Vancouver, BC V6A 2Z7
Phone: (604) 685-9695

#257
Omega Custom Framing
& Gallery
Category: Home Decor, Art Gallery
Area: Dunbar-Southlands
Address: 4290 Dunbar St
Vancouver, BC V6S 2E9
Phone: (604) 732-6778

#258
Centre A
Category: Art Gallery
Area: Chinatown, Strathcona
Address: 229 E Georgia Street
Vancouver, BC V6A 1Z6
Phone: (604) 683-8326

#259
Architectural Institute of B C
Category: Architects, Museum
Area: Downtown
Address: 440 Cambie St
Vancouver, BC V6B 2N5
Phone: (604) 683-8588

#260
Playwrights Theatre Centre
Category: Performing Arts
Area: Strathcona
Address: 202-739 Gore Ave
Vancouver, BC V6H 3R8
Phone: (604) 685-6228

#261
Blue Egg Studio
Category: Performing Arts,
Dance School
Area: Downtown
Address: 210-207 W Hastings Street
Vancouver, BC V6B 1H7
Phone: (604) 569-0326

#262
Austin-Tuck Studio
Category: Performing Arts, Art School
Area: Downtown, Gastown
Address: 68 Water Street
Vancouver, BC V6B
Phone: (604) 836-3422

#263
Catalog Gallery
Category: Art Gallery
Area: Gastown
Address: 100 - 56 Powell St
Vancouver, BC V6A
Phone: (604) 721-4266

#264
Interurban Gallery
Category: Art Gallery
Area: Downtown, Downtown Eastside
Address: 1 E. Hastings
Vancouver, BC V6A 0A7
Phone: (604) 629-8396

#265
Mascall Dance
Category: Performing Arts,
Dance School, Dance Studio
Area: West End
Address: 1130 Jervis Street
Vancouver, BC V6E 2C7
Phone: (604) 669-9337

#266
Rendez Vous
Category: Art Gallery
Area: Downtown
Address: 323 Howe St
Vancouver, BC V6C 2E5
Phone: (604) 687-7466

#267
New Image College of Fine Arts
Category: Performing Arts
Area: Downtown
Address: 510 Hastings St
Vancouver, BC V6B 1L8
Phone: (604) 685-8807

#268
Glass Onion Studio & Gallery
Category: Art Gallery, Jewelry
Average price: Modest
Area: Strathcona
Address: 1103 Union Street
Vancouver, BC V6A 2C7
Phone: (604) 258-4103

#269
Veronica Foster Arte Studio
Category: Art Gallery
Area: Strathcona
Address: 1000 Parker St
Vancouver, BC V6A 2H2
Phone: (604) 254-6612

#270
Quadro Photo & Framing
Category: Home Decor, Photography Store & Services, Art Gallery
Average price: Modest
Area: Point Grey
Address: 4396 W 10th Avenue
Vancouver, BC V6R 2H7
Phone: (604) 224-8773

#271
Kitsilano Showboat
Category: Performing Arts
Area: Kitsilano
Address: 2300 Cornwall St
Vancouver, BC V6K 1C3
Phone: (604) 734-7332

#272
Push Festival
Category: Festival
Area: Fairview Slopes
Address: 640 Broadway W
Vancouver, BC V5Z 1G4
Phone: (604) 605-8284

#273
Circle Craft Co-op
Category: Art Gallery, Art Supplies
Average price: Expensive
Area: Granville Island/False Creek
Address: 1666 Johnston St
Vancouver, BC V6H 3S2
Phone: (604) 669-8021

#274
Fox
Category: Music Venues, Venues & Event Space
Area: Mount Pleasant
Address: 2321 Main Street
Vancouver, BC V5T 3C9
Phone: (604) 874-3116

#275
Vancouver Cantata Singers
Category: Performing Arts
Area: Fairview Slopes
Address: 1254 7th Ave W
Vancouver, BC V6H 1B6
Phone: (604) 730-8856

#276
A Creative Arts Collective
Category: Performing Arts, Dance School
Area: Mount Pleasant
Address: 125 East 2nd Avenue
Vancouver, BC V5T 3B5
Phone: (604) 836-2787

#277
The Actors Chapel
Category: Performing Arts
Area: Mount Pleasant
Address: 225-196 W 3rd Avenue
Vancouver, BC V5T 1E9
Phone: (778) 891-5171

#278
Opera Di Concertisti e Meraviglie
Category: Opera & Ballet, Musicians
Area: Point Grey
Address: 1975 Alma Street
Vancouver, BC V6R 3P8
Phone: (604) 762-2330

#279
Musica Intima Vocal Ensemble
Category: Performing Arts
Area: Mount Pleasant
Address: 204-3102 Main Street
Vancouver, BC V5T 3G7
Phone: (604) 731-6618

#280
Federation of Canadian Artists
Category: Art Gallery
Average price: Exclusive
Area: Granville Island/False Creek
Address: 1241 Cartwright St
Vancouver, BC V6H 4B7
Phone: (604) 681-8534

#281
Gallery of B C Ceramics
Category: Art Gallery
Average price: Modest
Area: Granville Island/False Creek
Address: 1359 Cartwright St
Vancouver, BC V6H 3R7
Phone: (604) 669-3606

#282
Doctor Vigari Gallery
Category: Art Gallery
Average price: Expensive
Area: Grandview-Woodlands, The Drive
Address: 1816 Commercial Dr
Vancouver, BC V5N 4A5
Phone: (604) 255-9513

#283
Panache Antiques & Objets D'art
Category: Antiques, Art Gallery
Area: Fairview Slopes, South Granville
Address: 2212 Granville Street
Vancouver, BC V6H 4H7
Phone: (604) 732-1206

#284
Stone Age Art Company
Category: Art Gallery
Area: Granville Island/False Creek
Address: 1551 Johnston St
Vancouver, BC V6H 3R9
Phone: (604) 801-5108

#285
Creekhouse Gallery
Category: Art Gallery
Average price: Modest
Area: Granville Island/False Creek
Address: 1551 Johnston St
Vancouver, BC V6H 3R9
Phone: (604) 681-5016

#286
Gallery Indigena
Category: Art Gallery
Area: Granville Island/False Creek
Address: 1551 Johnston Street
Vancouver, BC V6H 3R9
Phone: (604) 681-5016

#287
Heffel Fine Art Auction House
Category: Art Gallery
Area: Fairview Slopes, South Granville
Address: 2247 Granville St
Vancouver, BC V6H 3G1
Phone: (604) 732-6505

#288
Debbie Lee Dance
Category: Dance Studio, Performing Arts, Opera & Ballet
Area: Downtown, Granville Entertainment District
Address: 677 Davie Street
Vancouver, BC V6B 2G6
Phone: (604) 312-4408

#289
Vancouver Opera
Category: Performing Arts
Area: Downtown
Address: 750 Cambie St
Vancouver, BC V6B 2P2
Phone: (604) 681-8712

#290
Stompers
Category: Winery
Area: Fairview Slopes
Address: 1529 4th Avenue W
Vancouver, BC V6J 1L6
Phone: (604) 731-1072

#291
Vetrova Art Studio & Gallery
Category: Art Gallery
Area: Downtown, Yaletown
Address: 11118 Homer St
Vancouver, BC
Phone: (604) 722-6987

#292
Elliott Louis Gallery
Category: Art Gallery
Area: Granville Island/False Creek, Fairview Slopes
Address: 1540 2nd Ave W
Vancouver, BC V6J 1H2
Phone: (604) 736-3282

#293
Vancouver Magician
Category: Performing Arts
Area: Fairview Slopes
Address: 630-1665 W Broadway
Vancouver, BC V6J 1X1
Phone: (604) 733-0037

#294
Lattimer Gallery
Category: Jewelry, Art Gallery
Area: Fairview Slopes
Address: 1590 2nd Ave W
Vancouver, BC V6J 1H2
Phone: (604) 732-4556

#295
Vancouver Civic Theatres
Category: Performing Arts
Area: Downtown
Address: 649 Cambie St
Vancouver, BC V6B 2P1
Phone: (604) 665-3050

#296
Grapevines Winemaking 99
Category: Winery
Area: Marpole
Address: 1314 Marine Drive SW
Vancouver, BC V6P 5Z6
Phone: (604) 261-2739

#297
Westbridge Fine Art Auction House
Category: Art Gallery
Area: Granville Island/False Creek, Fairview Slopes
Address: 1737 Fir Street
Vancouver, BC V6J 5J9
Phone: (604) 736-1014

#298
Latin Funk Dance
Category: Dance School
Area: Downtown
Address: 1211-933 Hornby Street
Vancouver, BC V6Z 3G4
Phone: (604) 764-1697

#299
Shudder Gallery
Category: Art Gallery
Area: Chinatown
Address: 433 Columbia Street
Vancouver, BC V6A 4J1
Phone: (604) 488-5477

#300
Dynamo Arts Assn
Category: Art Gallery
Area: Downtown, Downtown Eastside
Address: 142 Hastings St W
Vancouver, BC V6B 1G8
Phone: (604) 602-9005

#301
Djavad Mowafaghian Cinema
Category: Performing Arts
Area: Downtown, Downtown Eastside
Address: 149 W Hastings St
Vancouver, BC V6B 1G8
Phone: (778) 782-9149

#302
Scrap Arts Music
Category: Performing Arts
Area: Downtown
Address: 402 Pender Street W
Vancouver, BC V5L 2Z2
Phone: (604) 669-2112

#303
Satellite Gallery
Category: Art Gallery
Area: Downtown
Address: 560 Seymour St
Vancouver, BC V6B 3J5
Phone: (604) 681-8425

#304
Winsor Gallery
Category: Art Gallery
Area: Downtown
Address: 667 Howe St
Vancouver, BC V6C 2E5
Phone: (604) 681-4870

#305
Arts Off Main
Category: Art Gallery
Average price: Inexpensive
Area: Riley Park
Address: 216 28th Ave E
Vancouver, BC V5V 2M4
Phone: (604) 876-2785

#306
Trisko Talent Management
Category: Performing Arts
Area: Gastown, Downtown Eastside
Address: 1140 Homer Street
Vancouver, BC V6B 2X6
Phone: (604) 637-7009

#307
Jeffrey Boone Gallery
Category: Art Gallery
Area: Downtown, Gastown
Address: 1 E Cordova St
Vancouver, BC V6A 4H3
Phone: (604) 838-6816

#308
Baron Gallery
Category: Art Gallery
Area: Gastown, Downtown Eastside
Address: 293 Columbia Street
Vancouver, BC V6A 2R5
Phone: (604) 682-1114

#309
Dan's Bass Lessons
Category: Music Venues, Tutoring Center, Private Tutors
Area: Grandview-Woodlands
Address: 1890 Pandora St
Vancouver, BC V5L 1M5
Phone: (604) 817-8830

#310
Rendezvous Art Gallery
Category: Art Gallery
Area: Downtown
Address: 323 Howe Street
Vancouver, BC V6C 3L5
Phone: (604) 687-7466

#311
Wine Kitz
Category: Winery
Area: Kitsilano
Address: 3122 Blenheim Street
Vancouver, BC V6K 4J7
Phone: (604) 224-4445

#312
Oxygen Films Corp
Category: Cinema
Area: Coal Harbour, Downtown
Address: 999 Pl
Vancouver, BC V6C 3T4
Phone: (604) 216-2716

#313
Buschlen Mowatt Fine Arts
Category: Art Gallery
Area: Downtown
Address: 1445 Georgia St W
Vancouver, BC V6G 2T3
Phone: (604) 682-1234

#314
Dance Co
Category: Performing Arts, Dance School
Area: Shaughnessy
Address: 154-4255 Arbutus St
Vancouver, BC V6J 4R1
Phone: (604) 736-3394

#315
Pal Vancouver
Category: Performing Arts
Area: Coal Harbour, Downtown
Address: 581 Cardero St
Vancouver, BC V6G 3L3
Phone: (604) 255-4312

#316
Inventcorp Entertainment
Category: Performing Arts
Area: Coal Harbour, Downtown
Address: 699 Cardero Street
Vancouver, BC V6G 3H7
Phone: (604) 817-6462

#317
Darren Bersuk Vancouver Acrobat
Category: Performing Arts
Area: Coal Harbour, Downtown
Address: 699 Cardero Street
Vancouver, BC V6G 3H7
Phone: (604) 817-6462

Shops, Restaurants, Attractions & Nightlife / Vancouver Travel Guide

#318
Kitsilano Figure Skating Club
Category: Amateur Sports Team, Professional Sports Team
Area: Kitsilano
Address: 2690 Larch St
Vancouver, BC V6K 4K9
Phone: (604) 737-6000

#319
Smash Gallery of Modern Art
Category: Art Gallery
Area: Strathcona, Grandview-Woodlands
Address: 580 Clark Drive
Vancouver, BC V5L 3H7
Phone: (604) 251-3262

#320
Jungle Swing Productions
Category: Dance Studio, Party & Event Planning, Jazz & Blues
Area: Grandview-Woodlands, The Drive
Address: 2205 Commercial Dr
Vancouver, BC V5N 4B6
Phone: (604) 420-0087

#321
Jewish Community Centre
Category: Library, Fitness & Instruction, Performing Arts, Amateur Sports Teams
Area: Oakridge
Address: 950 41st Ave W
Vancouver, BC V5Z 2N7
Phone: (604) 257-5111

#322
Suna Studio
Category: Music Venues, Recording Studio
Area: Grandview-Woodlands
Address: 1585 E Pender
Vancouver, BC V5L 1V9
Phone: (604) 315-4863

#323
West Side Family Place
Category: Recreation Center, Social Club, Child Care & Day Care
Area: Kitsilano
Address: 2819 W 11th Avenue
Vancouver, BC V6K 2M2
Phone: (604) 738-2819

#324
Winemaster
Category: Kitchen & Bath, Winery
Area: Arbutus Ridge
Address: 4107 MacDonald St
Vancouver, BC V6L 2P1
Phone: (604) 731-9463

#325
4Cats Arts Studio
Category: Art School, Arts & Entertainment
Area: Dunbar-Southlands
Address: 4293 Dunbar Street
Vancouver, BC V6S 2G1
Phone: (604) 569-2426

#326
3Y Pictures & Frames
Category: Home Decor, Art Gallery
Area: Kitsilano
Address: 3075 Broadway W
Vancouver, BC V6K 2G9
Phone: (604) 732-4782

#327
Brockton Fields At Stanley Park
Category: Athletic Fields, Park
Area: Coal Harbour
Address: Stanley Park
Vancouver, BC V6B 6Y1
Phone: (800) 745-3000

#328
Old Hastings Mill Store Museum
Category: Museum
Area: Point Grey
Address: 1575 Alma Street
Vancouver, BC V6R 3P3
Phone: (604) 734-1212

#329
The Landing Dance Centre
Category: Performing Arts, Art School, Dance School
Area: Marpole
Address: 270 SW Marine Dr
Vancouver, BC V5X 2R5
Phone: (604) 325-8653

#330
Deeley Motorcycle Exhibition
Category: Museum, Venues
Area: Hastings-Sunrise
Address: 1875 Boundary Road
Vancouver, BC V5M 3Y7
Phone: (604) 293-2221

#331
The Vancouver Charity Horse Show
Category: Festival
Area: Hastings-Sunrise
Address: 2901 E Hastings Street
Vancouver, BC V5K 5J1
Phone: (778) 873-0996

#332
Press Box Pub
Category: Karaoke, Music Venues
Area: Hastings-Sunrise
Address: 2889 E Hastings
Vancouver, BC V5K 1Z9
Phone: (604) 252-2690

#333
Vancouver Tap Dance Academy
Category: Performing Arts
Area: Hastings-Sunrise
Address: 2775 E Hastings
Vancouver, BC V5K 1Z8
Phone: (604) 253-0293

#334
Green Thumb Theatre Studio
Category: Performing Arts
Area: Killarney, Renfrew-Collingwood
Address: 5560 McKinnon Street
Vancouver, BC V5R 0B6
Phone: (604) 254-4055

#335
Pacific Dancearts
Category: Dance School
Area: Hastings-Sunrise
Address: 3626 4th Ave E
Vancouver, BC V5M 1M3
Phone: (604) 738-8575

#336
B C Golf Museum
Category: Museum, Tours
Area: Point Grey
Address: 2545 Blanca St
Vancouver, BC V6R 4N1
Phone: (604) 222-4653

#337
Scotiabank Dance Centre
Category: Performing Arts, Venues & Event Space
Area: Downtown
Address: 677 Davie Street
Vancouver, BC V6B 2G6
Phone: (604) 606-6400

#338
Cambie Bar & Grill
Category: Pub, Dive Bar, Music Venues
Average price: Inexpensive
Area: Downtown, Gastown
Address: 300 Cambie St
Vancouver, BC V6B 2N3
Phone: (604) 684-6466

#339
Café for Contemporary Art
Category: Art Gallery, Mexican
Average price: Inexpensive
Area: Lower Lonsdale
Address: 140 E Esplanade North
Vancouver, BC V7L 4X9
Phone: (778) 340-3379

#340
Company-Art Gallery
Category: Art Gallery
Area: Oakridge
Address: 638 45th Ave W
Vancouver, BC V5Z 4R8
Phone: (604) 322-7713

#341
Sharman King Musical Services
Category: Performing Arts
Area: Fairview Slopes
Address: 632 Broadway W
Vancouver, BC V5Z 1G1
Phone: (604) 873-0661

#342
Neworld Theatre Society
Category: Performing Arts
Area: Fairview Slopes
Address: 640 Broadway W
Vancouver, BC V5Z 1G4
Phone: (604) 602-0007

#343
Great Canadian Casino
Category: Casino
Area: Fairview Slopes
Address: 709 Broadway W
Vancouver, BC V5Z 1J5
Phone: (604) 872-5543

#344
Fader Mountain Sound
Category: Music Venues, Musicians
Area: Mount Pleasant
Address: 201 W 7th Avenue
Vancouver, BC V5Y 1L9
Phone: (604) 628-7750

#345
Medallion Wine Marketing
Category: Winery
Area: Mount Pleasant
Address: 138 8th Ave W
Vancouver, BC V5Y 1N2
Phone: (604) 251-5030

#346
Denbigh Fine Art Services
Category: Art Supplies
Area: Mount Pleasant
Address: 169 7th Ave W
Vancouver, BC V5Y 1L8
Phone: (604) 876-3303

#347
Vancouver Musicians' Assn
Category: Performing Arts
Area: Fairview Slopes
Address: 925 8th Ave W
Vancouver, BC V5Z 1E4
Phone: (604) 737-1110

#348
Clarke Don
Category: Art Gallery
Area: Hastings-Sunrise
Address: 2828 Yale St
Vancouver, BC V5K 1C6
Phone: (604) 251-3079

#349
Buschlen Mowatt Fine Arts
Category: Art Gallery
Area: Mount Pleasant
Address: 290 3rd Ave W
Vancouver, BC V5Y 1G1
Phone: (604) 707-1109

#350
Buschlen-Mowatt Fine Arts
Category: Art Gallery
Area: Mount Pleasant
Address: 290 3rd Ave W
Vancouver, BC V5Y 1G1
Phone: (604) 629-1700

#351
Welch Douglas Design
Category: Performing Arts
Area: Mount Pleasant
Address: 1 7th Ave W
Vancouver, BC V5Y 1L4
Phone: (604) 874-0552

#352
Total Lighting Solutions
Category: Performing Arts
Area: Mount Pleasant
Address: 1 7th Ave W
Vancouver, BC V5Y 1L4
Phone: (604) 872-0552

#353
Douglas Welch Design
Category: Performing Arts
Area: Mount Pleasant
Address: 1 7th Ave W
Vancouver, BC V5Y 1L4
Phone: (604) 874-0552

#354
Free House Wine & Spirits
Category: Winery
Area: Mount Pleasant
Address: 29 6th Ave W
Vancouver, BC V5Y 1K2
Phone: (604) 269-9040

#355
Renaissance Wine Merchants
Category: Winery
Area: Mount Pleasant
Address: 29 6th Ave W
Vancouver, BC V5Y 1K2
Phone: (604) 709-8017

#356
Trans Pool Hall
Category: Pool Hall, Casino
Area: Mount Pleasant
Address: 42 Broadway E
Vancouver, BC V5T 1V6
Phone: (604) 874-3118

#357
Charton-Hobbs
Category: Winery
Area: Mount Pleasant
Address: 1880 Ontario St
Vancouver, BC V5T 2W6
Phone: (604) 420-5009

#358
Aion Art Gallery
Category: Art Gallery
Area: Mount Pleasant
Address: 2315 Main St
Vancouver, BC V5T 3C9
Phone: (604) 879-9900

#359
Bonsai Takamatsu Design
Category: Art Gallery
Area: Fairview Slopes
Address: 1233 Broadway W
Vancouver, BC V6H 1G7
Phone: (604) 736-4747

#360
Broadway Gallery
Category: Art Gallery
Area: Fairview Slopes
Address: 1233 Broadway W
Vancouver, BC V6H 1G7
Phone: (604) 736-4747

#361
Somos Music
Category: Performing Arts
Area: Mount Pleasant
Address: 150 3rd Ave E
Vancouver, BC V5T 1C8
Phone: (604) 709-4300

#362
Video Out International Distribution
Category: Art Gallery
Area: Mount Pleasant
Address: 1965 Main St
Vancouver, BC V5T 3C1
Phone: (604) 872-8449

#363
Edam Performing Arts Society
Category: Performing Arts
Area: Mount Pleasant
Address: 303 8th Avenue E
Vancouver, BC V5T 1S1
Phone: (604) 876-9559

#364
Flavorite Music
Category: Music Venues
Area: Mount Pleasant
Address: 2050 Scotia Street
Vancouver, BC V5T 4S2
Phone: (778) 839-8567

#365
Calibrium International
Category: Winery
Area: Downtown, Yaletown
Address: 1260 Hamilton St
Vancouver, BC V6B 2S8
Phone: (604) 320-0103

#366
Trialto Wine Group
Category: Winery
Area: Downtown, Yaletown
Address: 1260 Hamilton St
Vancouver, BC V6B 2S8
Phone: (778) 331-8999

#367
Winspeer International Group
Category: Winery
Area: Downtown, Yaletown
Address: 1260 Hamilton St
Vancouver, BC V6B 2S8
Phone: (604) 320-0049

#368
Liquid Art Fine Wines
Category: Winery
Area: Downtown, Yaletown
Address: 1260 Hamilton St
Vancouver, BC V6B 2S8
Phone: (604) 320-0295

#369
1230 Gallery
Category: Art Gallery
Area: Downtown, Yaletown
Address: 1230 Hamilton Street
Vancouver, BC V6B 2S8
Phone: (604) 910-7037

#370
International Cellars
Category: Winery
Area: Downtown, Yaletown
Address: 1122 Mainland St
Vancouver, BC V6B 5L1
Phone: (604) 689-5333

#371
Select Wine Merchants
Category: Winery
Area: Downtown, Yaletown
Address: 1152 Mainland Street
Vancouver, BC V6B 4X2
Phone: (604) 687-8199

#372
Opera Pro Cantanti
Category: Opera & Ballet
Area: Riley Park
Address: 215 E 17th Avenue
Vancouver, BC V5V 1A1
Phone: (604) 340-8545

#373
Arpzco Pictures & Print Frames
Category: Home Decor, Art Gallery
Area: Downtown, Yaletown
Address: 1025 Cambie St
Vancouver, BC V6B 5L7
Phone: (604) 683-8225

#374
Sorour's Art Gallery
Category: Art Gallery
Area: Downtown, Yaletown
Address: 1058 Mainland St
Vancouver, BC V6B 2T4
Phone: (604) 669-3505

#375
Modpod Art Gallery
Category: Art Gallery
Area: Downtown, Yaletown
Address: 1058 Mainland St
Vancouver, BC V6B 2T4
Phone: (604) 608-6706

#376
Headlines Theatre Company
Category: Cinema
Area: Mount Pleasant, Strathcona
Address: 350 2nd Ave E
Vancouver, BC V5T 4R8
Phone: (604) 871-0508

#377
The Office Billiards
Category: Pool Hall, Casino
Area: Fairview Slopes, South Granville
Address: 1409 Broadway W
Vancouver, BC V6H 1H6
Phone: (604) 734-9914

#378
Joyce Williams Gallery
Category: Antiques, Art Gallery
Area: Downtown, Yaletown
Address: 1118 Homer St
Vancouver, BC V6B 6L5
Phone: (604) 688-7434

#379
B C Sports Hall of Fame & Museum
Category: Museum
Area: Downtown
Address: 777 Pacific Blvd
Vancouver, BC V6B 4Y8
Phone: (604) 687-5520

#380
Touchstone Theatre Company
Category: Cinema
Area: Downtown, Yaletown
Address: 873 Beatty St
Vancouver, BC V6B 2M6
Phone: (604) 709-9973

#381
DanceHouse
Category: Performing Arts
Area: Mount Pleasant, Strathcona
Address: 104-336 E 1st Ave
Vancouver, BC V5T 1A4
Phone: (604) 801-6225

#382
Granville Island Cultural Society
Category: Performing Arts
Area: Granville Island/False Creek
Address: 1398 Cartwright St
Vancouver, BC V6H 3R8
Phone: (604) 687-3005

#383
Pi Theatre
Category: Cinema
Area: Granville Island/False Creek
Address: 1411 Cartwright Street
Vancouver, BC V6H 3R7
Phone: (604) 872-1861

#384
Axis Theatre Company
Category: Cinema
Area: Granville Island/False Creek
Address: 1405 Anderson St
Vancouver, BC V6H 3R5
Phone: (604) 669-0631

#385
Ruby Slippers Production
Category: Cinema
Area: Granville Island/False Creek
Address: 1405 Anderson St
Vancouver, BC V6H 3R5
Phone: (604) 602-0585

#386
Greater Vancouver Professional Theatre Alliance Society
Category: Cinema
Area: Granville Island/False Creek
Address: 1405 Anderson St
Vancouver, BC V6H 3R5
Phone: (604) 608-6799

#387
Boca Del Lupo
Category: Performing Arts
Area: Granville Island/False Creek
Address: 1405 Anderson St
Vancouver, BC V6H 3R5
Phone: (604) 684-2622

#388
Eye Candy Design Solutions
Category: Art Gallery, Home Decor
Area: Downtown
Address: 786 Beatty St
Vancouver, BC V6B 2M1
Phone: (778) 370-1904

#389
Lambert's Gallery & Shop
Category: Art Gallery
Area: Fairview Slopes, South Granville
Address: 2439 Granville St
Vancouver, BC V6H 3G5
Phone: (604) 263-1111

#390
Art Gallery
Category: Art Gallery
Area: Fairview Slopes, South Granville
Address: 2427 Granville St
Vancouver, BC V6H 3G5
Phone: (604) 736-7695

#391
Vesna's Fibre Art Studio
Category: Art Gallery
Area: Granville Island/False Creek
Address: 1551 Johnston St
Vancouver, BC V6H 3R9
Phone: (604) 605-1580

#392
Marilyn S Mylrea Studio Art Gallery
Category: Art Gallery
Area: Fairview Slopes, South Granville
Address: 2341 Granville St
Vancouver, BC V6H 3G4
Phone: (604) 736-2450

#393
Spirits of the North Gallery
Category: Art Gallery
Area: Fairview Slopes, South Granville
Address: 2327 Granville St
Vancouver, BC V6H 3G4
Phone: (604) 733-8516

#394
Heffel Gallery
Category: Art Gallery
Area: Fairview Slopes, South Granville
Address: 2247 Granville St
Vancouver, BC V6H 3G1
Phone: (604) 732-6505

#395
Uno Langmann
Category: Antiques, Art Gallery
Area: Fairview Slopes
Address: 2117 Granville St
Vancouver, BC V6H 3E9
Phone: (604) 736-8825

#396
Staneley Theatre
Category: Performing Arts
Area: Granville Island/False Creek
Address: 1585 Johnston St
Vancouver, BC V6H 3R9
Phone: (604) 687-1644

#397
Ballet British Columbia
Category: Performing Arts
Area: Downtown, Granville Entertainment District
Address: 677 Davie St
Vancouver, BC V6B 2G6
Phone: (604) 732-5003

#398
New Performance Works Society
Category: Performing Arts
Area: Downtown, Granville Entertainment District
Address: 677 Davie St
Vancouver, BC V6B 2G6
Phone: (604) 893-8807

#399
Malaspina Printmakers Society
Category: Art Gallery
Area: Granville Island/False Creek
Address: 1555 Duranleau St
Vancouver, BC V6H 3S3
Phone: (604) 688-1724

#400
Granville Island Museum
Category: Museum
Area: Granville Island/False Creek
Address: 1502 Duranleau St
Vancouver, BC V6H 3S4
Phone: (604) 683-1939

#401
Vinterra Wine Merchants
Category: Winery
Area: Downtown
Address: 1460 Howe St
Vancouver, BC V6Z
Phone: (604) 736-9497

#402
David Herman & Son
Category: Winery
Area: Fairview Slopes
Address: 1526 6th Ave W
Vancouver, BC V6J 1R2
Phone: (604) 737-0018

#403
Toni Onley
Category: Art Gallery
Area: Fairview Slopes
Address: 1529 6th Ave W
Vancouver, BC V6J 1R1
Phone: (604) 261-8557

#404
Theatre La Seizieme
Category: Performing Arts
Area: Fairview Slopes
Address: 1555 7th Ave W
Vancouver, BC V6J 1S1
Phone: (604) 736-2616

#405
Douglas Udell Gallery
Category: Art Gallery
Area: Fairview Slopes
Address: 1558 6th Ave W
Vancouver, BC V6J 1R2
Phone: (604) 736-8900

#406
Doug Udell Gallery
Category: Art Gallery
Area: Fairview Slopes
Address: 1558 6th Ave W
Vancouver, BC V6J 1R2
Phone: (604) 736-8931

#407
Lawrence Tracey Gallery
Category: Art Gallery
Area: Fairview Slopes
Address: 1531 4th Ave W
Vancouver, BC V6J 1L6
Phone: (604) 730-2875

#408
Aboriginal Arts
Category: Art Gallery
Area: Downtown, Granville Entertainment District
Address: 1044 Granville St
Vancouver, BC V6Z 1L5
Phone: (604) 682-4602

#409
Appleton Gallery
Category: Art Gallery
Area: Downtown
Address: 1451 Hornby St
Vancouver, BC V6Z 1W8
Phone: (604) 685-1715

#410
Bent Box First Nations Art
Category: Art Gallery
Area: Granville Island/False Creek, Fairview Slopes
Address: 1536 2nd Ave W
Vancouver, BC V6J 1H2
Phone: (604) 731-4874

#411
Fei and Milton Wong Experimental Theatre
Category: Performing Arts
Area: Downtown, Downtown Eastside
Address: 149 W Hastings St
Vancouver, BC V6B 1H4
Phone: (778) 782-9149

#412
Espana Gallery
Category: Art Gallery
Area: Downtown
Address: 689 Abbott Street
Vancouver, BC V6B 6B8
Phone: (778) 773-2861

#413
Bachata Vancouver
Category: Dance Studio, Dance School, Performing Arts
Area: Downtown
Address: 688 Abbott Street
Vancouver, BC V6B 0C1
Phone: (604) 874-0126

#414
Let's Dance Studio
Category: Performing Arts, Dance School
Area: Downtown, Granville Entertainment District
Address: 927 Granville St
Vancouver, BC V6Z 1L3
Phone: (604) 683-2300

#415
Main Dance
Category: Performing Arts, Dance School
Area: Downtown, Granville Entertainment District
Address: 927 Granville St
Vancouver, BC V6Z 1L3
Phone: (604) 258-0274

#416
Vancouver City
Category: Performing Arts
Area: Downtown
Address: 649 Cambie Street
Vancouver, BC V6B 2P1
Phone: (604) 665-3050

#417
Westbridge Publications
Category: Antiques, Art Gallery
Area: Granville Island/False Creek, Fairview Slopes
Address: 1737 Fir St
Vancouver, BC V6J 5J9
Phone: (604) 736-1014

#418
Westbridge Fine Art
Category: Antiques, Art Gallery
Area: Granville Island/False Creek
Address: 1737 Fir St
Vancouver, BC V6J 5J9
Phone: (604) 736-1014

#419
Mortal Coil Performance Society
Category: Performing Arts
Area: Mount Pleasant, Strathcona
Address: 555 Great Northern Way
Vancouver, BC V5T 1E2
Phone: (604) 874-6153

#420
Rock Paper Scissors Comedy Creation
Category: Cinema
Area: Riley Park
Address: 4120 Main St
Vancouver, BC V5V 3P7
Phone: (604) 730-9596

#421
Art Beatus Consultancy
Category: Art Gallery
Area: Downtown
Address: 808 Nelson St
Vancouver, BC V6Z 2H2
Phone: (604) 688-2633

#422
Art Beatus Gallery
Category: Art Gallery
Area: Downtown
Address: 808 Nelson St
Vancouver, BC V6Z 2H2
Phone: (604) 688-2685

#423
Medical Arts Building
Category: Performing Arts, Music Venues
Area: Downtown, Granville Entertainment District
Address: 825 Granville St
Vancouver, BC V6Z 1K9
Phone: (604) 681-8622

#424
Art Center
Category: Art Gallery
Area: Fairview Slopes
Address: 2060 Pine St
Vancouver, BC V6J 4P8
Phone: (604) 731-5412

#425
Gallery O
Category: Art Gallery
Area: Fairview Slopes
Address: 2060 Pine St
Vancouver, BC V6J 4P8
Phone: (604) 733-2662

Shops, Restaurants, Attractions & Nightlife / Vancouver Travel Guide

#426
Heaventree Gallery
Category: Art Gallery
Area: Mount Pleasant
Address: 661 15th Ave E
Vancouver, BC V5T 2R6
Phone: (604) 877-1000

#427
Framed Customer Framing
Category: Home Decor, Art Gallery
Area: Fairview Slopes
Address: 1969 Pine St
Vancouver, BC V6J 3E1
Phone: (604) 731-3089

#428
Canamera Entertainment Group
Category: Performing Arts
Area: Strathcona
Address: 4411 Hastings Street
Vancouver, BC V6A 4C1
Phone: (604) 689-1144

#429
C C Arts Gallery
Category: Home Decor, Art Gallery
Area: Chinatown
Address: 20 Pender St E
Vancouver, BC V6A 1T1
Phone: (604) 669-2601

#430
Bjornson Kajiwara Gallery
Category: Art Gallery
Area: Fairview Slopes
Address: 1727 3rd Ave W
Vancouver, BC V6J 1K7
Phone: (604) 738-3500

#431
Forufera Centre for Dance Joy & Well-Being
Category: Performing Arts, Dance School
Area: Downtown
Address: 505 Hamilton St
Vancouver, BC V6B 2R1
Phone: (604) 633-2623

#432
Dancers Dancing
Category: Performing Arts
Area: Riley Park
Address: 236 26th Ave E
Vancouver, BC V5V 2H3
Phone: (604) 874-3416

#433
Vancouver Ballroom Dance Club
Category: Dance School
Area: Strathcona
Address: 456 Prior St
Vancouver, BC V6A 2E5
Phone: (604) 688-0217

#434
Arista Custom Framing
Category: Art Gallery
Area: Chinatown
Address: 88 Pender St E
Vancouver, BC V6A 3X3
Phone: (604) 681-2232

#435
Alliance Atlantis Cinemas
Category: Cinema
Area: Fairview Slopes
Address: 1788 5th Ave W
Vancouver, BC V6J 1P2
Phone: (604) 734-8700

#436
Vancouver Centre For Contemporary Asian Art
Category: Art Gallery
Area: Downtown Eastside
Address: 2 Hastings St W
Vancouver, BC V6B 1G6
Phone: (604) 683-8326

#437
James Tan Gallery
Category: Art Gallery
Area: Chinatown, Downtown Eastside
Address: 437 Columbia St
Vancouver, BC V6A 2R9
Phone: (604) 677-4082

#438
Company Erasga Dance Society
Category: Performing Arts
Area: Downtown
Address: 207 Hastings St W
Vancouver, BC V6B 1H7
Phone: (604) 687-6185

#439
Turner Music & Events
Category: Performing Arts
Area: Downtown
Address: 207 Hastings St W
Vancouver, BC V6B 1H7
Phone: (604) 662-4144

#440
Rumble Productions
Category: Cinema
Area: Downtown
Address: 207 Hastings St W
Vancouver, BC V6B 1H7
Phone: (604) 662-3395

#441
Battery Opera
Category: Performing Arts
Area: Downtown
Address: 207 Hastings St W
Vancouver, BC V6B 1H7
Phone: (604) 688-8583

#442
La G Gallery
Category: Art Gallery
Area: Downtown
Address: 612- 207 W Hastings St
Vancouver, BC V6B 2N4
Phone: (604) 999-1252

#443
Kinesis Dance
Category: Performing Arts
Area: Downtown
Address: 207 Hastings St W
Vancouver, BC V6B 1H7
Phone: (604) 684-7844

#444
Elan Fine Art
Category: Art Gallery
Area: Kitsilano
Address: 1819 W 5th Ave
Vancouver, BC V6J 1P5
Phone: (604) 568-5709

#445
Dancing Cranes Oriental Arts
Category: Art Gallery
Area: West End, Downtown
Address: 909 Burrard St
Vancouver, BC V6Z 2N2
Phone: (604) 688-3835

#446
Buschlen Mowatt Annex
Category: Art Gallery
Area: Downtown
Address: 661 Howe St
Vancouver, BC V6C 2E5
Phone: (604) 682-7777

#447
Plank Gallery
Category: Art Gallery
Area: Downtown Eastside
Address: 165 E Hastings St
Vancouver, BC V6A
Phone: (778) 558-4389

#448
Presentation House Gallery
Category: Art Gallery
Area: Lower Lonsdale
Address: 333 Chesterfield Avenue North
Vancouver, BC V7M 3G9
Phone: (604) 986-1351

#449
Mark Anthony Brands
Category: Winery
Area: Mount Pleasant, Strathcona
Address: 887 Great Northern Way
Vancouver, BC V5T 1E1
Phone: (604) 263-9994

#450
Mission Hill Winery
Category: Winery
Area: Mount Pleasant, Strathcona
Address: 887 Great Northern Way
Vancouver, BC V5T 1E1
Phone: (604) 263-9994

#451
Mark Anthony Properties
Category: Winery
Area: Mount Pleasant, Strathcona
Address: 887 Great Northern Way
Vancouver, BC V5T 1E1
Phone: (604) 263-9994

#452
California Cooler
Category: Winery
Area: Mount Pleasant, Strathcona
Address: 887 Great Northern Way
Vancouver, BC V5T 1E1
Phone: (604) 263-9994

#453
Grosvenor Fine Arts
Category: Art Gallery
Area: Downtown
Address: 470 Granville St
Vancouver, BC V6C 1V5
Phone: (604) 684-4295

#454
**Canadian Craft
& Design Museum**
Category: Museum
Area: Downtown
Address: 639 Hornby St
Vancouver, BC V6C 2G3
Phone: (604) 687-8266

#455
Marion Scott Gallery
Category: Art Gallery
Area: Downtown, Gastown
Address: 308 Water Street
Vancouver, BC V6B 1B6
Phone: (604) 685-1934

#456
**Canada International
Film Festival**
Category: Festival
Area: Downtown
Address: 991 Hornby Street
Vancouver, BC V6Z 3B7
Phone: (604) 608-5522

#457
**Kermodi Living Art
Showroom / Gallery**
Category: Art Gallery, Interior Design
Area: Downtown, Gastown
Address: 115 Water St
Vancouver, BC V6B 1B2
Phone: (604) 630-3759

#458
342066 BC
Category: Art Gallery
Area: Downtown, Gastown
Address: 164 Water St
Vancouver, BC V6B 1B2
Phone: (604) 685-7046

#459
**D A Choboter & Sons
Fine Art Gallery**
Category: Art Gallery
Area: Downtown, Gastown
Address: 23 Alexander St
Vancouver, BC V6A 1B2
Phone: (604) 688-0145

#460
Mayne Brand Productions
Category: Cinema
Area: Kitsilano
Address: 1450 Chestnut Street
Vancouver, BC V6J 3K3
Phone: (604) 440-4871

#461
Vancouver Men's Chorus
Category: Performing Arts
Area: Kitsilano
Address: 1270 Chestnut St
Vancouver, BC V6J 4R9
Phone: (604) 669-7464

#462
Yasel Dancesport
Category: Performing Arts, Dance School
Area: Riley Park
Address: 4603 Main St
Vancouver, BC V5V 3R6
Phone: (604) 872-0304

#463
Native Spirits Arts Alliance
Category: Art Gallery
Area: Downtown
Address: 757 Hastings St W
Vancouver, BC V6C 1A1
Phone: (604) 438-1111

#464
Foster's Wine Estates
Category: Winery
Area: Downtown
Address: 510 Burrard St
Vancouver, BC V6C 3A8
Phone: (604) 630-0900

#465
Southcop Wines
Category: Winery
Area: Downtown
Address: 510 Burrard St
Vancouver, BC V6C 3A8
Phone: (604) 408-2900

#466
Swangard Stadium
Category: Stadium
Area: Downtown
Address: 3883 Imperial St
Burnaby, BC V5G 4H7
Phone: (604) 435-6862

#467
Preview the Gallery Guide
Category: Art Gallery
Area: Downtown
Address: PO Box 549
Vancouver, BC V6C 2N3
Phone: (604) 254-1405

#468
The Bill Reid Foundation
Category: Museum
Area: Downtown
Address: 505 Burrard St
Vancouver, BC V7X 1M4
Phone: (604) 682-3455

#469
Green Thumb Theatre
Category: Performing Arts
Area: Downtown, Gastown
Address: 309 W Cordova St
Vancouver, BC V6B 1E5
Phone: (604) 254-4055

#470
2002 Design Art Studio
Category: Art Gallery
Area: Mount Pleasant
Address: 1227 7th Ave E
Vancouver, BC V5T 1R1
Phone: (604) 874-6796

#471
Philippe Dandurand Wines
Category: Winery
Area: Coal Harbour, Downtown
Address: 1055 Hastings St W
Vancouver, BC V6E 2E9
Phone: (604) 324-4443

#472
Al Mozaico Flamenco
Category: Performing Arts, Dance School
Area: Downtown Eastside
Address: 828 Hastings St E
Vancouver, BC V6A 1R6
Phone: (604) 671-9182

#473
Cosmopolitan Wine Agents
Category: Winery
Area: Strathcona
Address: 680 Raymur Ave
Vancouver, BC V6A 3L2
Phone: (604) 254-4214

#474
Fainting Goat Studio
Category: Art Gallery
Area: Strathcona
Address: 1000 Parker Street
Vancouver, BC V6A 2H2
Phone: (778) 998-7894

#475
Kien Giang
Category: Pool Hall, Casino
Area: Kensington-Cedar Cottage
Address: 1210 Kingsway
Vancouver, BC V5V 3E1
Phone: (604) 873-1574

#476
In Graphic Detail
Category: Art Gallery
Area: Strathcona
Address: 1000 Parker St
Vancouver, BC V6A 2H2
Phone: (604) 253-8311

#477
S & B Art Studio
Category: Art Gallery
Area: Strathcona, Grandview-Woodlands
Address: 1283 Clark Dr
Vancouver, BC V5L 3K6
Phone: (604) 253-7338

#478
Buschlen Mowatt Fine Arts
Category: Art Gallery
Area: Downtown
Address: 1445 W Georgia St
Vancouver, BC V6G 2T3
Phone: (604) 682-1234

#479
World Artists Productions
Category: Performing Arts
Area: Riley Park
Address: 211 38th Ave E
Vancouver, BC V5W 1H3
Phone: (604) 324-8680

#480
Holly Winters Paintings
Category: Art Gallery
Area: West End
Address: 1655 Barclay Street
Vancouver, BC V6G 2Y1
Phone: (604) 694-1021

Shops, Restaurants, Attractions & Nightlife / Vancouver Travel Guide

#481
Raja Cinema
Category: Cinema
Area: Grandview-Woodlands, The Drive, Kensington-Cedar Cottage
Address: 1660 Broadway E
Vancouver, BC V5N 1W1
Phone: (604) 879-7252

#482
Ace Of Spades Limousinse
Category: Party & Event Planning, Social Club, Wedding Planning
Area: Kensington-Cedar Cottage
Address: 5069 Chester Street
Vancouver, BC V5W 3A7
Phone: (604) 780-6652

#483
Grandview Recreations
Category: Pool Hall, Casino
Area: Grandview-Woodlands, The Drive
Address: 1816 Commercial Dr
Vancouver, BC V5N 4A5
Phone: (604) 254-9115

#484
Hambleton Fine Art Services
Category: Home Decor, Art Gallery
Area: Grandview-Woodlands, The Drive
Address: 1497 Adanac Street
Vancouver, BC V5L 2C4
Phone: (604) 879-2415

#485
Devon Gallery
Category: Home Decor, Art Gallery
Area: West End
Address: 688 Denman St
Vancouver, BC V6G 2L4
Phone: (604) 685-8894

#486
Stile Enterprises
Category: Winery
Area: Grandview-Woodlands, The Drive
Address: 1528 Commercial Drive
Vancouver, BC V5L 3Y2
Phone: (604) 255-2518

#487
Harpers First Nations Art Gallery
Category: Art Gallery
Area: Grandview-Woodlands, The Drive
Address: 931 Commercial Dr
Vancouver, BC V5L 3W8
Phone: (604) 439-1421

#488
Raja Cinema
Category: Cinema
Area: Grandview-Woodlands, The Drive
Address: 639 Commercial Dr
Vancouver, BC V5L 3W3
Phone: (604) 253-0402

#489
Art Image Gallery
Category: Home Decor, Art Gallery
Area: Kensington-Cedar Cottage
Address: 3769 Commercial St
Vancouver, BC V5N 4G1
Phone: (604) 327-7554

#490
Axé Capoeira
Category: Performing Arts, Dance School, Martial Arts
Area: Downtown Eastside
Address: 45 W Hastings St
Vancouver, BC V6B 1G4
Phone: (604) 537-8943

#491
Black Pants Productions
Category: Performing Arts
Area: Grandview-Woodlands, The Drive
Address: 1204 Victoria Dr
Vancouver, BC V5L
Phone: (604) 219-6491

#492
Felix Culpa
Category: Cinema
Area: Grandview-Woodlands
Address: 1748 Pender St E
Vancouver, BC V5L 1W4
Phone: (604) 251-7889

#493
The Paper Museum Creative Studio
Category: Museum
Area: Kitsilano
Address: 2607 MacKenzie St
Vancouver, BC V6K 3Z9
Phone: (604) 731-4714

#494
Mido Framers
Category: Home Decor, Art Gallery
Area: Kitsilano
Address: 2931 4th Ave W
Vancouver, BC V6K 1R3
Phone: (604) 736-1321

Shops, Restaurants, Attractions & Nightlife / Vancouver Travel Guide

#495
The Gallery
Category: Home Decor, Art Gallery
Area: Kitsilano
Address: 2901 Broadway W
Vancouver, BC V6K 2G6
Phone: (604) 731-1214

#496
Electric Company Theatre
Category: Performing Arts
Area: Grandview-Woodlands, The Drive
Address: 1885 Venables St
Vancouver, BC V5L 2H6
Phone: (604) 253-4222

#497
The Little Chamber Music Series
Category: Performing Arts
Area: Grandview-Woodlands, The Drive
Address: 1885 Venables St
Vancouver, BC V5L 2H6
Phone: (604) 253-4222

#498
Scrap Arts Music
Category: Performing Arts
Area: Grandview-Woodlands
Address: 2047 Grant St
Vancouver, BC V5L 2Z2
Phone: (604) 669-2112

#499
Tamsa Frames
Category: Art Gallery
Area: Grandview-Woodlands
Address: 1879 Franklin St
Vancouver, BC V5L 1P9
Phone: (604) 215-0225

#500
Vancouver Youth Symphony Orchestra Society
Category: Performing Arts
Area: Kitsilano
Address: 3214 10th Ave W
Vancouver, BC V6K 2L2
Phone: (604) 737-0714

TOP 400 NIGHTLIFE SPOTS
The Most Recommended by Locals & Trevelers
(From #1 to #400)

Shops, Restaurants, Attractions & Nightlife / Vancouver Travel Guide

#1
Alibi Room
Category: Pub, Canadian
Average price: Modest
Area: Downtown, Yaletown
Address: 157 Alexander St
Vancouver, BC V6A 1B8
Phone: (604) 623-3383

#2
Kitty Nights
Category: Performing Arts, Adult Entertainment
Average price: Inexpensive
Area: Mount Pleasant
Address: 395 Kingsway
Vancouver, BC V5T 3J7
Phone: (604) 676 0541

#3
Commodore Ballroom
Category: Music Venues
Average price: Modest
Area: Downtown, Granville Entertainment District
Address: 868 Granville Street
Vancouver, BC V6Z 1K3
Phone: (604) 739-4550

#4
The Biltmore Cabaret
Category: Music Venues, Bar
Average price: Inexpensive
Area: Mount Pleasant
Address: 2755 Prince Edward Street
Vancouver, BC V5T 3J7
Phone: (604) 676-0541

#5
Revel Room
Category: Lounge, Southern, Music Venues
Average price: Modest
Area: Downtown, Gastown
Address: 238 Abbott St
Vancouver, BC V6B 2K8
Phone: (604) 687-4088

#6
Guilt & Co
Category: Music Venues, Lounge
Average price: Modest
Area: Downtown, Gastown
Address: 1 Alexander Street
Vancouver, BC V6A 1B2
Phone: (604) 288-1704

#7
The Refinery
Category: Wine Bar, Tapas Bar
Average price: Modest
Area: Downtown, Granville Entertainment District
Address: 1115 Granville Street
Vancouver, BC V6Z 1M1
Phone: (604) 687-8001

#8
Narrow Lounge
Category: Lounge
Average price: Modest
Area: Mount Pleasant
Address: 1898 Main St
Vancouver, BC V5T 3B7
Phone: (604) 839-5780

#9
The Diamond
Category: Lounge, Mexican
Average price: Modest
Area: Downtown, Gastown
Address: 6 Powell Street
Vancouver, BC V6A 1E7
Phone: (604) 568 8272

#10
Railway Club
Category: Bar, Music Venues
Average price: Modest
Area: Downtown
Address: 579 Dunsmuir Street
Vancouver, BC V6B 1Y4
Phone: (604) 681-1625

#11
The Union
Category: Asian Fusion, Bar
Average price: Modest
Area: Strathcona
Address: 219 Union Street
Vancouver, BC V6A 0B4
Phone: (604) 568-3230

#12
Raw Canvas
Category: Wine Bar, Tapas, Party & Event Planning
Average price: Modest
Area: Downtown, Yaletown
Address: 1046 Hamilton St
Vancouver, BC V6B 2R9
Phone: (604) 687-1729

#13
Club 23 West
Category: Dance Club
Average price: Inexpensive
Area: Downtown, Gastown
Address: 23 W Cordova Street
Vancouver, BC V6B 1C8
Phone: (604) 662-3277

#14
The Keefer Bar
Category: Lounge
Average price: Expensive
Area: Chinatown
Address: 135 Keefer Street
Vancouver, BC V6A 1X3
Phone: (604) 688-1961

#15
Orpheum
Category: Music Venues, Performing Arts
Average price: Modest
Area: Downtown, Granville Entertainment District
Address: 884 Granville St
Vancouver, BC V6Z 1K3
Phone: (604) 665-3050

#16
The Cascade Room
Category: Pub, Canadian
Average price: Modest
Area: Mount Pleasant
Address: 2616 Main Street
Vancouver, BC V5T 3E6
Phone: (604) 709-8650

#17
Salt Tasting Room
Category: Wine Bar, Tapas
Average price: Modest
Area: Downtown, Gastown
Address: 45 Blood Alley Square
Vancouver, BC V6B 1A4
Phone: (604) 633-1912

#18
The Fringe Café
Category: Dive Bar
Average price: Modest
Area: Kitsilano
Address: 3124 W Broadway
Vancouver, BC V6K 2H3
Phone: (604) 738-6977

#19
Backstage Lounge
Category: Music Venues, Lounge
Average price: Modest
Area: Granville Island/False Creek
Address: 1585 Johnston St
Vancouver, BC V6H 3R9
Phone: (604) 687-1354

#20
The Storm Crow Tavern
Category: Pub, Canadian
Average price: Inexpensive
Area: Grandview-Woodlands, The Drive
Address: 1305 Commercial Drive
Vancouver, BC V5L 3X5
Phone: (604) 566-9669

#21
Celebrities Nightclub
Category: Dance Club
Average price: Modest
Area: West End
Address: 1022 Davie St
Vancouver, BC V6E 1M3
Phone: (604) 681-6180

#22
The Morrissey Pub
Category: Pub, Irish
Average price: Modest
Area: Downtown, Granville Entertainment District
Address: 1227 Granville Street
Vancouver, BC V6Z 1M5
Phone: (604) 682-0909

#23
The Improv Centre
Category: Comedy Club
Average price: Modest
Area: Granville Island/False Creek
Address: 1502 Duranleau St
Vancouver, BC V6H
Phone: (604) 738-7013

#24
The Locus
Category: Lounge, Canadian
Average price: Modest
Area: Riley Park
Address: 4121 Main Street
Vancouver, BC V5V 3P6
Phone: (604) 708-4121

#25
Fortune Sound Club
Category: Dance Club
Average price: Modest
Area: Chinatown
Address: 147 E Pender St
Vancouver, BC V6A 1T6
Phone: (604) 569-1758

#26
Johnnie Fox's Irish Snug
Category: Irish, Pub
Average price: Modest
Area: Downtown, Granville Entertainment District
Address: 1033 Granville Street
Vancouver, BC V6Z 1L4
Phone: (604) 685-4946

#27
The Shameful Tiki Room
Category: Bar
Average price: Modest
Area: Riley Park
Address: 4362 Main Street
Vancouver, BC V5V 3P9
Phone: (604) 999-5684

#28
Uva Wine Bar
Category: Wine Bar, Italian, Cafe
Average price: Expensive
Area: Downtown, Granville Entertainment District
Address: 900 Seymour Street
Vancouver, BC V6B 2L9
Phone: (604) 632-9560

#29
Clough Club
Category: Lounge, Tapas
Average price: Modest
Area: Downtown, Gastown
Address: 212 Abbott Street
Vancouver, BC V6B 1B2
Phone: (604) 558-1581

#30
Cascades Lounge
Category: Lounge, Canadian
Average price: Expensive
Area: Downtown
Address: 999 Place
Vancouver, BC V6C 3B5
Phone: (604) 662-8111

#31
Bacchus Restaurant & Lounge
Category: French, Pub
Average price: Expensive
Area: Downtown
Address: 845 Hornby Street
Vancouver, BC V6Z 1T9
Phone: (604) 608-5319

#32
Libra Room Café
Category: Lounge, Pub
Average price: Modest
Area: Grandview-Woodlands, The Drive
Address: 1608 Commercial Dr
Vancouver, BC V5L 3Y4
Phone: (604) 255-3787

#33
The Wolf & Hound
Category: Pub, Irish
Average price: Modest
Area: Kitsilano
Address: 3617 W Broadway
Vancouver, BC V6R 2B8
Phone: (604) 738-8909

#34
The Parlour
Category: Pizza, Gluten-Free, Champagne Bar
Average price: Modest
Area: Downtown, Yaletown
Address: 1011 Hamilton Street
Vancouver, BC V6B 2W7
Phone: (604) 568-3322

#35
The New Oxford
Category: Pub
Average price: Modest
Area: Downtown, Yaletown
Address: 1144 Homer St
Vancouver, BC V6B 2X6
Phone: (604) 609-0901

#36
Xi Shi Lounge
Category: Bar
Average price: Expensive
Area: West End, Downtown
Address: 1128 West Georgia Street
Vancouver, BC V6E 4M3
Phone: (604) 689-1120

#37
Brickhouse
Category: Pool Hall, Dive Bar
Average price: Inexpensive
Area: Strathcona
Address: 730 Main Street
Vancouver, BC V6A 2V7
Phone: (604) 689-8645

#38
**Chill Winston
Restaurant & Lounge**
Category: Lounge, Canadian
Average price: Modest
Area: Downtown, Gastown
Address: 3 Alexander Street
Vancouver, BC V6A
Phone: (604) 288-9575

#39
The Comedy Mix
Category: Comedy Club
Average price: Inexpensive
Area: West End, Downtown
Address: 1015 Burrard St
Vancouver, BC V6Z 1Y5
Phone: (604) 684-5050

#40
St. Augustines
Category: Pub
Average price: Modest
Area: Grandview-Woodlands, The Drive
Address: 2360 Commercial Drive
Vancouver, BC V5N 4B7
Phone: (604) 569-1911

#41
The Roxy
Category: Music Venues, Dance Club
Average price: Modest
Area: Downtown, Granville
Entertainment District
Address: 932 Granville Street
Vancouver, BC V6Z 1L2
Phone: (604) 331-7999

#42
Earls
Category: Bar, Canadian
Average price: Modest
Area: West End
Address: 1185 Robson Street
Vancouver, BC V6E 1B5
Phone: (604) 669-0020

#43
Score on Davie
Category: Sports Bar
Average price: Modest
Area: West End
Address: 1262 Davie St
Vancouver, BC V6J 5L1
Phone: (604) 632-1646

#44
Venue Nightclub
Category: Music Venues, Dance Club
Average price: Modest
Area: Downtown, Granville
Entertainment District
Address: 881 Granville St
Vancouver, BC V6Z 1K7
Phone: (604) 646-0064

#45
The Distillery Bar
Category: Bar
Average price: Modest
Area: Downtown, Yaletown
Address: 1131 Mainland Street
Vancouver, BC V6B 2S2
Phone: (604) 669-2255

#46
Toby's Pub
Category: Pub, Canadian
Average price: Modest
Area: Kensington-Cedar Cottage
Address: 2733 Commercial Drive
Vancouver, BC V5N 4C5
Phone: (604) 879-2099

#47
The Pumpjack Pub
Category: Gay Bar
Average price: Inexpensive
Area: West End
Address: 1167 Davie St
Vancouver, BC V6E 1N2
Phone: (604) 685-3417

#48
Killjoy
Category: Tapas, Lounge
Average price: Expensive
Area: Downtown, Yaletown
Address: 1120 Hamilton Street
Vancouver, BC V6B 5P6
Phone: (604) 669-4604

#49
Brandi's
Category: Adult Entertainment
Average price: Expensive
Area: Downtown
Address: 595 Homby Street
Vancouver, BC V6C 2E8
Phone: (604) 684-2000

#50
George Lounge
Category: Lounge
Average price: Expensive
Area: Downtown, Yaletown
Address: 1137 Hamilton St
Vancouver, BC V6B 5P6
Phone: (604) 628-5555

#51
Portland Craft
Category: Pub, Gastropub
Average price: Modest
Area: Riley Park
Address: 3835 Main Street
Vancouver, BC V5V 3N9
Phone: (604) 569-2494

#52
Famous Warehouse
Category: Pub
Average price: Inexpensive
Area: Downtown, Granville Entertainment District
Address: 989 Granville St
Vancouver, BC V6Z 1L2
Phone: (604) 677-8080

#53
1067 Jazz Club
Category: Music Venues
Average price: Inexpensive
Area: Downtown, Granville Entertainment District
Address: 1067 Granville Street
Vancouver, BC V6Z 1L4

#54
Back Forty
Category: Pub, Barbeque
Average price: Modest
Area: Downtown
Address: 118 Robson Street
Vancouver, BC V6B 2M1
Phone: (604) 688-5840

#55
New Amsterdam Café
Category: Hookah Bar
Average price: Modest
Area: Downtown
Address: 301 Hastings Street W
Vancouver, BC V6B 1H6
Phone: (604) 682-8955

#56
Corduroy
Category: Pizza, Lounge
Average price: Modest
Area: Kitsilano
Address: 1943 Cornwall Ave
Vancouver, BC V6J
Phone: (604) 733-0162

#57
Pourhouse Restaurant
Category: Lounge, Canadian, Cocktail Bar
Average price: Expensive
Area: Downtown, Gastown
Address: 162 Water Street
Vancouver, BC V6B 1B2
Phone: (604) 568-7022

#58
Yuk Yuk's Comedy Club
Category: Comedy Club
Average price: Inexpensive
Area: Fairview Slopes
Address: 2837 Cambie Street
Vancouver, BC V5Z 1N6
Phone: (604) 696-9857

#59
OPUS Bar
Category: Lounge
Average price: Exclusive
Area: Downtown, Yaletown
Address: 350 Davie St
Vancouver, BC V6J 5L1
Phone: (604) 642-0557

#60
Chaise Lounge Restaurant
Category: Lounge, American
Average price: Modest
Area: Riley Park
Address: 4444 Main St
Vancouver, BC V5V 3R3
Phone: (604) 874-7114

#61
Shine
Category: Dance Club
Average price: Modest
Area: Downtown, Gastown
Address: 364 Water St
Vancouver, BC V6B 1B6
Phone: (604) 408-4321

#62
The Media Club
Category: Lounge, Music Venues
Average price: Modest
Area: Downtown
Address: 695 Cambie St
Vancouver, BC V6B 2P1
Phone: (604) 608-2871

#63
Cats Socialhouse
Category: Lounge
Average price: Modest
Area: Granville Island/False Creek
Address: 1540 Old Bridge St
Vancouver, BC V6H 3S6
Phone: (604) 647-2287

#64
Wise Hall
Category: Venues & Event Spaces, Performing Arts, Music Venues
Average price: Inexpensive
Area: Grandview-Woodlands, The Drive
Address: 1882 Adanac Street
Vancouver, BC V5L 2E2
Phone: (604) 254-5858

#65
Lobby Lounge at the Fairmont Pacific Rim
Category: Lounge, Sushi Bar, Piano Bar
Average price: Expensive
Area: Coal Harbour, Downtown
Address: 1038 Place
Vancouver, BC V6C 0B9
Phone: (604) 695-5502

#66
LanaLou's
Category: Music Venues, Canadian
Average price: Inexpensive
Area: Downtown Eastside
Address: 362 Powell Street
Vancouver, BC V6A 1G4
Phone: (604) 563-5055

#67
Caffe Barney
Category: Bar, Breakfast & Brunch
Average price: Modest
Area: Fairview Slopes, South Granville
Address: 2975 Granville Street
Vancouver, BC V6H 3J6
Phone: (604) 731-6446

#68
The Sandbar Seafood Restaurant
Category: Seafood, Sushi Bar, Music Venues
Average price: Expensive
Area: Granville Island/False Creek
Address: 1535 Johnston Street
Vancouver, BC V6H 3R9
Phone: (604) 669-9030

#69
Electric Owl Social Club
Category: Music Venues, Bar
Average price: Modest
Area: Strathcona
Address: 928 Main Street
Vancouver, BC V6A 2W1
Phone: (604) 558-0928

#70
Prohibition Brewing
Category: Bar
Average price: Modest
Area: Downtown, Yaletown
Address: 1269 Hamilton Street
Vancouver, BC V6B 6K3
Phone: (604) 563-9494

#71
Red Room Ultra Bar
Category: Dance Club, Music Venues
Average price: Expensive
Area: Downtown
Address: 398 Richards Street
Vancouver, BC V6B 4Y2
Phone: (604) 687-5007

#72
The Bottleneck
Category: Pub, Canadian
Average price: Modest
Area: Downtown, Granville Entertainment District
Address: 870 Granville Street
Vancouver, BC V6B 2C9
Phone: (604) 739-4540

#73
The Mod Club
Category: Music Venues
Average price: Expensive
Area: Downtown Eastside
Address: 455 Abbott St
Vancouver, BC V6B 2N3
Phone: (604) 685-7777

#74
FanClub
Category: Dance Club, Cocktail Bar, Music Venues, Cocktail Bar
Average price: Modest
Area: Downtown, Granville Entertainment District
Address: 1050 Granville Street
Vancouver, BC V6Z 1L5
Phone: (604) 689-7720

#75
Elwood's
Category: Pub, Canadian
Average price: Modest
Area: Kitsilano
Address: 3145 W Broadway
Vancouver, BC V6K 2H2
Phone: (604) 736-4301

#76
Ginger 62
Category: Dance Club, Lounge
Average price: Modest
Area: Downtown, Granville Entertainment District
Address: 1219 Granville Street
Vancouver, BC V6Z 1M6
Phone: (604) 688-5494

#77
The Lamplighter Public House
Category: Pub, Gastropub
Average price: Modest
Area: Downtown, Gastown
Address: 92 Water Street
Vancouver, BC V6B 2K8
Phone: (604) 687-4424

#78
Dover Arms
Category: Sports Bar
Average price: Modest
Area: West End
Address: 961 Denman Street
Vancouver, BC V6G 2M3
Phone: (604) 683-1929

#79
1181
Category: Gay Bar, Lounge
Average price: Modest
Area: West End
Address: 1181 Davie St
Vancouver, BC V6E 1N2
Phone: (604) 787-7130

#80
Original Joe's Restaurant & Bar
Category: Pub, Canadian
Average price: Modest
Area: Fairview Slopes
Address: 2525 Cambie Street
Vancouver, BC V5Z 3Y6
Phone: (604) 434-5636

#81
The Pint Public House
Category: Sports Bar, Pub
Average price: Modest
Area: Downtown Eastside
Address: 455 Abbott Street
Vancouver, BC V6B 1S5
Phone: (604) 684-0258

#82
The Bayside Lounge
Category: Lounge
Average price: Modest
Area: West End
Address: 1755 Davie Street
Vancouver, BC V6G 1W5
Phone: (604) 682-1831

#83
Vancouver Alpen Club
Category: German, Venues, Event Spaces, Dance Club
Average price: Modest
Area: Kensington-Cedar Cottage
Address: 4875 Victoria Drive
Vancouver, BC V5N 4P3
Phone: (604) 874-3811

#84
The Royal Canadian Legion
Category: Dive Bar
Average price: Inexpensive
Area: Grandview-Woodlands, The Drive
Address: 2205 Commercial Drive
Vancouver, BC V5N 4B6
Phone: (604) 253-1181

Shops, Restaurants, Attractions & Nightlife / Vancouver Travel Guide

#85
The Ascot Lounge
Category: Lounge, Tapas Bar
Average price: Modest
Area: Downtown
Address: 420 W Pender
Vancouver, BC V6B 1T1
Phone: (604) 566-9599

#86
Ceili's Modern Irish Pub
Category: Pub, Irish
Average price: Modest
Area: Kitsilano, Fairview Slopes
Address: 1774 W 7th Street
Vancouver, BC V6J 4T3
Phone: (604) 732-0010

#87
Granville Room
Category: Bar, Canadian
Average price: Modest
Area: Downtown, Granville Entertainment District
Address: 957 Granville Street
Vancouver, BC V6Z 1L3
Phone: (604) 633-0056

#88
Cambie Bar & Grill
Category: Pub, Dive Bar, Music Venues
Average price: Inexpensive
Area: Downtown, Gastown
Address: 300 Cambie St
Vancouver, BC V6B 2N3
Phone: (604) 684-6466

#89
Hidden Tasting Bar & Social Lounge
Category: Wine Bar, Canadian
Average price: Modest
Area: Downtown
Address: 433 Robson St
Vancouver, BC V6B 6L9
Phone: (604) 647-2521

#90
The Wicklow Public House
Category: Pub
Average price: Modest
Area: Granville Island/False Creek
Address: 610 Stamps Landing
Vancouver, BC V5Z 3Z1
Phone: (604) 879-0821

#91
Darby's Pub
Category: Pub, American
Average price: Modest
Area: Kitsilano
Address: 2001 MacDonald Street
Vancouver, BC V6K 3Y2
Phone: (604) 731-0617

#92
Steamworks Brewing Company
Category: Pub, Canadian
Average price: Modest
Area: Downtown, Gastown
Address: 375 Water Street
Vancouver, BC V6B 5C6
Phone: (604) 689-2739

#93
The Hastings Warehouse
Category: Pub, Burgers
Average price: Inexpensive
Area: Downtown, Downtown Eastside
Address: 156 W Hastings Street
Vancouver, BC V6B 1G8
Phone: (604) 558-1560

#94
Rowan's Roof Restaurant & Lounge
Category: American, Lounge
Average price: Modest
Area: Kitsilano
Address: 2340 W 4th Ave
Vancouver, BC V6K 1P4
Phone: (604) 733-0330

#95
Five Sixty
Category: Bar, Dance Club
Average price: Modest
Area: Downtown
Address: 560 Seymour Street
Vancouver, BC V6B 3J5
Phone: (604) 678-6322

#96
The Stable House
Category: Tapas Bar, Wine Bar
Average price: Modest
Area: Fairview Slopes, South Granville
Address: 1520 W 13th Avenue
Vancouver, BC V6J 2G4
Phone: (604) 736-1520

#97
Seventeen89
Category: Seafood, Steakhouse, Lounge
Average price: Expensive
Area: West End
Address: 1789 Comox Street
Vancouver, BC V6G 2M5
Phone: (604) 428-0705

#98
Displace Hashery
Category: Pub, Comedy Club, Canadian
Average price: Modest
Area: Kitsilano
Address: 3293 W 4th Avenue
Vancouver, BC V6K 1R8
Phone: (604) 736-0212

#99
Bar None Nightclub
Category: Bar, Music Venues
Average price: Expensive
Area: Downtown, Yaletown
Address: 1222 Hamilton St
Vancouver, BC V6B 2S8
Phone: (604) 689-7000

#100
The Kings Head
Category: Pub, Sports Bar, American, Breakfast & Brunch
Average price: Inexpensive
Area: Kitsilano
Address: 1618 Yew Street
Vancouver, BC V6K 3E7
Phone: (604) 738-6966

#101
Hyde
Category: Lounge, Burgers
Average price: Modest
Area: Mount Pleasant
Address: 2960 Main Street
Vancouver, BC V5T 3G3
Phone: (604) 709-6215

#102
Pub 340
Category: Pub
Average price: Inexpensive
Area: Downtown
Address: 340 Cambie Street
Vancouver, BC V6B 2N3
Phone: (604) 602-0644

#103
Army Navy & Airforce Veterans Unit 298 Canteen
Category: Bar, Social Club
Average price: Inexpensive
Area: Riley Park
Address: 3917 Main St
Vancouver, BC V5V
Phone: (604) 879-1020

#104
The Portside Pub
Category: Pub, Sandwiches
Average price: Modest
Area: Downtown, Gastown
Address: 7 Alexander Street
Vancouver, BC V6A 1E9
Phone: (604) 559-6333

#105
Funky Winker Beans
Category: Dive Bar, Karaoke
Average price: Inexpensive
Area: Downtown, Downtown Eastside
Address: 37 W Hastings Street
Vancouver, BC V6B 1G4
Phone: (604) 569-3515

#106
BierCraft Bistro
Category: Tapas Bar, Lounge
Average price: Modest
Area: South Cambie, Riley Park
Address: 3305 Cambie Street
Vancouver, BC V5Z 2W6
Phone: (604) 874-6900

#107
Hooker's Green
Category: Pub
Average price: Modest
Area: Downtown, Yaletown
Address: 1141 Hamilton Street
Vancouver, BC V6B 5P6
Phone: (604) 669-4848

#108
Cedar Cottage Neighbourhood Pub
Category: Pub
Average price: Modest
Area: Kensington-Cedar Cottage
Address: 3728 Clark Drive
Vancouver, BC V5V 4Y6
Phone: (604) 876-1411

#109
Chapel Arts
Category: Music Venues, Art Gallery
Average price: Modest
Area: Downtown Eastside
Address: 304 Dunlevy St
Vancouver, BC V6A
Phone: (778) 371-9210

#110
The Metropole Community Pub
Category: Pub
Average price: Inexpensive
Area: Downtown Eastside
Address: 320 Abbott St
Vancouver, BC V6B 2K9
Phone: (604) 408-5822

#111
Red Card Sports Bar
Category: Italian, Sports Bar
Average price: Modest
Area: Downtown
Address: 560 Smithe Street
Vancouver, BC V6Z 1X9
Phone: (604) 689-4460

#112
Mr Brownstone Bar & Grill
Category: Gastropub, Bar
Average price: Modest
Area: Mount Pleasant
Address: 2904 Main Street
Vancouver, BC V5T 3G3
Phone: (604) 876-1236

#113
The Rickshaw Theatre
Category: Music Venues, Venues & Event Spaces
Average price: Inexpensive
Area: Downtown Eastside
Address: 254 E Hastings St
Vancouver, BC V6A 1A1
Phone: (604) 681-8915

#114
Doolin's Irish Pub
Category: Irish, Pub
Average price: Modest
Area: Downtown, Granville Entertainment District
Address: 654 Nelson St
Vancouver, BC V6B 6K4
Phone: (604) 605-4343

#115
Falconetti's East Side Grill
Category: Dive Bar, Breakfast & Brunch
Average price: Modest
Area: Grandview-Woodlands, The Drive
Address: 1812 Commercial Drive
Vancouver, BC V5N 4A5
Phone: (604) 251-7287

#116
Numbers Cabaret
Category: Dance Club, Gay Bar
Average price: Modest
Area: West End
Address: 1042 Davie St
Vancouver, BC V6E 1M3
Phone: (604) 685-4077

#117
London Pub
Category: Pub
Average price: Modest
Area: Strathcona
Address: 700 Main St
Vancouver, BC V6A 2V4
Phone: (604) 563-5053

#118
The Yard Cafe
Category: Pub, Sandwiches
Average price: Modest
Area: Marpole
Address: 8482 Granville Street
Vancouver, BC V6P 4Z7
Phone: (604) 569-1353

#119
1927 Lobby Lounge
Category: Lounge
Average price: Modest
Area: Downtown
Address: 801 W Georgia Street
Vancouver, BC V6C 1P7
Phone: (604) 682-5566

#120
Coppertank Grill
Category: Sports Bar, Music Venues, Canadian
Average price: Modest
Area: Kitsilano
Address: 3135 W Broadway
Vancouver, BC V6K 2H2
Phone: (604) 731-6565

#121
The Press Box
Category: Lounge, American
Average price: Modest
Area: Hastings-Sunrise
Address: 2889 Hastings St E
Vancouver, BC V5K
Phone: (604) 252-2690

#122
Whet Kitchen.Bar.Patio
Category: Bar, Seafood, Gluten-Free
Average price: Modest
Area: Granville Island/False Creek
Address: 1517 Anderson St
Vancouver, BC V6H 3S2
Phone: (604) 696-0739

#123
Milestones Grill + Bar
Category: Canadian, Bar
Average price: Modest
Area: Fairview Slopes
Address: 2425 Cambie St
Vancouver, BC V5Z 4M5
Phone: (604) 678-8488

#124
The Academic Public House
Category: Pub, Gastropub
Average price: Modest
Area: Fairview Slopes
Address: 1619 W Broadway
Vancouver, BC V6J 1W9
Phone: (604) 733-4141

#125
Wings Restaurants &Pub
Category: Chicken Wings, Sports Bar
Average price: Modest
Area: Downtown, Granville Entertainment District
Address: 1162 Granville Street
Vancouver, BC V6Z 1L8
Phone: (604) 682-3473

#126
Dunlevy Snack Bar
Category: Cocktail Bar
Average price: Modest
Area: Downtown Eastside
Address: 433 Dunlevy Avenue
Vancouver, BC V6A 3A7
Phone: (604) 569-0454

#127
The Yale Hotel
Category: Music Venues
Average price: Expensive
Area: Downtown, Granville Entertainment District
Address: 1300 Granville St
Vancouver, BC V6Z 1M7
Phone: (604) 681-9253

#128
Gringo
Category: Mexican, Pub
Average price: Modest
Area: Mount Pleasant
Address: 27 Blood Alley Square
Vancouver, BC V6B 1A4
Phone: (604) 721-0607

#129
Fets Whisky Kitchen
Category: Bar, Southern, Canadian
Average price: Modest
Area: Grandview-Woodlands, The Drive
Address: 1230 Commercial Drive
Vancouver, BC V5L 3X4
Phone: (604) 255-7771

#130
Oscar's Pub
Category: Pub
Average price: Modest
Area: Burnaby Heights, Hastings-Sunrise
Address: 3684 Hastings Street E
Vancouver, BC V5K
Phone: (604) 298-5825

#131
Malone's Urban Drinkery Downtown
Category: Sports Bar, Pub
Average price: Modest
Area: Downtown
Address: 608 W Pender Street
Vancouver, BC V6B 1V8
Phone: (604) 684-9977

#132
LIFT Bar Grill View
Category: Seafood, Bar
Average price: Expensive
Area: Coal Harbour
Address: 333 Menchions Mews
Vancouver, BC V6G 3H5
Phone: (604) 689-5438

#133
Astoria Hotel
Category: Hotel, Pub
Average price: Inexpensive
Area: Downtown Eastside
Address: 769 Hastings St E
Vancouver, BC V6A 1R3
Phone: (604) 254-3355

#134
Wildebeest
Category: Wine Bar, Canadian
Average price: Expensive
Area: Downtown, Downtown Eastside
Address: 120 W Hastings Street
Vancouver, BC V6B 1G8
Phone: (604) 687-6880

#135
Jackalope's Neighbourhood Dive
Category: Dive Bar
Average price: Modest
Area: Grandview-Woodlands
Address: 2257 E Hastings Street
Vancouver, BC V5L 1V3
Phone: (604) 568-6674

#136
Comox Street Long Bar
Category: Sports Bar, Lounge, American
Average price: Modest
Area: West End
Address: 1763 Comox Street
Vancouver, BC V6G 1P6
Phone: (604) 688-7711

#137
Ivanhoe Pub
Category: Pub
Average price: Inexpensive
Area: Downtown, Strathcona
Address: 1038 Main St
Vancouver, BC V6A 2W1
Phone: (604) 608-1444

#138
JOEY Burrard
Category: Canadian, Lounge
Average price: Modest
Area: Downtown
Address: 820 Burrard Street
Vancouver, BC V6C 0B6
Phone: (604) 683-5639

#139
Notturno
Category: Italian, Wine Bar
Average price: Modest
Area: Downtown, Gastown
Address: 280 Carrall Street
Vancouver, BC V6B 2J2
Phone: (604) 720-3145

#140
The Bimini Public House
Category: Gastropub, Lounge, Pub
Average price: Modest
Area: Kitsilano
Address: 2010 W 4th Aveune
Vancouver, BC V6J 1M7
Phone: (604) 733-7116

#141
Beyond Restaurant & Lounge
Category: Lounge, Canadian
Average price: Modest
Area: West End, Downtown
Address: 1015 Burrard Street
Vancouver, BC V6Z
Phone: (604) 684-3474

#142
Jimmy's Tap House
Category: Pub, Canadian
Average price: Modest
Area: Downtown
Address: 783 Homer Street
Vancouver, BC V6B 2W1
Phone: (604) 689-2800

#143
Regal Beagle
Category: Gastropub, Music Venues
Average price: Modest
Area: Kitsilano
Address: 2283 Broadway W
Vancouver, BC V6K 2E4
Phone: (604) 739-0677

#144
Gerard Lounge
Category: Lounge
Average price: Expensive
Area: Downtown
Address: 845 Burrard St
Vancouver, BC V6Z 2K7
Phone: (604) 682-5511

#145
Cavino
Category: Italian, Tapas, Wine Bar
Average price: Modest
Area: Downtown
Address: 1234 Hornby Street
Vancouver, BC V6Z 1W2
Phone: (604) 688-1234

#146
Reflections
Category: Canadian, Lounge
Average price: Expensive
Area: Downtown
Address: 801 W Georgia Street
Vancouver, BC V6C 1P7
Phone: (604) 682-5566

#147
The Charlatan
Category: American, Pub
Average price: Modest
Area: Grandview-Woodlands, The Drive
Address: 1447 Commercial Dr
Vancouver, BC V5L 3X8
Phone: (604) 253-2777

#148
Vogue Theatre
Category: Performing Arts, Music Venues, Venues & Event Spaces
Average price: Modest
Area: Downtown, Granville Entertainment District
Address: 918 Granville St
Vancouver, BC V6Z 1L2
Phone: (604) 569-1144

#149
Highlife Records & Music
Category: Music & DVDs
Average price: Modest
Area: Grandview-Woodlands, The Drive
Address: 1317 Commercial Dr
Vancouver, BC V5L 3X5
Phone: (604) 251-6964

#150
Cheshire Cheese Inn
Category: Pub, Canadian
Average price: Modest
Area: Dunbar-Southlands
Address: 4585 Dunbar Street
Vancouver, BC V6S 2G7
Phone: (604) 224-2521

#151
Sunset Grill Taphouse and Whiskey Bar
Category: American, Pub
Average price: Modest
Area: Kitsilano
Address: 2204 York Avenue
Vancouver, BC V6K 1C6
Phone: (604) 732-3733

#152
No5 Orange
Category: Adult Entertainment
Average price: Modest
Area: Downtown Eastside
Address: 205 Main St
Vancouver, BC V6A 2S7
Phone: (604) 687-3483

#153
Fahrenheit 212
Category: Adult Entertainment, Day Spa, Leisure Centers
Average price: Modest
Area: West End
Address: 1048 Davie Street
Vancouver, BC V6E 1M3
Phone: (604) 689-9719

#154
Shark Club Bar & Grill
Category: Bar
Average price: Modest
Area: Downtown
Address: 180 W Georgia St
Vancouver, BC V6B 4P4
Phone: (604) 687-4275

#155
Lickerish Restaurant & Lounge
Category: Tapas Bar, Music Venues
Average price: Modest
Area: Downtown
Address: 903 Davie Street
Vancouver, BC V6Z 2E9
Phone: (604) 696-0725

#156
The Sin Bin
Category: Sports Bar
Average price: Modest
Area: Mount Pleasant
Address: 295 W 2nd Avenue
Vancouver, BC V5Y
Phone: (604) 677-3515

#157
The Cove Neighborhood Pub
Category: American, Pub
Average price: Modest
Area: Kitsilano
Address: 3681 W 4th Avenue
Vancouver, BC V6R 1P1
Phone: (604) 734-1205

#158
The Shack
Category: Pub, Canadian
Average price: Modest
Area: Kitsilano
Address: 3189 W Broadway
Vancouver, BC V6K 2H2
Phone: (604) 738-0242

#159
Tap and Barrel
Category: Comfort Food, Bar
Average price: Modest
Area: Granville Island/False Creek
Address: 1 Athletes Way
Vancouver, BC V5Y 0B1
Phone: (604) 685-2223

#160
The Locker Room Pub
Category: Pub
Average price: Inexpensive
Area: Mount Pleasant
Address: 395 Kingsway
Vancouver, BC V5T 3J7
Phone: (604) 620-6283

#161
Shenanigans
Category: Pub, Canadian
Average price: Inexpensive
Area: West End
Address: 1225 Robson Street
Vancouver, BC V6E 1C2
Phone: (604) 688-1411

#162
Vinyl Retro Dance Lounge
Category: Dance Club
Average price: Modest
Area: Downtown Eastside
Address: 455 Abbott Street
Vancouver, BC V6B 1S5
Phone: (778) 980-2852

#163
Charqui Grill
Category: Bar, Soup, Tapas Bar
Average price: Modest
Area: Kitsilano
Address: 1955 Cornwall Avenue
Vancouver, BC V6J 1C9
Phone: (604) 733-3323

#164
Library Square Public House
Category: Pub, Music Venues
Average price: Modest
Area: Downtown
Address: 300 W Georgia St
Vancouver, BC V6B 6B4
Phone: (604) 633-9644

#165
V Yaletown
Category: Canadian, Lounge, Venues & Event Spaces
Average price: Modest
Area: Mount Pleasant
Address: 1095 Mainland Street
Vancouver, BC V6B 2T5
Phone: (604) 688-5954

#166
The Forum Sports Bar
Category: Sports Bar
Average price: Modest
Area: Downtown, Granville Entertainment District
Address: 1161 Granville Street
Vancouver, BC V6Z 0B4
Phone: (604) 605-1163

#167
Oyster Express
Category: Seafood, Bar
Average price: Modest
Area: Chinatown, Strathcona
Address: 296 Keefer Street
Vancouver, BC V6A 1X5
Phone: (604) 684-3300

#168
Black Frog Eatery
Category: Pub, American
Average price: Modest
Area: Downtown, Gastown
Address: 108 Cambie Street
Vancouver, BC V6B 2M8
Phone: (604) 602-0527

#169
The Bunker At The Barclay
Category: Bar
Average price: Inexpensive
Area: West End
Address: 1348 Robson St
Vancouver, BC V6E 1C5
Phone: (604) 688-8850

#170
Fairview Vancouver Pub
Category: Hotel, Pub
Average price: Modest
Area: Fairview Slopes
Address: 898 Broadway W
Vancouver, BC V5Z 1J8
Phone: (604) 872-1262

#171
Yaletown Brewing Company
Category: American, Pub
Average price: Modest
Area: Downtown, Yaletown
Address: 1111 Mainland Street
Vancouver, BC V6B 2T9
Phone: (604) 681-2739

#172
Exile Bistro
Category: Cafe, Bar
Average price: Modest
Area: West End
Address: 1220 Bute Street
Vancouver, BC V6E 1Z8
Phone: (604) 563-8633

#173
The Oasis Pub
Category: Pub
Average price: Modest
Area: West End
Address: 1240 Thurlow Street
Vancouver, BC V6E 1X5
Phone: (604) 685-1724

#174
The Capital
Category: Pub, Canadian
Average price: Inexpensive
Area: West End
Address: 1178 Davie Street
Vancouver, BC V6E 1N1
Phone: (604) 620-2201

#175
The Penthouse
Category: Adult Entertainment
Average price: Modest
Area: Downtown, Granville
Entertainment District
Address: 1019 Seymour St
Vancouver, BC V6B 3M4
Phone: (604) 683-2111

#176
Bogart's Bar and Restaurant
Category: Cocktail Bar, Italian
Area: Downtown
Address: 121 Robson Street
Vancouver, BC V6B 2A8
Phone: (604) 336-3578

#177
Abigail's Party
Category: Lounge, Canadian,
Breakfast & Brunch
Average price: Modest
Area: Kitsilano
Address: 1685 Yew St
Vancouver, BC V6K 3E6
Phone: (604) 739-4677

#178
Gargoyles Bar & Grill
Category: Bar, Canadian
Average price: Modest
Area: Kitsilano
Address: 3357 Broadway W
Vancouver, BC V6R 2B1
Phone: (604) 733-1159

#179
Ironwork Studio Productions
Category: Art Gallery, Music Venues
Area: Downtown Eastside
Address: 235 Alexander St
Vancouver, BC V6A 1C2
Phone: (604) 681-5033

#180
West Hotel & Bar
Category: Hotel, Dive Bar
Average price: Inexpensive
Area: Chinatown
Address: 488 Carrall St
Vancouver, BC V6B 2J7
Phone: (604) 681-8374

#181
Caprice Night Club
Category: Dance Club
Average price: Expensive
Area: Downtown, Granville Entertainment District
Address: 967 Granville Street
Vancouver, BC V6Z 1L3
Phone: (604) 685-3288

#182
The Cobalt
Category: Bar, Music Venues
Average price: Modest
Area: Downtown, Strathcona
Address: 917 Main Street
Vancouver, BC V6A
Phone: (778) 918-3671

#183
Icy Bar
Category: Bar
Average price: Inexpensive
Area: Killarney
Address: 3618 Kingsway
Vancouver, BC V5R 5M2
Phone: (604) 500-8922

#184
Joseph Richard Nightclub
Category: Dance Club, Bar
Average price: Expensive
Area: Downtown, Granville Entertainment District
Address: 1082 Granville Street
Vancouver, BC V6Z 1L5
Phone: (604) 488-1333

#185
The Whip Restaurant Gallery
Category: Bar, American
Average price: Modest
Area: Mount Pleasant
Address: 209 6th Avenue E
Vancouver, BC V5T 1J7
Phone: (604) 874-4687

#186
Stages Bistro & Lounge
Category: Lounge
Average price: Modest
Area: Fairview Slopes
Address: 711 Broadway W
Vancouver, BC V5Z 3Y2
Phone: (604) 879-0511

#187
The Brighton
Category: Pub, Canadian
Average price: Modest
Area: Hastings-Sunrise
Address: 2471 E Hastings Street
Vancouver, BC V5K
Phone: (604) 428-8822

#188
Ahwaz Hookah House
Category: Hookah Bar
Average price: Inexpensive
Area: West End, Downtown
Address: 1322 W Georgia St
Vancouver, BC V6J 5L1
Phone: (604) 696-9376

#189
Good Wolfe Kitchen & Bar
Category: Bar
Average price: Modest
Area: Downtown, Yaletown
Address: 1043 Mainland Street
Vancouver, BC V6B 1A9
Phone: (604) 428-1043

#190
Barcelona Ultra Lounge
Category: Dance Club, Lounge
Average price: Expensive
Area: Downtown, Granville Entertainment District
Address: 1180 Granville St
Vancouver, BC V6Z 1L8
Phone: (604) 249-5151

#191
Pne Forum
Category: Music Venues
Average price: Modest
Area: Hastings-Sunrise
Address: 100 N. Renfrew St.
Vancouver, BC V5K 4W3
Phone: (604) 253-2311

#192
Speakeasy On Granville
Category: Dive Bar, Sports Bar
Average price: Modest
Area: Downtown, Granville Entertainment District
Address: 921 Granville Street
Vancouver, BC V6Z 1L3
Phone: (604) 685-5531

#193
BLVD22 Nightclub
Category: Dance Club, Music Venues
Average price: Expensive
Area: Downtown
Address: 750 Pacfic Blvd
Vancouver, BC V6B

#194
Armoury Studio
Category: Music Venues
Area: Fairview Slopes
Address: 1688 W 1st Avenue
Vancouver, BC V6J 1G1
Phone: (604) 737-1687

#195
Tunnel Nightclub
Category: Dance Club
Average price: Exclusive
Area: Downtown
Address: 620 W Pender St
Vancouver, BC V6B 1V8
Phone: (604) 568-8022

#196
The Bourbon
Category: Pub
Average price: Modest
Area: Gastown, Downtown Eastside
Address: 50 Cordova Street W
Vancouver, BC V6B 1C9
Phone: (604) 684-4214

#197
Six Acres
Category: Pub, Canadian, Cafe
Average price: Modest
Area: Downtown, Gastown
Address: 203 Carrall Street
Vancouver, BC V6B 2J2
Phone: (604) 488-0110

#198
The Cellar Nightclub
Category: Dance Club
Average price: Modest
Area: Downtown, Granville Entertainment District
Address: 1006 Granville Street
Vancouver, BC V6Z 1L5
Phone: (604) 605-4340

#199
Bismarck Bar
Category: Bar
Average price: Expensive
Area: Downtown
Address: 526 Abbot Street
Vancouver, BC V6B 6N7

#200
Avanti's Neighbourhood Pub
Category: Pub
Average price: Inexpensive
Area: Grandview-Woodlands, The Drive
Address: 1601 Commercial Dr
Vancouver, BC V5L 3Y3
Phone: (604) 254-5466

#201
Pondok Indonesia
Category: Karaoke, Indonesian
Average price: Modest
Area: Fairview Slopes
Address: 950 W Broadway
Vancouver, BC V5Z 1K7
Phone: (604) 732-7608

#202
Prontino
Category: Cocktail Bar, Italian
Average price: Modest
Area: South Cambie, Riley Park
Address: 3475 Cambie Street
Vancouver, BC V5Z 2W7
Phone: (604) 722-9331

#203
Lounge at Caprice
Category: Lounge
Area: Downtown, Granville Entertainment District
Address: 965 Granville Street
Vancouver, BC V6Z 1L2
Phone: (604) 685-3288

#204
The Butcher & Bullock
Category: Canadian, Bar
Average price: Modest
Area: Downtown
Address: 911 W Pender Street
Vancouver, BC V6C 3B2
Phone: (604) 662-8866

#205
Ten Ten Tapas
Category: Tapas, Jazz & Blues
Average price: Modest
Area: Downtown
Address: 1010 Beach Avenue
Vancouver, BC V6E 1T7
Phone: (604) 689-7800

#206
Northern Tickets
Category: Music Venues
Area: Downtown, Granville Entertainment District
Address: 918 Granville Street
Vancouver, BC V6B 2C9
Phone: (604) 569-1144

#207
Blarney Stone
Category: Dance Club, Pub, Music Venues
Average price: Modest
Area: Downtown, Gastown
Address: 216 Carrall St
Vancouver, BC V6B 2J1
Phone: (604) 687-4322

#208
YEW Seafood + Bar
Category: Seafood, Wine Bar
Average price: Expensive
Area: Downtown
Address: 791 W Georgia Street
Vancouver, BC V6C 2T4
Phone: (604) 692-4939

#209
The Shebeen Whisky House
Category: Bar
Average price: Modest
Area: Downtown, Gastown
Address: 210 Carrall St
Vancouver, BC V6B 2J2
Phone: (604) 688-9779

#210
Village Pub
Category: Pub
Average price: Modest
Area: Killarney, Champlain Heights
Address: 7725 Champlain Crescent
Vancouver, BC V5S 4J6
Phone: (604) 433-1111

#211
Manchester Public Eatery
Category: Pub, Sports Bar
Average price: Modest
Area: Kitsilano
Address: 1941 W Broadway
Vancouver, BC V6J 1Z3
Phone: (604) 568-6867

#212
Spencer's Resto Lounge
Category: Lounge, Canadian
Average price: Modest
Area: Downtown
Address: 550 W Hastings St
Vancouver, BC V6B 1L6
Phone: (604) 689-8188

#213
Mosaic Arts Academy
Category: Performing Arts, Jazz & Blues
Area: Point Grey
Address: 4511 W 10th Ave
Vancouver, BC V6R 2J2
Phone: (604) 568-9840

#214
The Bachelor Plan
Category: Adult Entertainment, Event Planning & Services
Average price: Exclusive
Area: Downtown, Yaletown
Address: Lower Mainland
Vancouver, BC V6Z 2Y3
Phone: (604) 696-2424

#215
Joe Fortes Seafood & Chop House
Category: Seafood, Steakhouse, Bar
Average price: Expensive
Area: West End
Address: 777 Thurlow Street
Vancouver, BC V6E 3V5
Phone: (604) 669-1940

#216
Kanaka
Category: Bar
Average price: Inexpensive
Area: Downtown, Gastown
Address: 332 Water Street
Vancouver, BC V6B 1E5
Phone: (604) 725-8157

#217
Campagnolo Bar and Caffé
Category: Bar, Italian
Average price: Modest
Area: Downtown, Strathcona
Address: 1020 Main Street
Vancouver, BC V6A 2W1
Phone: (604) 484-6018

#218
Jaguars Pub
Category: Pub
Average price: Modest
Area: Killarney, Renfrew-Collingwood
Address: 3483 Kingsway
Vancouver, BC V5R 5L5
Phone: (604) 434-5240

#219
Princeton Pub
Category: Dive Bar
Area: Grandview-Woodlands
Address: 1901 Powell St
Vancouver, BC V5L 1J2
Phone: (604) 253-6645

#220
Joe's Apartment Bar
Category: Bar
Average price: Modest
Area: Downtown, Granville Entertainment District
Address: 919 Granville St
Vancouver, BC V6B 2C9
Phone: (604) 563-5030

#221
Gossip Nightclub
Category: Dance Club
Average price: Exclusive
Area: Downtown
Address: 750 Pacific Blvd
Vancouver, BC V6B
Phone: (604) 780-5485

#222
Milltown Bar & Grill
Category: Bar, Burgers, Sandwiches
Average price: Modest
Area: Marpole
Address: 9191 Bentley Street
Vancouver, BC V6P 6G2
Phone: (604) 269-2348

#223
The Fountainhead Pub
Category: Pub, Gastropub, Gay Bar
Average price: Modest
Area: West End
Address: 1025 Davie Street
Vancouver, BC V6E 1M5
Phone: (604) 687-2222

#224
Jolly Alderman
Category: Hotel, Pub
Area: Fairview Slopes
Address: 500 12th Avenue W
Vancouver, BC V5Z 1M2
Phone: (604) 873-1811

#225
Whiskey Dix
Category: Bar
Average price: Inexpensive
Area: Downtown, Gastown
Address: 303 Columbia St
Vancouver, BC V6A 4J1
Phone: (604) 558-1124

#226
Gorgomish
Category: Dance Club
Area: Downtown, Granville Entertainment District
Address: 695 Smithe St
Vancouver, BC V6B
Phone: (604) 694-9007

#227
Heavens Door Lounge
Category: Music Venues, Lounge
Area: West End
Address: 1216 Bute Street
Vancouver, BC V6E 1Z8
Phone: (604) 428-0602

#228
J-Lounge
Category: Tapas Bar, Lounge
Average price: Modest
Area: West End
Address: 1216 Bute St
Vancouver, BC V6E 1Z8
Phone: (604) 609-6665

#229
Oasis Ultra Lounge
Category: Lounge, Canadian
Area: West End
Address: 1240 Thurlow Street
Vancouver, BC V6E 1N7
Phone: (604) 685-1724

#230
Crush Champagne Lounge
Category: Dance Club
Area: Downtown, Granville Entertainment District
Address: 1180 Granville Street
Vancouver, BC V6Z 1L8
Phone: (604) 684-0355

#231
Speakeasy on DAVIE
Category: Pub, Canadian
Average price: Modest
Area: West End
Address: 1239 Davie Street
Vancouver, BC V6E 2N4
Phone: (604) 685-5761

#232
Bellaggio Cafe
Category: Bar, Italian, Breakfast & Brunch
Average price: Modest
Area: Downtown
Address: 1055 Place
Vancouver, BC V6C 0C3
Phone: (604) 647-7523

#233
Lux Lounge
Category: Lounge
Average price: Modest
Area: Downtown
Address: 1180 Howe Street
Vancouver, BC V6Z 1R2
Phone: (604) 559-5533

#234
Pop Opera
Category: Dance Club
Average price: Expensive
Area: Downtown
Address: 686 W Hastings Street
Vancouver, BC V6B 1M8
Phone: (604) 683-0315

#235
Bayside Lounge
Category: Bar
Area: West End
Address: 1184 Denman Street
Vancouver, BC V6G 2M9
Phone: (800) 661-7887

#236
Soho Cafe & Billiards
Category: Pool Hall, Bar
Average price: Modest
Area: Downtown, Yaletown
Address: 1283 Hamilton Street
Vancouver, BC V6B 6K3
Phone: (604) 688-1180

#237
StackHouse Burger Bar
Category: Burgers, Canadian, Cocktail Bar
Average price: Modest
Area: Downtown, Granville Entertainment District
Address: 1224 Granville Street
Vancouver, BC V6B 2G6
Phone: (604) 558-3499

#238
La Casa del Artista
Category: Music Venues
Average price: Inexpensive
Area: Mount Pleasant
Address: 150 E 3rd Ave
Vancouver, BC V5T 1C8
Phone: (604) 709-4300

#239
Plaza of Nations
Category: Performing Arts, Music Venues
Average price: Modest
Area: Downtown
Address: 750 Pacific Blvd
Vancouver, BC V6B 5E7
Phone: (604) 682-0777

#240
The Fox Cabaret
Category: Music Venues
Average price: Modest
Area: Mount Pleasant
Address: 2321 Main Street
Vancouver, BC V5T 3C9

Shops, Restaurants, Attractions & Nightlife / Vancouver Travel Guide

#241
Vivo Media Centre
Category: Music Venues
Area: Mount Pleasant
Address: 1965 Main St
Vancouver, BC V5T 3B9
Phone: (604) 872-8337

#242
Cravings Restaurant + Lounge
Category: Lounge, Comfort Food
Average price: Modest
Area: Marpole
Address: 8808 Osler Street
Vancouver, BC V6P 4G2
Phone: (604) 261-7779

#243
Skyline Restaurant & Lounge
Category: Lounge, Mediterranean
Average price: Modest
Area: Downtown
Address: 88 W Pender St
Vancouver, BC V6B 6N9
Phone: (604) 558-2188

#244
Persian Teahouse
Category: Hookah Bar
Average price: Expensive
Area: Downtown, Granville Entertainment District
Address: 668 Davie St
Vancouver, BC V6B 2G5
Phone: (604) 681-6672

#245
Tavern at The New Oxford
Category: Lounge
Area: Downtown, Yaletown
Address: 1141 Hamilton Street
Vancouver, BC V6B 5P6
Phone: (604) 669-4848

#246
Space Lounge
Category: Lounge
Average price: Modest
Area: Downtown, Granville Entertainment District
Address: 1149 Granville St
Vancouver, BC V6Z 1M1
Phone: (604) 568-7842

#247
ARC
Category: Canadian, Cocktail Bar
Average price: Expensive
Area: Downtown
Address: 900 Place
Vancouver, BC V6C 3L5
Phone: (604) 691-1818

#248
ABODE Restaurant & Coffee Bar
Category: Breakfast & Brunch, Comfort Food, Lounge
Average price: Modest
Area: West End
Address: 1225 Robson Street
Vancouver, BC V6E 1C2
Phone: (800) 663-1333

#249
The JEM Gallery
Category: Music Venues, Art Gallery
Area: Mount Pleasant
Address: 225 Broadway E
Vancouver, BC V5T 1W4
Phone: (604) 879-5366

#250
Red Gate Collective
Category: Music Venues
Average price: Inexpensive
Area: Downtown Eastside
Address: 855 E Hastings
Vancouver, BC V6A 3Y1

#251
The Alexander
Category: Lounge
Average price: Modest
Area: Downtown, Gastown
Address: 99 Powell Street
Vancouver, BC V6B 2J1

#252
Jeremiah's Neighbourhood Pub
Category: Pub
Average price: Modest
Area: Kitsilano
Address: 3681 4th Ave W
Vancouver, BC V6R 1P2
Phone: (604) 734-1205

#253
Romer's Burger Bar
Category: Burgers, Bar
Average price: Modest
Area: Downtown, Yaletown
Address: 1039 Mainland Street
Vancouver, BC V6B 1A9
Phone: (604) 559-7210

#254
Showcase Restaurant & Bar
Category: Seafood, Bar
Area: Coal Harbour, Downtown
Address: 1128 W Hastings Street
Vancouver, BC V6E 4R5
Phone: (604) 639-4040

#255
Hudson's Landing Pub
Category: Lounge, Canadian
Average price: Modest
Area: Marpole
Address: 1041 SW Marine Drive
Vancouver, BC V6P 6L6
Phone: (604) 263-5445

#256
Fantacity
Category: Karaoke
Average price: Expensive
Area: West End
Address: 1133 Robson Street
Vancouver, BC V6E 1B5
Phone: (604) 899-0006

#257
Gotham Steakhouse & Cocktail Bar
Category: Steakhouse, Cocktail Bar
Average price: Exclusive
Area: Downtown
Address: 615 Seymour Street
Vancouver, BC V6B 3K3
Phone: (604) 605-8282

#258
Taste Resto Lounge
Category: Wine Bar, Champagne Bar
Area: Downtown
Address: 560 Seymour Street
Vancouver, BC V6B 3J5
Phone: (604) 235-6060

#259
The Hastings Warehouse
Category: Sports Bar
Area: Downtown, Downtown Eastside
Address: 156 W Hastings Street
Vancouver, BC V6A 4J1
Phone: (604) 558-1560

#260
Regent Hotel
Category: Dive Bar
Average price: Inexpensive
Area: Downtown Eastside
Address: 160 Hastings St E
Vancouver, BC V6A 1N4
Phone: (604) 681-7435

#261
Bingo For Life
Category: Gay Bar
Area: West End
Address: 1022 Davie Street
Vancouver, BC V6E 1N2
Phone: (604) 681-6180

#262
Boss Night Club
Category: Dance Club
Average price: Modest
Area: Downtown
Address: 1320 Richards Street
Vancouver, BC V6B
Phone: (604) 662-7707

#263
Moulin Rouge Bar & Grill
Category: Bar, American
Average price: Inexpensive
Area: Hastings-Sunrise
Address: 2828 E Hastings Street
Vancouver, BC V5K 5C5
Phone: (604) 251-4141

#264
PHAT Sports Bar & Restaurant
Category: Delis, Sports Bar
Average price: Modest
Area: Downtown, Yaletown
Address: 1055 Mainland St
Vancouver, BC V6B
Phone: (604) 684-6239

Shops, Restaurants, Attractions & Nightlife / Vancouver Travel Guide

---

#265
The Lennox Pub
Category: Pub, Irish, Canadian
Average price: Modest
Area: Downtown, Granville
Entertainment District
Address: 800 Granville Street
Vancouver, BC V6Z 1K3
Phone: (604) 408-0881

#266
Serotonin Afterhours
Category: Music Venues
Area: Downtown, Granville
Entertainment District
Address: 1058 Granville Street
Vancouver, BC V6Z 1L2
Phone: (604) 688-8151

#267
Live Bait Yacht Club Marine Pub
Category: Pub
Area: Coal Harbour, Downtown
Address: 1583 Coal Harbour Quay
Vancouver, BC V6G 3E7
Phone: (604) 669-7666

#268
Cottage Bistro
Category: Jazz & Blues, Asian Fusion
Average price: Modest
Area: Riley Park
Address: 4468 Main Street
Vancouver, BC V5V 3R3
Phone: (604) 876-6138

#269
The Denman Taphouse
Category: Sports Bar, Pub
Average price: Modest
Area: West End
Address: 1184 Denman Street
Vancouver, BC V6G 2N1
Phone: (604) 568-3437

#270
The Queen's Republic
Category: Dance Club
Average price: Modest
Area: Downtown, Granville
Entertainment District
Address: 958 Granville Street
Vancouver, BC V6B 2C9
Phone: (604) 669-3266

#271
Mr Dance
Category: Social Club, Dance Club
Area: Kensington-Cedar Cottage
Address: 4875 Victoria Drive
Vancouver, BC V5N 4P3
Phone: (604) 436-4436

#272
Hippo's Sports Bar & Grill
Category: Karaoke
Area: Sunset
Address: 725 SE Marine Drive
Vancouver, BC V5X 2T9
Phone: (604) 321-6611

#273
Yaletown L'Antipasto
Category: Tapas, Italian, Wine Bar
Average price: Modest
Area: Downtown, Yaletown
Address: 1127 Mainland Street
Vancouver, BC V6B 5P2
Phone: (604) 558-1174

#274
Mahony & Sons Burrard Landing
Category: Irish, Pub, Burgers
Average price: Modest
Area: Coal Harbour, Downtown
Address: 1055 Pl
Vancouver, BC V6C 0C3
Phone: (604) 647-7513

#275
Gam Gallery
Category: Art Gallery, Music Venues
Average price: Inexpensive
Address: 110 E Hastings Street
Vancouver, BC V6A 1N4
Phone: (778) 235-6928

#276
The Balmoral
Category: Bar
Area: Downtown Eastside
Address: 159 E Hastings St
Vancouver, BC V6A 1N6
Phone: (778) 828-8742

#277
The Afrika Shrine
Category: Music Venues
Area: Grandview-Woodlands, The Drive
Address: 2205 Commercial Drive
Vancouver, BC V5N 4B6
Phone: (778) 552-8238

#278
Sidecar
Category: Pub, Tapas Bar
Average price: Modest
Area: Downtown, Granville Entertainment District
Address: 1163 Granville Street
Vancouver, BC V6Z 1L8

#279
Cabana Lounge
Category: Lounge, Music Venues
Average price: Exclusive
Area: Downtown, Granville Entertainment District
Address: 1159 Granville Street
Vancouver, BC V6Z 1L8
Phone: (778) 251-3335

#280
The Shack Eatery & Watering Hole
Category: Pub
Area: Kitsilano
Address: 3189 W Broadway
Vancouver, BC V6K 2H2
Phone: (604) 738-0242

#281
Red Door
Category: Adult Entertainment
Area: Downtown, Granville Entertainment District
Address: 1210 Granville Street
Vancouver, BC V6B 2G6
Phone: (604) 559-7007

#282
Platinum Club
Category: Adult Entertainment, Massage
Area: Downtown
Address: 426 Homer Street
Vancouver, BC V6B 2V5
Phone: (604) 683-2582

#283
The Winking Judge Pub
Category: Pub
Average price: Modest
Area: Downtown
Address: 888 Burrard Street
Vancouver, BC V6Z 1X9
Phone: (604) 684-9465

#284
Colony Bar
Category: Bar
Average price: Modest
Area: Kitsilano
Address: 3255 W Broadway Street
Vancouver, BC V6K 4N7
Phone: (604) 559-6070

#285
Summer Latin Cruises
Category: Dance Club, Tours
Area: Downtown
Address: 750 Pacific Boulevard
Vancouver, BC V6B 5E7
Phone: (604) 722-1559

#286
Elephant & Castle
Category: Pub, British
Area: Downtown
Address: 298 Robson Street
Vancouver, BC V6B 6A1
Phone: (604) 689-4499

#287
Vancouver Latin Fever
Category: Dance Club
Area: Downtown
Address: 398 Richards Street
Vancouver, BC V5R 3T9
Phone: (604) 722-1559

#288
The Swedish Touch
Category: Adult Entertainment, Massage
Area: Downtown
Address: 595 Hornby Street
Vancouver, BC V6C 2E8
Phone: (604) 681-0823

#289
The Three Brits Public House
Category: Pub
Average price: Modest
Area: West End
Address: 1780 Davie Street
Vancouver, BC V6G 1W2
Phone: (604) 801-6681

#290
The Roof Restaurant & Bar
Category: Bar
Area: Downtown
Address: 900 W Georgia Street
Vancouver, BC V6C 2W6
Phone: (604) 443-1816

Shops, Restaurants, Attractions & Nightlife / Vancouver Travel Guide

#291
Stagmen
Category: Adult Entertainment
Area: West End
Address: 1315 Broughton Street
Vancouver, BC V6G 2B6
Phone: (604) 720-3667

#292
The Royal Canadian Legion
Category: Bar, Karaoke
Area: Kerrisdale
Address: 2177 42nd Avenue W
Vancouver, BC V6M 2B7
Phone: (604) 261-8848

#293
Novo Pizzeria & Wine Bar
Category: Wine Bar, Pizza, Italian
Average price: Modest
Area: Fairview Slopes
Address: 2118 Burrard Street
Vancouver, BC V6J 3H6
Phone: (604) 736-2220

#294
DMC Gentlemen
Category: Adult Entertainment
Area: Mount Pleasant
Address: 169 E 12th Avenue
Vancouver, BC V5T 2G8
Phone: (604) 499-4752

#295
Creekside Restaurant & Lounge
Category: Bar, Canadian
Area: Downtown, Granville
Entertainment District
Address: 1335 Howe Street
Vancouver, BC V6Z 1R7
Phone: (604) 682-0229

#296
The Lido
Category: Music Venues
Area: Mount Pleasant
Address: 518 E Broadway
Vancouver, BC V5T 1X5
Phone: (604) 879-5436

#297
Haze Public House
Category: Pub
Area: Downtown
Address: 1180 Howe Street
Vancouver, BC V6Z 1P6
Phone: (604) 722-1559

#298
Grain Tasting Bar
Category: Lounge
Area: Downtown
Address: 750 Burrard Street, Suite 730
Vancouver, BC V6Z 2V6
Phone: (604) 683-4749

#299
Host Consulting
Category: Bar
Area: Chinatown
Address: 88 E Pender St
Vancouver, BC V6A 1S9
Phone: (604) 558-2571

#300
Brandiz Pub
Category: Dive Bar
Average price: Modest
Area: Downtown Eastside
Address: 122 Hastings St E
Vancouver, BC V6A 1N4
Phone: (604) 687-3241

#301
Prohibition
Category: Bar
Average price: Modest
Area: Downtown
Address: 801 W Georgia St
Vancouver, BC V6C 3G1

#302
Boogie Shoes DJ & Karaoke
Category: Karaoke, DJs
Area: West End
Address: 125A - 1030 Denman St
Vancouver, BC V6G 2M6
Phone: (604) 816-7727

#303
Fox
Category: Music Venues
Area: Mount Pleasant
Address: 2321 Main Street
Vancouver, BC V5T 3C9
Phone: (604) 874-3116

#304
Azure Lounge & Grill
Category: Bar
Average price: Expensive
Area: Downtown
Address: 770 Pacific Blvd
Vancouver, BC V6B 5E7
Phone: (604) 633-1611

Shops, Restaurants, Attractions & Nightlife / Vancouver Travel Guide

#305
Abitibi Boat
Category: Bar, Boat Charter
Area: Downtown, Yaletown
Address: 750 Plaza Of Nations
Vancouver, BC V6Z 2R8
Phone: (604) 669-4604

#306
Mda Sys
Category: Bar
Area: Downtown
Address: 350 West Georgia Street
Vancouver, BC V6B 6B1
Phone: (604) 669-1543

#307
Olympia Bar and Grill
Category: Greek, Bar
Area: Downtown, Granville Entertainment District
Address: 911 Granville Street
Vancouver, BC V6Z 1L3
Phone: (604) 568-3454

#308
Oasis Restaurant and Bar
Category: Bar
Area: West End
Address: 1240 Thurlow Street
Vancouver, BC V6E 1N7
Phone: (604) 685-1724

#309
Malone's Second Door
Category: Lounge
Area: Downtown
Address: 520 Seymour St
Vancouver, BC V6B 3K4
Phone: (604) 684-9977

#310
Dan's Bass Lessons
Category: Music Venues, Tutoring Centers, Private Tutors
Area: Grandview-Woodlands
Address: 1890 Pandora St
Vancouver, BC V5L 1M5
Phone: (604) 817-8830

#311
Robson Karaoke Box
Category: Karaoke
Area: West End
Address: 1238 Robson Street
Vancouver, BC V6E 1C1
Phone: (604) 688-0611

#312
Tokyo Lounge
Category: Lounge
Area: West End, Downtown
Address: 1050 Alberni Street
Vancouver, BC V6E 1A3
Phone: (604) 689-0003

#313
Muse Karaoke
Category: Karaoke
Area: Kensington-Cedar Cottage
Address: 1050 Kingsway Street
Vancouver, BC V5V 3C6
Phone: (604) 336-2918

#314
East End Billards
Category: Pool Hall
Area: Grandview-Woodlands
Address: 2305 Hastings Street E
Vancouver, BC V5L 1V6
Phone: (604) 251-4071

#315
Jungle Swing Productions
Category: Dance Studio, Party & Event Planning, Jazz & Blues
Area: Grandview-Woodlands, The Drive
Address: 2205 Commercial Dr
Vancouver, BC V5N 4B6
Phone: (604) 420-0087

#316
Al Diwan
Category: Mediterranean, Karaoke
Area: Kensington-Cedar Cottage
Address: 1440 Kingsway
Vancouver, BC V5N 2R5
Phone: (604) 336-0933

#317
Waldorf Grove Pub
Category: Pub
Area: Grandview-Woodlands
Address: 1489 Hastings Street E
Vancouver, BC V5L 1S4
Phone: (604) 253-7141

#318
Suna Studio Inc.
Category: Music Venues
Area: Grandview-Woodlands
Address: 1585 E Pender
Vancouver, BC V5L 1V9
Phone: (604) 315-4863

#319
Pierre's Champagne Lounge
Category: Lounge
Area: Downtown, Yaletown
Address: 1035 Mainland Street
Vancouver, BC V6B 1A9
Phone: (604) 123-4567

#320
Charqui Grill
Category: Bar, Soup, Tapas Bar
Area: Bakırköy, Zeytinlik
Address: 200 - 8168 Granville Street
Vancouver, BC V6P 4Z4
Phone: (778) 231-8888

#321
Press Box Pub
Category: Karaoke, Music Venues, Pub
Area: Hastings-Sunrise
Address: 2889 E Hastings
Vancouver, BC V5K 1Z9
Phone: (604) 252-2690

#322
The Blackbird Pub & Oyster Bar
Category: Bar, Canadian
Average price: Modest
Area: Downtown
Address: 905 Dunsmuir Street
Vancouver, BC V6C 2G2
Phone: (604) 899-4456

#323
Lions Pub
Category: Pub
Average price: Modest
Area: Downtown
Address: 888 West Cordova St
Vancouver, BC V6C 3N8
Phone: (604) 488-8602

#324
Rodney's Oyster Bar
Category: Bar
Average price: Expensive
Area: Downtown, Yaletown
Address: 1228 Hamilton Street
Vancouver, BC V6B

#325
Mark Igonia Ticket Broker
Category: Music Venues
Area: Downtown, Yaletown
Address: 1133 Homer Street
Vancouver, BC V6B 0B1
Phone: (604) 782-9961

#326
Burgoo Bistro
Category: Bar, Soup, Canadian
Average price: Modest
Area: Kitsilano
Address: 2272 W 4th Avenue
Vancouver, BC V6K 1P2
Phone: (604) 734-3478

#327
Commodore Lanes & Billiards
Category: Pool Hall, Bowling, Casino
Average price: Modest
Area: Downtown, Granville Entertainment District
Address: 838 Granville St
Vancouver, BC V6Z 1K3
Phone: (604) 681-1531

#328
Lola Cabaret
Category: Bar
Average price: Inexpensive
Area: Kitsilano
Address: 2291 Broadway W
Vancouver, BC V6K 2E4
Phone: (604) 733-7989

#329
Kien Giang
Category: Pool Hall, Casino
Area: Kensington-Cedar Cottage
Address: 1210 Kingsway
Vancouver, BC V5V 3E1
Phone: (604) 873-1574

#330
Polynesian Dining Room
Category: Hotel, Bar
Area: Grandview-Woodlands
Address: 1489 Hastings Street E
Vancouver, BC V5L 1S4
Phone: (604) 253-7141

#331
East Side Craft House
Category: Sports Bar, Pub, Burgers
Average price: Modest
Area: Fraserview
Address: 1445 E 41st Street
Vancouver, BC V5P 2Y3
Phone: (604) 324-1400

#332
Army Navy & Air Force Veterans
Category: Dive Bar
Area: Sunset
Address: 5896 Fraser St
Vancouver, BC V5W 2Z5
Phone: (604) 327-1421

#333
Penny Lane Neighbourhood Pub
Category: Pub
Area: Fraserview
Address: 6509 Victoria Drive
Vancouver, BC V5P 3X8
Phone: (604) 321-9189

#334
Grandview Recreations
Category: Pool Hall, Casino
Area: Grandview-Woodlands, The Drive
Address: 1816 Commercial Dr
Vancouver, BC V5N 4A5
Phone: (604) 254-9115

#335
The Office Billiards
Category: Pool Hall, Casino
Area: Fairview Slopes, South Granville
Address: 1409 Broadway W
Vancouver, BC V6H 1H6
Phone: (604) 734-9914

#336
Rack Billiards
Category: Pool Hall
Area: Grandview-Woodlands, The Drive
Address: 2155 Commercial Dr
Vancouver, BC V5N 4B3
Phone: (604) 251-5055

#337
Fader Mountain Sound
Category: Music Venues, Musicians
Area: Mount Pleasant
Address: 201 W 7th Avenue
Vancouver, BC V5Y 1L9
Phone: (604) 628-7750

#338
Trans Pool Hall
Category: Pool Hall, Casino
Area: Mount Pleasant
Address: 42 Broadway E
Vancouver, BC V5T 1V6
Phone: (604) 874-3118

#339
Flavorite music
Category: Music Venues
Area: Mount Pleasant
Address: 2050 Scotia Street
Vancouver, BC V5T 4S2
Phone: (778) 839-8567

#340
Vibes Lounge
Category: Lounge
Area: Downtown
Address: 555 Davie Street
Vancouver, BC V6B 5B6
Phone: (604) 688-5559

#341
Center Ice Grill
Category: Sports Bar
Area: Downtown
Address: 800 Griffiths Way
Vancouver, BC V6B 6G1
Phone: (604) 899-7525

#342
Milan's Bistro
Category: Bar Bristo
Area: Downtown, Yaletown
Address: 1223 Hamilton Street
Vancouver, BC V6B 6K3
Phone: (604) 915-7225

#343
Medical Arts Building
Category: Performing Arts, Music Venues
Area: Downtown, Granville Entertainment District
Address: 825 Granville St
Vancouver, BC V6Z 1K9
Phone: (604) 681-8622

#344
F212 Steam
Category: Gay Bar
Area: West End
Address: 1048 Davie Street
Vancouver, BC V6Z 1Y9
Phone: (604) 689-9719

#345
Vancouver Vapor Lounge
Category: Lounge
Area: Chinatown
Address: 138 East Pender
Vancouver, BC V6A 2V2
Phone: (604) 668-3334

#346
The Majestic Restaurant & Lounge
Category: Bar, Lounge
Area: West End
Address: 1138 Davie Street
Vancouver, BC V6E 1N1
Phone: (604) 669-2013

#347
Vintropolis Wine Bar & Bistro
Category: Wine Bar
Area: Kitsilano
Address: 1809 1st Ave W
Vancouver, BC V6J 5B8
Phone: (604) 732-8877

#348
Metro Coffee Bar & Billiards
Category: Pool Hall, Casino
Area: Renfrew-Collingwood
Address: 3175 Kingsway
Vancouver, BC V5R 5K2
Phone: (604) 437-9613

#349
Pat's Pub & Brewhouse
Category: Music Venues, Pub
Average price: Modest
Area: Downtown Eastside
Address: 403 E Hastings Street
Vancouver, BC V6A 1P6
Phone: (604) 255-4301

#350
Ferguson Billiards
Category: Pool Hall, Casino
Area: Grandview-Woodlands
Address: 2305 Hastings St E
Vancouver, BC V5L 1V6
Phone: (604) 253-9961

#351
L'ufficio
Category: Wine Bar, Italian, Tapas
Area: Point Grey, Kitsilano
Address: 3687 W 4th Avenue
Vancouver, BC V6R 1P2
Phone: (604) 676-1007

#352
Adanoi Pub
Category: Pub
Area: Downtown, Gastown
Address: 303 Columbia Street
Vancouver, BC V6A 2R7
Phone: (604) 605-1076

#353
Moose's Down Under
Category: Pub, Australian
Average price: Modest
Area: Downtown
Address: 830 Pender Street W
Vancouver, BC V6C 1J8
Phone: (604) 683-3300

#354
Elephant & Castle
Category: British, Pub
Average price: Modest
Area: Downtown
Address: 385 Burrard Street
Vancouver, BC V6C 2G8
Phone: (604) 696-6730

#355
Cavo Bar and Kitchen
Category: Bar, Mediterranean
Average price: Modest
Area: Downtown, Granville Entertainment District
Address: 911 Granville Street
Vancouver, BC V6B 2C9
Phone: (604) 568-3454

#356
Milestone's Grill & Bar
Category:Bar
Average price: Modest
Area: West End
Address: 1210 Denman St
Vancouver, BC V6G 2N2
Phone: (604) 662-3431

#357
The Junction Public House
Category: Gay Bar
Average price: Modest
Area: West End
Address: 1138 Davie St
Vancouver, BC V6E 1N1
Phone: (604) 669-2013

#358
Pasha Lounge
Category: Middle Eastern, Hookah Bar
Average price: Modest
Area: Lower Lonsdale
Address: #210-150 West Esplanade North
Vancouver, BC V7M 1A3
Phone: (778) 318-4483

#359
In the Mood
Category: Adult Entertainment
Average price: Expensive
Area: Lower Lonsdale
Address: 123 Carrie Cates Court North
Vancouver, BC V7M 3K7
Phone: (604) 990-0580

#360
Milestone's Grill & Bar
Category: Bar
Average price: Modest
Area: West End
Address: 1145 Robson St
Vancouver, BC V6E 1B5
Phone: (604) 682-4477

#361
TWB The Wine Bar
Category: Wine Bar
Average price: Expensive
Area: Downtown, Yaletown
Address: 1167 Marinaside Crescent
Vancouver, BC V6Z 2V4
Phone: (604) 681-4144

#362
Yagger's Kits Restaurant & Sports Bar
Category: Fast Food, Sports Bar
Average price: Modest
Area: Kitsilano
Address: 2884 West Broadway
Vancouver, BC V6K 2G7
Phone: (604) 733-3002

#363
Coco Rico Cafe
Category: Bar
Average price: Modest
Area: West End
Address: 1290 Robson St
Vancouver, BC V6E 1C1
Phone: (604) 687-0424

#364
Hoang Tat Billiards
Category: Pool Hall, Casino
Area: Kensington-Cedar Cottage
Address: 2123 Kingsway
Vancouver, BC V5N 2T4
Phone: (604) 431-7771

#365
Krazy Kangaroo
Category: Bar
Area: Killarney, Champlain Heights
Address: 7725 Champlain Cres
Vancouver, BC V5S 4J6
Phone: (604) 433-1111

#366
Paper Rock Bar & Grill
Category: Bar
Area: Mount Pleasant
Address: 395 Kingsway
Vancouver, BC V5T 3J7
Phone: (604) 872-5252

#367
Tom Lee Music
Category: Music Venues
Average price: Expensive
Area: Downtown, Granville Entertainment District
Address: 929 Granville St
Vancouver, BC V6Z 1L3
Phone: (604) 685-8471

#368
The Keg Steakhouse + Bar
Category: Seafood, Steakhouse, Bar
Average price: Modest
Area: Downtown
Address: 688 Dunsmuir Street
Vancouver, BC V6B 1N3
Phone: (604) 685-7502

#369
Viti Wine and Lager
Category: Wine Bar
Average price: Modest
Area: Downtown, Granville Entertainment District
Address: 900 Seymour Street
Vancouver, BC V6B 3L9
Phone: (604) 683-3806

#370
131 Water Kitchen & Bar
Category: Pub, Tapas
Average price: Modest
Area: Downtown, Downtown Eastside
Address: 131 Water Street
Vancouver, BC V6B 1B2
Phone: (604) 669-7219

#371
The Lobby
Category: Lounge, Canadian
Average price: Expensive
Area: Lower Lonsdale
Address: 138 Victory Ship Way North
Vancouver, BC V7L 0B1
Phone: (604) 986-7437

#372
The Keg Steakhouse + Bar
Category: Steakhouse, Bar, Seafood
Average price: Expensive
Area: Downtown, Yaletown
Address: 1011 Mainland Street
Vancouver, BC V6B 5P9
Phone: (604) 633-2534

#373
Stanley's Park Bar & Grill
Category: Bar, American
Average price: Modest
Area: Coal Harbour
Address: 610 Pipeline Road
Vancouver, BC V6G 1Z4
Phone: (604) 602-3088

#374
Ceili's Modern Irish Pub
Category: Pub, Irish
Average price: Modest
Area: Downtown, Granville Entertainment District
Address: 670 Smithe Street
Vancouver, BC V6B 1E3
Phone: (604) 697-9199

#375
Jack Lonsdale's Public House
Category: Canadian, Pub
Average price: Modest
Area: Central Lonsdale
Address: 1433 Lonsdale Ave North
Vancouver, BC V7M 2H9
Phone: (604) 986-7333

#376
900 West Lounge & Wine Bar
Category: Wine Bar
Average price: Expensive
Area: Downtown
Address: 900 Georgia St W
Vancouver, BC V6C 2W6
Phone: (604) 669-9378

#377
Homer St. Cafe And Bar
Category: Bar, Cafe
Average price: Expensive
Area: Downtown, Yaletown
Address: 898 Homer Street
Vancouver, BC V6B 5S3
Phone: (604) 428-4299

#378
The Charles Bar
Category: Bar
Average price: Modest
Area: Downtown, Gastown
Address: 136 W Cordova St
Vancouver, BC V6B 1G1
Phone: (604) 568-8040

#379
The Squarerigger Neighbourhood Pub
Category: Pub
Average price: Inexpensive
Area: Ambleside
Address: 1425 Marine Dr West
Vancouver, BC V7T 1B9
Phone: (604) 926-3811

#380
The Rusty Gull Neighbourhood Pub
Category: Pub
Average price: Modest
Area: Lower Lonsdale
Address: 175 1st St E North
Vancouver, BC V7L 1B2
Phone: (604) 988-5585

#381
Sailor Hagar's Brew Pub
Category: Pub
Average price: Modest
Area: Lower Lonsdale
Address: 221 1st St W North
Vancouver, BC V7M 1B3
Phone: (604) 984-3087

#382
BC Place
Category: Music Venues
Average price: Modest
Area: Downtown
Address: 777 Pacific Blvd.
Vancouver, BC V6B 4Y8
Phone: (604) 669-2300

#383
G Sports Bar & Grill
Category: Sports Bar
Average price: Modest
Area: Downtown, Granville Entertainment District
Address: 1208 Granville Street
Vancouver, BC V6Z 1M4
Phone: (604) 687-7684

#384
El Matador
Spanish Tapas & Drinks
Category: Bar, Spanish, Canadian
Average price: Modest
Area: Lower Lonsdale
Address: 131 W Esplanade North
Vancouver, BC V7M 3H9
Phone: (604) 770-1717

#385
Two Parrots Perch & Grill
Category: Pub, American
Average price: Modest
Area: Downtown, Granville Entertainment District
Address: 1202 Granville Street
Vancouver, BC V6Z 1M4
Phone: (604) 685-9657

#386
Vino Volo
Category: Wine Bar, Tapas
Average price: Expensive
Area: YVR
Address: Vancouver International Airport Richmond, BC V7B 1Y7
Phone: (604) 279-1836

#387
Guys & Dolls Billiards
Category: Pool Hall, Casino
Average price: Expensive
Area: Mount Pleasant
Address: 2434 Main St
Vancouver, BC V5T 3E2
Phone: (604) 879-4433

#388
Au Bar
Category: Dance Club
Average price: Expensive
Area: Downtown
Address: 674 Seymour Street
Vancouver, BC V6B 3K4
Phone: (604) 648-2227

#389
Sailor Hagar's Brew Pub
Category: Pub
Average price: Exclusive
Area: Lower Lonsdale
Address: 86 Semisch Avenue North
Vancouver, BC V7M 3H8
Phone: (604) 984-3087

#390
Cloud 9 Bodycare
Category: Adult Entertainment, Massage
Area: Burnaby Heights
Address: 3849 Hastings Street
Burnaby, BC V5C 2H7
Phone: (604) 299-0872

#391
Tableau Bar Bistro
Category: French, Wine Bar
Average price: Expensive
Area: Downtown
Address: 1181 Melville St
Vancouver, BC V6E 2S8
Phone: (604) 639-8692

#392
La Tasca
Category: Lounge
Average price: Inexpensive
Area: Lower Lonsdale
Address: 144 Lonsdale Avenue North
Vancouver, BC V7M 2E8
Phone: (604) 349-1941

#393
The Brew House Grill
Category: Pub
Area: Downtown
Address: 800 Griffiths Way
Vancouver, BC V6B 6G1
Phone: (604) 899-7525

#394
Brix Restaurant
Category: Wine Bar, French
Average price: Expensive
Area: Downtown, Yaletown
Address: 1138 Homer Street
Vancouver, BC V6B 2X6
Phone: (604) 915-9463

#395
Centennial Theatre Centre
Category: Music Venues, Performing Arts
Area: Central Lonsdale
Address: 2300 Lonsdale Ave North
Vancouver, BC V7M 3L1
Phone: (604) 984-4484

#396
The Keg Steakhouse + Bar
Category: Steakhouse, Bar, Seafood
Average price: Expensive
Area: Granville Island/False Creek
Address: 1499 Anderson Street
Vancouver, BC V6H 3R5
Phone: (604) 685-4735

#397
The Queen Elizabeth Theatre
Category: Music Venues, Performing Arts
Average price: Expensive
Area: Downtown
Address: 600 Hamilton St
Vancouver, BC V6B 2P1

#398
One12 Restaurant & Lounge
Category: Lounge
Area: Central Lonsdale
Address: 112 13th Street W North
Vancouver, BC V7M 1N6
Phone: (604) 980-1092

#399
Subeez Cafe
Category: Pub, Canadian
Average price: Modest
Area: Downtown, Yaletown
Address: 891 Homer Street
Vancouver, BC V6B 2W2
Phone: (604) 687-6107

#400
SIP Resto-Lounge
Category: Wine Bar, Tapas Bar
Average price: Modest
Area: Downtown, Granville Entertainment District
Address: 1117 Granville Street
Vancouver, BC V6Z 1M1
Phone: (604) 687-7474

Made in the USA
Monee, IL
10 February 2022